Social Problems in the UK

Social Problems in the UK: An introduction is the first textbook on contemporary social issues to contextualise social problems within the disciplines of sociology, social policy, criminology and applied social science. Drawing on the research and teaching experience of academics in these areas, this much-needed textbook brings together a comprehensive range of expertise. *Social Problems in the UK* discusses the strengthening and changing character of social construction, providing a new and invigorated way of studying the issues for all social science students. This clear, accessible textbook guides students in approaching the methodology, theory and research of social problems, and introduces the key topics in the area:

- migration and 'race';
- education, work and unemployment;
- poverty;
- drugs, violence and policing;
- youth, and sub-culture and gangs; and
- childhood and education.

Social Problems in the UK provides a number of helpful pedagogical features for ease of teaching and learning, including: case studies; links to data sources; textboxes highlighting examples, key figures, etc.; study questions; and tips on how to undertake literature reviews and use journals and databases.

Stuart Isaacs is a Senior Lecturer in Social Policy and Sociology at London Metropolitan University. He is the co-author of *Contemporary Political Theorists in Context*

(2009) and *Political Theorists in Context* (2004), as well as the sole author of *The Politics and Philosophy of Michael Oakeshott* (2006), all published by Routledge. His research interests are in political and social theory. He has recently been made a University Teaching Fellow in recognition of his outstanding contribution to teaching and learning.

David Blundell worked as a primary school teacher and then taught education students at South Bank and North London universities. David established community sport clubs with young people in Hackney before joining London Metropolitan University as Principal Lecturer in the School of Social Sciences in 2006.

Anne Foley is an Academic Liaison Librarian and has worked with students and staff in the Faculty of Applied Social Sciences and Humanities at London Metropolitan University for several years. Her research interests are in the areas of information literacy, digital literacy, problem-based learning and learning transfer.

Norman Ginsburg has been Professor of Social Policy at London Metropolitan University since 1996. His research interests are the comparative impact of social policy on social injustice and inequality, and the social effects of urban regeneration and housing policy. He is the author of *Divisions of Welfare: An Introduction to Comparative Social Policy* (1992). Recent publications include articles on globalisation and the liberal welfare states, social policy in Sweden, social aspects of urban regeneration, the privatisation of council housing, and on globalisation and racism.

Brian McDonough is Senior Lecturer and Course Leader of Sociology and Associate Director of the International Centre for Community Development at London Metropolitan University. His doctoral research involved an ethnographic study of experts' use of technology at work. His research interests include work and the use of information and communication technologies.

Daniel Silverstone is Principal Lecturer and overall course leader for Criminology in the School of Social Science at London Metropolitan University. His expertise is in the area of organised crime, drugs and the night-time economy and illegal firearms use. He has published widely in the field for a number of scholarly journals including, *Global Crime, Criminology and Criminal Justice* and *Policy Studies*.

Tara Young is a Senior Research Fellow in the Faculty of Humanities and Applied Social Sciences at London Metropolitan University. She has expertise in qualitative research and is currently undertaking research into interpersonal relationships between gang members and their intimate others (e.g. partners, parents, carers, siblings). She has published academic papers on gang violence and the experiences of women in UK gangs and completed studies related to violence against women, multiple perpetrator rape, and the role of the family in facilitating gang membership, criminality and desistance.

Social Problems in the UK

An introduction

*Stuart Isaacs, David Blundell,
Anne Foley, Norman Ginsburg,
Brian McDonough, Dan Silverstone
and Tara Young*

Routledge
Taylor & Francis Group

LONDON AND NEW YORK

First published 2015
by Routledge
2 Park Square, Milton Park, Abingdon, Oxon OX14 4RN

and by Routledge
711 Third Avenue, New York, NY 10017

Routledge is an imprint of the Taylor & Francis Group, an informa business

British Library Cataloguing-in-Publication Data
A catalogue record for this book is available from the British Library

Library of Congress Cataloging-in-Publication Data
Isaacs, Stuart.
  Social problems in the UK : an introduction / by Stuart Isaacs,
  David Blundell, Anne Foley, Norman Ginsberg, Brian McDonough,
  Dan Silverstone, Tara Young
     pages cm
  1. Social problems—Great Britain. 2. Great Britain—Social policy. I. Title.
  HN390.I83 2014
  303.30941—dc23   2014003956

ISBN: 978-0-415-71997-1 (hbk)
ISBN: 978-0-415-71999-5 (pbk)
ISBN: 978-1-315-86722-9 (ebk)

Typeset in Scala
by Sunrise Setting Ltd, Paignton, UK

MIX
Paper from
responsible sources
FSC
www.fsc.org   FSC® C013604

Printed and bound by CPI Group (UK) Ltd, Croydon, CR0 4YY

For all our students, past, present and future.

Contents

Illustrations

Figures

Tables

Acknowledgement

It is with deep gratitude that we acknowledge the help of Janet Ransom for her thorough review and edit of some of the material presented in this book.

chapter 1

Introduction

'Social problems, no thanks!' Ten years ago, this was the response of most academics to the idea that we could usefully investigate UK society through the lens of social problems. Although this way of investigating the social was common in the US, in Britain approaching society as a 'problem' was taken as wrongly implying that all social issues could be 'solved'. It was also argued that this point of view was a negative and simplistic way of examining complex social institutions, structures and circumstances. Fast-forward ten years, and now most social science departments in the UK have some sort of Social Problems module on their first-year undergraduate courses.

So, why the change?

Well, there are a number of reasons, but the first has to be that it came to be seen that a social problems perspective was a lot more useful and sophisticated than was initially thought. This change was in no small part due to the publication of a social policy textbook produced by academics at London Metropolitan University (then the University of North London). In May et al. (2001), *Understanding Social Problems: Issues in Social Policy*, a way of studying social problems was set out that avoided the trap of treating society as one big pathological problem that could be remedied. In particular, the framework of social construction was used to study social issues in an appropriate methodological manner. This also satisfied a second concern of those who were sceptical about a social problems perspective, namely that it individualised social issues, moving away from a critique about broader social inequalities and social justice. In fact the approach used by May et al. illustrated that, far from looking at social problems merely in terms of discrete social groups, intensely political and ideological arguments could be presented. A social problems perspective enabled both academics and students to articulate strong positions relating to fundamental social values without undermining the academic rigour of investigating a range of issues.

Social Problems in the UK: An Introduction builds upon the platform laid by our former colleagues at London Metropolitan University at the beginning of this century, but with one big change. A social problems perspective is now no longer associated only with social policy. Throughout the UK social problems is taught on sociology, social policy, criminology and applied social science degree courses. This textbook is the first on contemporary social issues to situate social problems within all of these subject areas. Drawing from the research and teaching experience of academics in these areas, this textbook brings together a comprehensive range of expertise to guide students and to aid lecturers in their teaching.

The central aim of our text, then, is to contextualise contemporary social problems in the broader social sciences, using the methodology of social construction. At the same time a key motivation for this book is to bring teaching to the page. That is, to be an accessible study aid to students that introduces them to applying a methodological perspective to familiar issues. You will find within these pages a great deal of pedagogic content. Rather than relating reams of quantitative material in relation to each of the social problems, further readings are used to direct the student to sources that will help them keep up to date. Examples that relate to classic works in the field, important historical moments, key figures and key concepts are also highlighted in text boxes. At the end of each chapter there are revision notes, coursework questions, seminar tasks and further readings. All this draws from over a decade of teaching social problems. At the heart of this teaching has been the desire to lead students from a 'common sense' experienced-based way of thinking, to a more critically engaged approach that relies upon social research and social theory.

In Chapter 2 the book opens with a general methodological and theoretical chapter on understanding and defining social problems. This chapter introduces students to the 'common sense' view, the social construction approach and related sociological theories. Practical examples are given whenever possible. This is an on-going feature of the book, to tie theory and practice in order to guide students towards the applied character of this type of study. The overall purpose of this chapter on definitions and approaches is to try to convey to the student the importance of using methodological and theoretical tools, rather than the over-elaborate explanation and evaluation of such tools.

Chapter 3 is of critical importance to the pedagogic aims of this book. Foley has been working as an academic librarian in the social sciences for many years. She understands the difficulties first-year students experience when given coursework. This is often related to a lack of understanding of the sources available and of how to find and evaluate those sources.

Understanding the types of material available, as well as learning how to locate, evaluate and use these materials in their studies and coursework is crucial to student success. However, the skills and knowledge necessary to learn these are all too often taught in isolated library induction sessions. Research has shown that embedding this knowledge and skill within a subject context, in a seamless union of learning and researching, has a higher chance of success. In this chapter Foley combines the core areas of subject knowledge with the library research skills necessary for students to confidently and independently research social problems.

Common problems addressed in this chapter include: the confusion that often arises about journals and journal articles; citing and referencing sources; plagiarism; and how to transfer the skills learned when researching one area to researching another. Finally, teaching staff may also find this chapter useful as a readymade resource to guide their students when they are searching for material.

Chapter 4 begins the engagement with material situated around a particular set of social problems. In keeping with the rest of the book, Isaacs examines the social construction of poverty. He argues that debates about poverty often demonise the poor themselves, blaming them for their own circumstances, as well as sometimes wider economic and social welfare failings. The chapter moves on to analyse New Labour's social exclusion policies. It looks at the assumptions embedded in those policies and whether or not they had any success in alleviating poverty. New Labour's policies are the most recent example of a comprehensive, reasonably resourced government initiative to try to deal with the manifold issues associated with low income and underachievement. Analysing their success and failures helps us to think more clearly about this social problem. As a case study the chapter ends with a discussion on homelessness. The main question here is: to what extent is homelessness caused by poverty and social exclusion? Isaacs maintains that, rather than being a social problem for the few, homelessness is a fundamental social issue that affects the whole of society.

In Chapter 5, McDonough looks at work as a social problem by setting out its social construction from a number of different perspectives. He discusses the underlying discourses which create assumptions about our role as workers. In particular he examines why the 'work ethic' seems to be such a strong moral imperative in the UK. Following this examination the author offers alternative ways of understanding what we might mean by 'work'. Closely related to work is, of course, unemployment. As with the notion of work, what we characterise as 'unemployment' cannot merely be taken at face value, as a 'common sense' given. The ways in which unemployment is socially constructed are therefore analysed. This throws some light on the stratified character of work and how it affects various social groups in different ways in relation to gender, social class and ethnicity. McDonough concludes that unemployment and the responsibility for finding work are often constructed in political and media debates as the responsibility of the individual alone. In contrast, he maintains that, in fact, they relate to a whole set of social circumstances, often beyond the individual's capabilities to control.

Professor Ginsburg has been teaching, researching and publishing in the area of migration and 'race' for over three decades. Unlike straightforward sociology of 'race' approaches, Chapter 6 looks at the issues of migration, asylum and 'race' through the perspective of various socially constructed debates in the UK. These are set out very clearly and thoroughly in a series of case studies. The chapter highlights the links between politicised debates about migration and racism. For example, indicating how tough talk from politicians and sections of the print media on limiting immigration may have a negative effect on discourses around 'race'. In this way the chapter explores the sub-text of integrationist policies and hardening attitudes to immigration. On the other hand, Ginsburg also points out the burgeoning ethnic diversity in the UK and the more widespread acceptance, awareness and sensitivity to issues of 'race'. He goes on to highlight the way in which recent debates have shifted towards the migration of EU citizens from Central and Eastern Europe. Arguments regarding overcrowding, increased pressure on public services, reduced employment opportunities for British workers and so on have all been deployed to construct an anti-immigration discourse. However, Ginsburg argues that these arguments do not stand up to critical scrutiny, despite the portrayal of migration as a threat to British culture. The reality on the ground is also different, in that new migrants have often experienced a tolerant and friendly welcome, particularly from employers who understand the value of their contribution.

In Chapter 7, on childhood and education, Blundell starts by stating that 'No social group figures as consistently or frequently in the discussion of social problems as do children'. In this way the author points to one of the main ways in which the social construction approach helps us to take one step back from 'common sense' arguments. Rather than immediately situate his account of education in disputes about standards, policies, issues of class, gender or ethnicity, Blundell insightfully pieces together how it is that 'the child' is constituted in various ways. As he points out, these constructions of childhood are part of a historical legacy that constitutes powerful ideological assumptions which underlie many current education policies. Blundell explores the impact this has upon young people themselves as well as the wider policy implications. He argues that children are overly burdened as a source of hope in the search for solutions to many social problems. It is in the system of education and the institutions of schooling where many issues of social concern are presumed to be 'solvable'. This includes not only educational achievement but the future of the UK's economic success, health problems, issues relating to social cohesion and crime, youth gangs and drug-related crime. Fundamentally, then, this chapter explores where our ideas about children and childhood come from and why childhood and education have become so closely identified as means to solve society's 'ills'.

The criminology dimension of the book is writ large in Chapters 8 and 9. In the first of these Silverstone, who is a leading expert on issues of drug use and drug dealing within the night-time economy, looks at the social construction of so-called 'organised crime'. This involves enquiring into the social construction of criminal issues, including discussions in relation to trafficking, measuring crime and the 'moral panics' that are sometimes created around international criminal syndicates. He notes how policing strategies often ignore issues of 'race' and poverty in their attempted solutions. Although this penultimate chapter is situated on the territory of criminology, by highlighting these social issues it serves to illustrate how social problems can be used to unify studies across the social sciences.

The final chapter looks at the various constructions of youth gangs, in the media and public debates. Young begins the chapter by giving an overview of the theoretical discussions regarding the character of gangs. This begins in the US but quickly relates to the UK, which has an altogether different tradition of analysis. Young moves on to discuss the experience of 'gang formation' and whether or not there is a phenomenon we might call 'gang culture'. She looks at how the problem of gangs is constructed in contemporary society and reviews how government and policy makers respond to the issues. Young argues that political viewpoints influence the way in which debates about gangs as well as 'gun and knife culture' are disseminated in society. Moreover, the construction of 'gang culture' in the UK is itself a means of social control which engenders a widespread fear of young people and a growth in punitive sanctions against them. Finally, Young looks at the issue of girl gangs. This is a focus that is often marginalised in the literature on youth gangs.

Reference

May, M., Page, R. and Brunsden, E. (eds), *Understanding Social Problems: issues in social policy*, Oxford: Blackwell, 2001

chapter 2

Understanding and defining social problems

Stuart Isaacs

2.1 Introduction

To engage with social problems is to decide to think about issues that affect millions of people. Most of us have already had some kind of experience of these issues. This might be from a distance, for example, seeing a rough sleeper on the street. Or it could be more personal, as someone who has been homeless. Social problems are, unfortunately, part of all of our problems. To illustrate this we can start by understanding their relationship to other types of problems, namely, individual, economic and political problems.

When you wake up not wanting to go to school or college or work this may be because you are hung-over, or want to avoid someone or simply because you're feeling drained. This is a problem for you, but it's not a social problem. Not unless what you were going to do was of national importance!

Individual difficulties to do with personal trauma, psychological conditions, relationship problems, financial troubles and other such private concerns are not in themselves social problems. But they could be, if looked at from a broader, more generalised social context. Psychological issues would normally fall outside of the remit of social problems. But if any of the personal problems listed above were in some way tied to poverty, homelessness, social exclusion, racism, sexism, homophobia, unemployment, lack of educational achievement and so on, then they could be brought into an analysis of social problems.

On the whole we can maintain that social problems may be differentiated from individual problems, except where they form part of a collective issue.

Social problems ought also to be distinguished from economic problems. There is a commonplace view that all political and social issues are reducible to questions of resources and money. If this were the case then all we would have to do to alleviate illness or crime would be find the right economic model to use for the National Health Service (NHS) or the police force. But this would be a rather ahistorical understanding and one that lacked sociological knowledge. Most social problems have existed for some time. They have a history to them. A range of government policies have usually already been tried, giving rise to a complex array of bureaucratic and organisational structures. For example, policies regarding immigration are tied to a long history of Immigration Acts that span the twentieth century and into our own age. This complex set of laws has spawned central and local government agencies, incorporating UK Visas and Immigration and the Border Force, through to small refugee help centres. Economic models alone cannot help us to analyse how these organisations work, how policy is implemented within them and their own particular histories.

The organisations and agencies that address social problems through policy making and implementation cannot be analysed from a purely economic point of view. Nor can economic models help us to understand the social attitudes that have already grown around these issues. Since the first wave of post-war migrants came to the UK a varied range of social attitudes towards immigration can be observed. These attitudes span inclusive and sympathetic discourses, through to outright hostility and racism. Economics may well be a part of some of these attitudes, such as the argument that immigrants are a burden on the welfare system. But economic ideas alone cannot help us to interpret these opinions, assumptions or actions. Furthermore, the success or otherwise of integrationist policies or the work of organisations helping new immigrants is not solely reliant on what resources they have. It will be a matter of policy strategies, wider social circumstances and acceptability, as well as how each individual project is implemented on the ground.

Economic issues, such as the unequal distribution of wealth, may well be part of a discussion of social problems. But social problems are by no means determined by economics alone.

When it comes to distinguishing social problems from political problems this is a much more difficult task. If we think, for the moment, of political issues as only those that government is concerned with, then a distinction is fairly straightforward. Some social problems may be publicly debated as on-going issues, such as drug abuse. However, they may not necessarily impress themselves upon government to act even where public debate is clearly evident. In this sense, if we are thinking of politics as only what government does, social problems may be distinguished from political problems.

There is, however, only a very minimal definition of politics underlying this argument. To reduce politics to merely central or local government activity would actually be to de-politicise the very idea. Politics is conventionally defined as involving the participation of citizens in debates about public issues. Ideology, power relations, conflict and the struggle over rights are one side of this public dialogue. Compromise, tolerance and responsibility are the other side. Politics is about debating rights and wrongs, justice and injustice, the good life and the bad. In this sense, exploring social problems is, arguably, one of the most politicised areas of debate in the social sciences, as it involves making judgements about social rights and social wrongs.

Social problems may be distinguished from political problems in that government might not always be involved in acting on an issue that is publicly debated. But social problems are inherently political in that they are debates about the kind of society that we believe is just.

2.2 The private sphere and the public sphere

Like all concepts in the social sciences, there are no transparent or absolutely fixed boundaries to what may or may not be a social problem. We have already seen that although individual, economic and political problems may be distinguished from a social problem, we cannot entirely discount them from our definition. This is not to say that there are no parameters at all. There are. But they are not simply given or self-evident. There is no national authority that determines *this* or *that* is a social problem and everyone must agree. If there were, it would make studying the subject much easier! What we must do in the absence of an absolute authority is make a case: construct a reasonable definition and argument.

 Key thinker: Charles Wright Mills (1916–62)

For Mills, the main task of social research was to investigate how our personal troubles are often tied to wider social problems. Through the collection of empirical material and by applying social theory, the role of the social scientist was to uncover the broader, collective social factors that underlay individual, particular problems. See his famous book, *The Sociological Imagination* (1959), for these ideas.

understanding and defining social problems

To make a case we have a whole history of debate about concepts in the social sciences to help us. We do not have to start from scratch. Thankfully, many great minds have taken it upon themselves to do a lot of the work for us. C. Wright Mills, one of the most well-known social thinkers of the twentieth century, famously made a distinction between 'personal troubles' and 'public interest' to define a social concern. For our purposes we can take this as meaning that to be a social problem, an issue has to move from being private to public.

These two categories of our practical lives are often understood as the 'private sphere' and the 'public sphere'. Traditionally, in liberal democracies like that of the UK, the private sphere is where the state leaves us alone. It is where we interact with our families and choose our friends. It may also be where we pursue a hobby or interest or passion. Romantic love is arguably the most intense of our experiences in the private sphere, when we are most completely wrapped up in just one other individual and ourselves. Hannah Arendt (1958: 242) has argued that we are in our most private state when we are in love. If we have a lovers' tiff no one else is interested and it affects very few people (although, as we shall see, scale does not necessarily help us to define a social problem).

On the other hand, the public sphere is where we are known by strangers, students in the class, shopkeepers, parents at your child's school, in political or community organisations. Most commonly we are in the public sphere when we are doing our job, and this is often the most widely known aspect of our identities.

When a concern is discussed in the public sphere it becomes located in the broad territory where we find social problems. These might be issues that are timely and capture the public imagination for a short period. What are sometimes called 'moral panics' that occasionally break out, for example, over the behaviour of teenagers and young people.

FAST FORWARD >>>>> 9.4

For an example of 'moral panics' in relation to youth gangs.

Or they might be social problems which are on-going from generation to generation, such as debates about poverty.

2.3 How do social problems emerge?

Social problems are, then, issues that arise in the public sphere and become the site for general debate. The obvious next question is how do these issues emerge?

The first thing to dismiss is that social problems become a public concern because of the *scale* of the problem; that is, because a large number of people might be directly affected. If they did, we would not be concerned with drug addicts or asylum seekers or many other relatively small groups of people. Rough sleepers, for example, account for only a fraction of the overall number of people who are homeless. In 2011 the homeless campaigning organisation and charity Crisis estimated that 2,181 people were sleeping rough during a single night in England. Yet a huge amount of government resources, paid and voluntary workers and charity organisations are involved in trying to alleviate the problem of rough sleeping. This group are also often the focal point for media reporting, documentaries and discussion. If you look at videos about homelessness on YouTube almost all of them cover rough sleepers, rather than the millions of people who are not sleeping rough but are still homeless.

FAST FORWARD >>>>> 4.5

For a more detailed account of homelessness.

If it is not scale that gives rise to a social problem, then what is it?

Social problems come and go for a variety of immediate, contemporary reasons: as a result of government policy, because of a newsworthy event or due to a noticeable social change. There is no end to the number of reasons why a particular issue becomes a debate in the public sphere, and there will always be an incalculable number of them at the same time.

On the whole there will never be just one single reason why a social problem emerges: a number of factors tend to come together to highlight a problem. No one cause is ever at play. Rather like a major accident, there is never one factor that leads to the incident but a whole host of causes that happen to collide at a particular moment. Poverty, for example, might become a high-profile issue not because it has ever gone away, but because it is highlighted by prominent public figures. These figures may have been speaking on the issue for years but their voices are heard because there may be an economic downturn. This might coincide with new statistical evidence or a widely publicised report of increased poverty, as well as a growing perception that life is simply harder. Watching human-interest stories on the TV about struggling families might add to this. All these factors – publicity, wider political or economic circumstances, people's perceptions and media coverage – might collide to establish the prominence of a particular social problem.

The immediate reasons why a social problem emerges may not have anything to do with it being new or that it has returned. Like death and taxes, most social problems are always with us, or at least with us for a very long time. There will be immediate causes such as the ones given above that we can identify to help us understand this. However, the fact that social problems persist over time means that we can associate their emergence not just with immediate causes but to our social structures.

In the social sciences, social structures are understood as the fundamental organisational features of our society. Society is made up of social institutions that create social structures; if it were not, then there could not be a 'society', as such. The social institutions and social structures that are most commonly identified are the family, the education system, the type of socio-economic stratification, cultural practices, the state and the legal system. These are the bedrock of our social realm. They consist of repeated patterns of organisation and behaviour that make society identifiable. If we think of social problems in relation to social structures (rather than as a collection of discrete individual behaviours), then we can come to appreciate that social problems emerge because they are part of the on-going examination of the most important social institutions that make up our social world.

If we take what might appear as a relatively new social problem, that of anti-social behaviour, and look at it in this way we find that although the language surrounding anti-social behaviour is new, the issue is not. The term, 'anti-social behaviour' really only became widely used to denote a type of harassment against individuals in the 1990s. This culminated in the first legislation to prevent it in 1998, the centrepiece being the notorious Anti-Social Behaviour Orders or ASBOs. On the surface of it, anti-social behaviour became a public concern because it was associated with a new form of persistent, aggravated attacks on individuals. In other words, it was quite frightening because it highlighted how vulnerable we were as individuals or defenceless families. But if we think about the issue in relation to social structures we can argue that it emerged as a social problem because it also fed into various fears about the changing character of the family. A great deal of the debate surrounding anti-social behaviour was associated with the state of the family. Public concern was as much about anti-social behaviour being a symptom of family breakdown, or too many single-parent families, or lack of family guidance, or childhood poverty, as about the individual incidents themselves.

The point here is that social problems emerge because they appear to carry a *threat* to the stability of our social institutions and structures. Underlying public concern with anti-social behaviour is a fundamental anxiety about the threat to what is perceived as a normal model of the family. Competing arguments about anti-social behaviour tend to have at their core differing ideas about the desirable make-up of contemporary family life.

We can maintain from this discussion that social problems emerge from a variety of different immediate and contemporary causes which bring them to public attention. But they do so only because underlying these particular timely events, social problems are part of the ever-present social dialogue about the character of our most important social structures.

Key points: what are social problems?

- Social problems are not fixed or given, and they change over time.
- Social problems can be distinguished from individual, economic and political problems, but not completely.
- Our judgements about social problems are always politicised.
- To be a social problem, an issue must move from the private to the public sphere.
- The scale of an issue does not determine the importance of a social problem.
- Social problems emerge for a variety of immediate reasons. But underlying the concern is usually the perception of a threat to our social structures.

2.4 Threat and perception

In a limited investigation, such as in your college essay, it may not be possible to trace every social problem back to its historical construction in fine detail. Nor to address every aspect of the relationship between social structures and social problems. However, both of these features are important and should be recognised in any analysis, great or small.

Another feature that should also be ever-present is an investigation into the extent to which the social problem is perceived as a threat. This ought to be undertaken in terms of any immediate and explicit threat, as well as one that may be implicit in its relationship to social structures. At stake here is not whether the problem is 'real', as such, but how it might be taken as potentially harmful to social stability or social values or norms.

There is no need to enter into a philosophical debate about whether the problem *really* exists. If social problems were about scale we might be able to do this. Then we could use a purely quantitative measure – using statistics and factual data – to say whether it was real in this empirical sense. Yet, even this would be difficult, as there would be differences of opinion about what number of people an issue had to affect before it became 'real'.

Fortunately we do not need to get into such complex debates. Social problems are defined by our perception of them and the degree to which they are understood as a threat in different ways by different social groups.

Facts and figures may inform us about the extent of a social problem but they are not sufficient alone to create a convincing case of what issues are the most urgent.

Statistics may, for example, inform us of how many people are unemployed and how this might compare to the previous year or decade. The collection of factual information might tell us that a great many of the unemployed are young people, or from a particular minority ethnic group, or are physically impaired. But the figures alone cannot tell us *why* this is the case. They require interpretation and sociological explanations.

Sociological research involves trying to understand people's perceptions and assumptions not only from measurable data but by drawing from a normative position and a selected theoretical framework. When we look at unemployment we not only want to know how many and who, but also if the trends relate to, say, inequalities or social injustice. Is high unemployment among certain minority ethnic groups due to racism? Are so many young people unemployed because of government policy? Is there enough support for disabled people in the workplace?

FAST FORWARD >>>>> 5.4

For a more detailed discussion of unemployment.

These are questions that can be addressed only through social research and investigation using a methodology, theory and quantitative and qualitative methods.

Of course perceptions of a social problem will differ. Social scientists collate these views and come up with *perspectives* which they attribute to different social groups. These perspectives are knowingly generalised and 'ideal'. This means that social scientists understand that it is impossible to transfer the opinions expressed by discrete individuals in their practical lives and package them up into neat little parcels of absolutely accurate views. As soon as you start to take society as an object of study, you change it. The inevitable act of generalising individual opinions into social attitudes turns what is concrete in our experience into something abstract. Sociological concepts cannot capture the infinite refinements of every individual's thought. However, in order to be able to say something worthwhile it is possible, through good quantitative and qualitative research, to bring together a convincing, coherent argument that reflects, in a general way, the observed opinions held by specific social groups. When social scientists construct perspectives on social problems they mainly do so not under the misguided belief that they are 'real', in the sense that they completely and transparently transmit the views held by individuals in practical experience, but they are constructs or 'ideal types'. These are *models*, used for the purposes of comparison, analysis and to help us make sense of the observed discourses in practical experience.

 Key thinker: Max Weber's 'ideal types'

Weber (1864–1920) is one of the so-called founding fathers of sociology. His notion of ideal types is important to grasp in order to understand what it is we are doing when we investigate a social problem. Weber argued that social scientists gather together related social phenomena under one heading. This makes possible generalised, meaningful statements about the world. So it is that when we talk of 'capitalism' everyone understands its general traits, that it is based around a market economy. Weber argued that ideal types were not only useful for important concepts like capitalism, but could also be used to understand and interpret emotions and behaviour. It is in all of these ways that we use them to investigate social problems. Using social research, we construct generalised categories of social attitudes and attribute them to particular social groups, themselves 'ideal types'. So it is that we might try to argue that there is a *conservative* perspective on law and order, and a *liberal* one. The attributes of these perspectives would be set out and examples given of the social groups that might represent these views. In this way, what we have to say on crime comes from observed reality but is formed into an artificial, coherent whole for purposes of analysis.

The job of the social scientist is, then, not to record exactly what every individual thinks but to construct an argument that holds together as accurately as possible for particular 'idealised' social groups. It needs to be theoretically consistent and reflect the social views expressed in quantitative and qualitative research.

In the reading that you will undertake for your classes in social problems you will find that academic authors will present you with various ways of constructing the social problem, using different ideal types abstracted from practical experience. It will be up to you to read these accounts and to understand their arguments and to contrast them. Don't expect these to link together easily. It will be up to you to make the connections. This will be at the centre your own analysis of the social problem.

2.5 Methodology

It has been maintained that an enquiry into social problems is not an exact match to the experiences we have of them in our practical lives. Rather, we

understanding and defining social problems

identify social problems by bringing together general traits of that social experience to construct ideal types. These are categories of social groups and social attitudes that, it can be argued, are significant models that bring together consistent patterns of belief, behaviour and emotions. By establishing these we can then analyse the way that a social problem is perceived as a threat in different ways by different people.

This method does not rely on scale alone or on other empirical measures to denote a social problem. Nor do we have to get into philosophical debates about the reality or otherwise of the problem. If an argument can be made, this is sufficient for us to identify a social problem and to investigate it.

This open-ended way of defining social problems is an approach that can be associated with a particular methodology, that of social construction, which is discussed below.

In the social sciences we use a methodology in order to justify the way that we abstract from social experience in order to explain it. A methodology is an overarching way by which to understand a topic. It enables us to analyse everyday circumstances from another point of view, that of the social scientist. There wouldn't be much point in studying at university if we were merely going to replicate everything that we experienced in practical life. Just as barristers have to have points of law at their fingertips to argue a case, or a doctor the basics of human biology to make a diagnosis, a social scientist has to have a range of methodologies (and theories) to make sense of the world. This is not to 'cure' society of its social ills, as a doctor might with a patient. Neither is it to find a definitive conclusion or solution, as a court might when a person is found guilty or innocent of a crime. As social scientists we use methodologies to try to clear some of the mental fog from our everyday thinking, to bring coherence to what appears in experience: what is normally tied to assumptions, emotions, prejudices, kindly thoughts, stereotypes, common-sense generalisations and other unreflective opinions.

When a natural scientist uses water in an experiment they do not understand it as something to drink. For them it is hydrogen oxide (H_2O), a chemical compound. It is a familiar substance viewed from a different point of view. Similarly, as social scientists we take the experiences and social groups that are familiar to us, but use a different *language* to make sense of them. If you expected to transplant all the opinions and ideas you already have about society into an essay you would have the wrong idea of what studying sociology, social policy, criminology and the social sciences is all about. Just like any other form of study, looking at social problems should make you stop and think. By coming to university you create a halting-station in your experience, a place where there is a chance to reflect. These topics, of drugs and crime, lone parents, poverty, homelessness, migration, unemployment and so on may be familiar to you. But you are coming to study them in an unfamiliar manner, to learn how to enquire into them through the discipline of the social sciences. While thinking of familiar issues in this way may not replace your existing views, it may refine them or cause you to rethink in a more rigorous, reflective, thought-through way.

Although we might make a comparison between the social sciences and the natural sciences we can go only so far. As stated above, when we discuss social problems we are making judgements about what is right and wrong. It is impossible, and not even desirable, to try to be totally objective in what we do. We are studying ourselves and the lives of others. We all come loaded with ideas about the social world. We make normative judgements all the time. Judgements about what we feel are the most important principles upon which to base our actions.

A methodology, such as social construction, helps us to use a coherent and reflective method of investigation. At the same time it allows us to express normative arguments. Debates about social problems can be political, ideological and ethical. But there must be a legitimate way to reach these conclusions. In this sense, for you as students, your conclusions are not the most important part of your work. More important is to make sure that you can illustrate that you understand how to think as a social scientist: how to use methodologies and apply them. As you will see later, you will also need to deploy theory, as well as the right content, to indicate that you know how to use the whole of the 'language' appropriate to investigating social problems.

2.6 Social construction

The methodology that is most suited to an analysis of social problems is that of social construction. This is because it captures most about what we have already said in our search for the meaning of the term 'social problem'. Social problems are fluid, not fixed, even though usually tied to historical debates and fundamental aspects of our social institutions and structures. At its heart social construction maintains that knowledge of the world is a result of the interaction of individuals with their social environment. That environment is made up of family, school, peers, popular culture and sub-cultures, religious belief or non-belief, state institutions and the law. This interaction can be shown to construct a consistency of collective attitudes that is stable enough to translate into perspectives on social problems using qualitative as well as quantitative material.

In this way social problems are constructed in different ways depending upon the social position of the groups articulating them. For an asylum seeker given leave to remain in the UK, immigration is certainly a problem. It means dealing with a strange culture, possibly hostility and racism, and more than likely dirty, dangerous and difficult jobs. For those we might

understanding and defining social problems

describe as conservative on immigration, who would like to see strong immigration controls, asylum seekers may be a social problem because they do not easily integrate into the existing culture, or because they are perceived as a drain on the welfare system, or because they over-extend the population. In different ways these groups, 'asylum seekers' and 'conservatives', construct the problem of immigration very differently. In order to attribute a position to 'asylum seekers' and 'conservatives' in the first place we would have to precede the arguments we wished to associate with them by drawing them out as appropriate social models or ideal types. We would need to bring together quantitative and qualitative information to express what we meant by asylum seekers. This ought to be fairly straightforward, as a great deal of debate has taken place about this particular group.

FAST FORWARD >>>>> 6.5

For a debate about the social construction of political migrants.

Fortunately for you, as students, you (usually) don't have to do the primary research yourselves on this or any of the social problems you will come across. The content of your essays will be based on relating the research already undertaken by academics and, in some, cases campaigning groups, charities, media commentators and policy makers. You will take material from academic sources (textbooks, journals), government statements and policy, media reporting and relevant websites.

Although it may seem daunting to use a methodology to study social problems it is not as difficult as it may at first seem. In the lecture programmes and classes that you will have at university your tutors will highlight the important social groups and the varied social constructions that exist around them. For you as an undergraduate your job is to bring together this existing material. Remember, you do not have to do the actual constructing yourself! Rather, you need be able to show that you comprehend the underlying methodology and theories at play when analysing social problems, as well as wade through the particular content appropriate to your topic.

2.7 Theory

Each topic you will come across will also involve theory. If, as we have acknowledged, we artificially construct social types ('the working-class', 'asylum seekers', 'a conservative perspective') for the purposes of analysis, we then have to have a way of talking about them which is meaningful. This is the 'theory paradox': the categories we work with are *subjective* ones established through argument that may involve normative and politicised judgements. But we also use quantitative and qualitative research to try to be as *objective* as possible in order to have legitimate and significant things to say about contemporary British social problems. We work through this subjective–objective dichotomy by deploying theory. Theory is the conduit for legitimating what we have to say in terms of our subjective arguments and our evidence-based social research.

There are many theories that academics use to unpick the categories constructed from the empirical and qualitative evidence. For example, we may approach the issue of poverty by using a theory of social exclusion, a theory of welfare dependency, a feminist theory, a neo-liberal theory, a theory of the under-class and so it may go on. In the reading that you undertake you will find a whole range of such theories that authors use. In your own work you can decide which of these theories or collections of them you find persuasive. You do not have to come up with your own theories – not unless you are thinking of starting a PhD!

The theory that you use will always be second hand. At an undergraduate level of study it is enough to try to get to grips with other people's theories and to try to nurture your own ability to compare and contrast them. This is the stuff of *analysis* that so often confuses students. When you compare and contrast various authors' theories, this *is* analysis. Pointing out conflicting theories is good analysis. You do not necessarily have to say which theories are 'best'. As stated above, it is the process of reasoning through arguments, not your conclusions, which is most important at this stage.

2.8 Social research: an example

In order to illustrate further the kind of methods, theories and forms of analysis that you will come across in your studies of social problems, below is a brief summary of one particular highly focused piece of social research. This research concerns higher education and minority ethnic students. It is the sort of material you might be guided to read, for example, on the social problem of inequalities relating to some minority ethnic groups and education.

FAST FORWARD >>>>> 7.1

This chapter relates debates about education to the social construction of childhood.

In 'Ethnic Choosing', Ball et al. (2002) undertook a set of interviews (a qualitative study) with minority ethnic students in London. The researchers wanted to find out why these students chose their university. In particular

understanding and defining social problems

they were concerned to understand if the 'ethnic mix' (the degree of cultural diversity among the students) of their university played a part in this choice.

The interview sample group consisted of 30 men and 35 women. There was a wide range of ethnicities, 16 were Jewish, 8 described themselves as Black-British, 7 as mixed race, there were 4 Chinese and a range from different African, West Indian and Asian families. Interviews were also conducted with parents and a questionnaire was answered by a further 502 students.

From gathering all this research material the authors argued that there were two ideal types of higher education students among ethnic minority groups in London. These were *contingent choosers* and *embedded choosers*. These two categories of students represented, in a general way, the main sets of reasons why minority ethnic students chose particular universities. The authors acknowledged that these were hypothetical divisions, not representing an exact fit of any single individual, but 'a step away from reality' (Ball et al., 2002: 217). However, they maintained that the construction of the problem in this way laid the groundwork for more detailed analysis.

For the *contingent choosers* finance was a big issue and choices were made without much information or awareness of differences on offer. Because of a lack of a family tradition in higher education, parental support for choices was weak and at a distance. *Contingent choosers* did see the ethnic mix of the university as a factor in their decision.

For the *embedded choosers* finance was not an issue and choices were based around extensive and diverse sources of information. Parents were heavily involved in the decision making and there was an embedded cultural practice in the family as to how the choice would be made. The choice of university was based around long-term goals and aspirations. The ethnic mix of the university played almost no part in their decision.

Overall the study found that there was not a white/ethnic minority divide in choosing a university. Even when given as a factor for their choice, ethnic mix was only one variable among many. In fact, the study found that social class and educational achievement were more important factors for student choices. In other words, *contingent choosers* tended to be from working-class backgrounds (those from families with little or no higher education experience) and ethnic mix was part of a rather vague and unfocused set of criteria that students used. This contrasted with the more middle-class *embedded choosers* (with a family history of higher education), who were singularly focused upon the university's status and how their choice might impact on their future careers.

The importance of this study for us is not so much the conclusions of the authors but that it is a very good example of the type of social research you will be reading when you study social problems. From this example we hope that you can see the way in which social scientists construct arguments based upon their objective social research and form subjective judgements in the way that they put this research together; in this example arguing that social class is key.

The research that the authors present also has embedded into it a number of the methodological features we have already discussed. The authors explicitly use 'ideal types' as a way of constructing their two social groups. These 'ideal types' are grounded on sound, quantitative and qualitative research. It will not always be the case in the academic texts that you come across that this will be so explicit, even if it is what is happening. But in this study we can clearly see that a particular social construction of minority ethnic students is taking place. *Embedded* and *contingent* choosers are one way of bringing together a range of individuals who come from diverse backgrounds. These categories are based upon an accentuation of particular features that can be legitimately argued to bring them together as sharing collective attitudes.

In this study there are also aspects relating to social institutions and social structures. The conclusion of the research is that family background and social class are more important than ethnicity in relation to choice of university. In this respect even amongst the *contingent choosers* ethnic mix is only one among many factors. This, the authors argued, was a reflection of a working-class background that did not have the necessary knowledge (what is sometimes called 'cultural capital') to understand which factors might be the most important to consider when choosing a university. As we have seen above, social class and the family can be considered part of the fabric upon which our society is built. Part, that is, of our social structures and institutions that give rise to social problems when they are challenged.

Finally, theories of 'race' and racism might be said to underlie this issue. This is not an explicit discussion in the research but can be extrapolated as a matter of analysis. Although the study concludes that ethnic mix is not a prominent issue for most students, many of those interviewed stated that they did want a more diverse university and that was why they were attracted to London. Extrapolating from these comments, it could be argued that further investigation is needed to elicit whether or not this desire for diversity was attached to any kind of perceived threat of racism.

2.9 Newsworthiness

If an area of study is topical, as most of the social problems you come across will be, you may find that during the course of your studies it will be reported in the media. This is one of the advantages of studying social problems. They are contemporary issues and you can expect that new

understanding and defining social problems

material which you can use will arise in at least some of your areas of study. This may be government reports, or reports from campaigning organisations or pressure groups or the police authorities. New policy might also be talked about or implemented around your social problem. Or perhaps a new incident occurs: a vicious knife crime, a rise in unemployment among young adults, greater homelessness or some other newsworthy account that triggers a public debate. Although this media reporting may be beneficial to you in providing you with up-to-date material for your coursework, there are also some pitfalls to watch out for in respect of the newsworthiness of social problems.

We have to be very careful when looking at the media. We have to be particularly careful about media determinism, that is, stating 'the media says' and assuming that what is read, or listened to, or watched totally shapes what people think. Given the multimedia environment in which we live, where information is available from a whole range of visual, printed and internet sources, this is a point of view that cannot easily be sustained. If you were doing a media studies course you would very soon be alerted to the difficulty of translating media opinions into actual effects on attitudes and behaviour (Curran and Seaton 2003: Pt. 4, Ch. 20).

Not least of all this is because each one of us has a distinct social experience. So, if you read a newspaper article that implies most lone parents are committing fraud on the benefit system, but you have been brought up by a hard-working single mum, you are unlikely to believe this type of reporting.

In some cases newsworthiness may be an important factor in making an issue a social problem. Famously, the documentary *Cathy Come Home* was viewed by millions of TV viewers in the 1960s. This single programme is credited with having had the enormous effect of raising people's awareness of homelessness. However, the reliability of media presentations of factual information is variable. The way that statistics, or government policy, or a particular event are reported may not be entirely accurate. A social policy, for example, will tend to be highlighted for what is most sensational or headline grabbing. But this might not be the most important part of that particular policy as far as welfare research is concerned.

It is important to be aware that debates started because they are newsworthy always need to be examined in more detail. Take the case of one social problem that has been debated in the UK over the last few years, the issue of so-called binge drinking among young people. TV programmes have been produced about this, pages of newspaper copy devoted to the revelations and medical experts brought in to discuss the implications for the future health problems of a generation. Yet all the credible research indicates that while the health- and socially related problems of alcohol may be a concern among the under-24s, it is a problem that is more than *ten times* greater for the affluent and those aged over 55 (Alcohol Harm Map 2012). Yet there are no sensationalist fly-on-the-wall documentaries made about middle-aged, middle-income drinkers having a bottle or two of wine every evening with their dinner. It wouldn't make for very exciting TV. Yet this is a better image of where these problems lie than the falling-over, puking young people that appear on our small screens.

2.10 Summary

In this chapter we have defined and understood social problems in three main ways: from the point of view of the discipline of social science; from the point of view of you, the student; and from the point of view of other social actors.

The understanding of social problems set out here from the point of view of the discipline of social science is that there is no fixed or absolute way of defining the term. When a sociologist or criminologist wants to identify a social problem they have to do so by arguing their case. This case has to be based on primary research, either their own or that of other academics. The social research will normally involve some statistics or data (quantitative analysis) and some form of collating together social attitudes (qualitative analysis). Even though this kind of rigorous academic technique is employed, there is no pretence that the endeavour is without subjective judgements. The reason why university lecturers are drawn to research social problems is because they have a social concern, they care passionately about social issues. This may not always reveal itself in the way that they write, as the discipline requires a highly tuned technical knowledge and ability. However, even if the writing can sometimes seem dull, academics will always bring something of themselves into their work. Political, social and ethical judgements will be made to state an argument about the social problem that is identified. These arguments have to be sustained in the methodology that they use and the coherence of the theories which they draw upon. Competing arguments have to be engaged with. The whole purpose of the scholarly exploration is to try to genuinely engage with the social evidence, to think through its many different aspects and ultimately construct a point of view. However, the goal is not to 'solve' the problem. This is not something that academics (or anyone) can realistically achieve. All that those working from this disciplinary approach can hope for is to add their voice to public debate.

For you as a student, your job is to read and try to understand the methodologies, theories and social research of social scientists as they apply to various social problems. Through the lecture and seminar programme at your university you should come to understand that there is a body of literature, written in another language – that of social science – that you need to learn. The topics you come across may be ones that you are familiar with, but the way that you will need to come to think about them will have to be altered if you are to succeed. This is not an easy task. It is not only the descriptive detail of particular topics that a student needs to grapple with, but also you have to acquire the tools of the social scientist's trade in order to explain and analyse them. You need to indicate in your coursework that you understand that social problems can be constructed in different ways, that there are competing perspectives, but also that there may be similarities that can be identified. And all this in an essay that is usually only around 1500/2000 words long!

As well as the academic analysis, statements about social problems come from other social actors: politicians, various media, pressure groups, campaigning organisations, charities, interested public figures, think-tanks and so on. All these voices may legitimately feature as part of your research. Of all of these other sources of commentary, policy content and media coverage will almost always be a part of any analysis. How government policy, past and present, has responded to a social problem will be an important component, and as it is generally newsworthy there will also tend to be media coverage of social problems. These accounts, from government in terms of policy making, or the media in terms of reporting, may not be situated on the same ground as academic concerns. For example, whereas politicians and the popular press might generally emphasise *standards* in education debates, academics might argue that *inequalities* and underlying differences in educational achievement are more important. The social construction of the problem by other social actors will generally not be based on such rigorous research material as that used by scholars. Rather, ideology, opinion, prejudice and personal experience will inform these points of view.

Revision notes

Social problems are distinct and yet tied to other types of problems. Social problems are a particular way of understanding the social issues that emerge in public life. They may be distinguished from individual problems which are largely a matter for the private sphere. However, private matters can become public concerns if a collective threat is perceived. Social problems may also be distinguished from economic issues. Economic models and theories cannot explain the historical and sociological reasons for social problems. However, significant economic change can be part of the reasons for the emergence of a social problem, such as poverty. Social problems are not necessarily associated with government intervention. But discussing social problems does involve making political judgements about the kind of society we believe is just.

Social problems are contemporary and culturally embedded. Social problems come and go as public discussion shifts. These changes may be tied to what is currently going on in British society, cultural shifts such as greater ethnic diversity or the rise of insecurity in the workplace. However, social problems almost always have a history to them. They are connected in some way to on-going debates about key social structures and institutions.

Threat and perception. Identifying social problems cannot be done using a purely empirical measure. The scale of the problem is no indication of its public importance. This means that the significance of a particular social problem becomes a matter of argument and debate. The most convincing arguments are based on social research, where the assumptions of the author are made explicit.

Social construction. This is the methodological perspective that is most conducive to the study of social problems. Social scientists abstract collective identities from practical experience. To these identities (be they 'asylum seekers', 'lone parents', 'liberals', 'contingent choosers' or whatever) they ascribe particular social attitudes. This is done in order to make meaningful statements about the social world. However, social scientists undertake this task using a clear methodology and theoretical framework. Other social actors (politicians, media commentators, pressure group representatives and so on) tend to do so in a less self-reflective and analytical mode.

The role of social science. As students of criminology, social policy, sociology or any of the social sciences, our task is to try to identify the assumptions built into the discourses surrounding social problems; that is, to attempt to explain the way that the meanings and definitions implied in the language used about certain social groups are loaded with assumptions; and to try to construct more rigorous explanations of social problems using the tools of social science. In short, to turn what is an unexamined social problem into an examined one.

Seminar tasks

Social construction

1 Issue:
There is a common-sense view of social problems and issues, that somehow problems and issues are clearly understood and have a single meaning. However, from the discussion above we can see that this is not the case. Different social groups will have varied assumptions about the people and issues involved in a particular social problem.

understanding and defining social problems

Coursework questions

How can we define a social problem?

In what ways does social construction help us to analyse social problems?

What normative judgements are made when identifying a social problem?

References

Arendt, H., *The Human Condition*, London: University of Chicago Press, 1958

Ball, S.J., Reay, D. and David, M., '"Ethnic Choosing": minority ethnic students, social class and higher education choice', *Race Ethnicity and Education*, 2003, 5(4): 333–57, in *Education Policy and Social Class: the selected works of Stephen J. Ball*, London: Routledge, 2002

Curran, J. and Seaton, J., *Power Without Responsibility* (6th edn), London: Routledge, 2003

Mills, C. Wright, *The Sociological Imagination*, London: Oxford University Press, 1959

Crisis, n.d. *The National Charity for Single Homeless People*, http://www.crisis.org.uk/pages/rough-sleeping.html

Alcohol Harm Map, 2012, *Age Concern*, http://www.alcoholconcern.org.uk/campaign/alcohol-harm-map

Further reading

There are very few books that cover the issues discussed in this section, hence the need for this textbook! In fact, there is only one chapter in one single UK centred text that covers the methodological issues outlined here.

May, M., Page, R., Brunsden, E. (eds), 'Social Problems: sociological perspectives', John Clarke in *Understanding Social Problems: issues in social policy*, Oxford: Blackwell, 2001

Other than that, this further reading section is really a 'don't further read' section. There are a great many American texts on social problems. Very few employ an approach that would be compatible to the way the subject is taught in British universities. For example, Kornblum, W. and Julian, J., *Social Problems* (Pearson 2011), now in its 14th edition, is heavily situated in an American tradition which is not very helpful for UK centred social problems. However, with cautious reading there are one or two chapters in a few textbooks that touch on basic methodological and theoretical issues that might be useful.

Horsfall, S.A., 'What Is a Social Problem?' Section 1, Chapter 1, in *Social Problems: an advocate group approach*, Colorado: Westfield Press, 2012.

Macionis, J.J., 'Sociology: studying social problems', Chapter 1, in *Social Problems* (4th edn), London: Pearson, 2010.

Rubington, E. and Weinberg, M., 'Social Problems and Sociology,' Part 1, Chapter 1, and 'Social Constructionism', Part 2, Chapter 8, in *The Study of Social Problems: seven perspectives*, London: Oxford University Press, 2002.

chapter 3

Researching social problems

Anne Foley

3.1 Introduction

Research is central to life at university and it is important to learn the basics early in your studies in order to get off to a good start. Essentially, research is the systematic investigation into phenomena with the aim of establishing facts and reaching new conclusions. There are many different levels of research which this chapter will not describe in any depth, as numerous excellent guides to research in general are published every year. A number of these are listed in the Further Reading section at the end of this chapter.

The role of research in the area of social problems is to attempt to understand the assumptions surrounding social problems, to describe the issues, to look for causal relationships between particular factors and to begin to outline a more thorough explanation of the construction of social problems. Having done this, the research can lead towards, if not solutions, then a more comprehensive appreciation of why and how social problems emerge into the public sphere and how government and other agencies respond.

3.2 Primary and secondary research

Primary research involves the researcher directly collecting original data by methods such as interviews, surveys, questionnaires and focus groups. Before carrying out primary research, the researcher will usually have done some secondary research into their topic by carrying out a literature review. A literature review is an appraisal of published works in a topic area and the scope of the review is dependent on the extent of the enquiry being carried out. The literature review informs and supports the research.

In order to carry out a rigorous literature review, it is necessary to develop the ability to plan and execute effective literature searches. Undergraduate students may be required to carry out a limited amount of primary research during their studies but, typically, secondary research in the form of literature searches for essays and literature reviews is more common. For essays and other coursework, regardless of the scope, students need to carry out literature searches to identify literature that will inform and underpin their analysis of an issue and provide evidence for claims and arguments. This chapter focuses on the skills and knowledge necessary to carry out effective literature searches, as well as outlining the range of literature students are likely to encounter during their studies.

3.3 Introduction to literature types and uses

Success in assessments and study develops from critical interaction with a wide range of literature. To begin this process, it is necessary to become familiar with the types of literature available in, and appropriate to, academic contexts.

The literature is made up of a broad range of material, available either in print or online, written by individuals and/or groups. The literature can be divided into two general areas, academic literature (also called scholarly literature) and non-academic, which comprises popular literature and trade or professional literature. The main sources of literature are:

> Books: textbooks, readers, monographs
> Journal articles
> Conference papers
> Grey literature: reports, white papers, policy documentation
> News media

Academic books are not all the same; they have various features and purposes, depending on the category to which they belong. This section will help in learning to identify the characteristics and intended use of different types of book.

Textbooks. Textbooks provide a comprehensive overview of a subject and are written for student readers. They are useful for those unfamiliar with a specific subject or topic and provide introductions to key theories and context. As the purpose of textbooks is mainly introductory, and therefore general in nature, they are best used as launchpads for more in-depth study. Textbooks contain comprehensive reading lists and references to original works in topic areas. Example: Giddens, A. (2013) *Sociology*. 7th edn. Cambridge: Polity Press.

Readers/handbooks. These provide an in-depth view of a subject and are the work of several authors. They provide different perspectives on topics and are essential for critical examination of these topics. Handbooks are compiled by an editor or editors, who choose the handbook's content. Editors may or may not contribute chapters but always provide an introduction. Example: Greve, B. (2012) *Routledge Handbook of the Welfare State*. London: Routledge.

Subject-specific and general reference books. Reference books are used for precise information such as the correct spelling and meaning of a word, the exact meaning of a phrase within a specific discipline or synonyms (alternative words) and similar words. Examples:

Language dictionaries (e.g. *Oxford English Dictionary*)
Subject-specific dictionaries (e.g. *Dictionary of Social Policy* or *Dictionary of Sociology*)
Thesauri (e.g. *The Oxford Thesaurus*).

In the study of social problems other reference books may be useful; these include directories, which give details of organisations and people. An example of a directory is the *DWP Public Bodies Directory* published by the UK Department of Work and Pensions (DWP), which gives details of public bodies sponsored by the DWP. Also, public groups publish directories and/ or handbooks. For example, *Welfare Benefits and Tax Credits Handbook* produced annually by the Child Poverty Action Group.

Monographs. In an academic context, the word monograph usually refers to a scholarly work that covers a single topic in depth, usually reporting the findings of primary research carried out by the author. Monographs are written mainly for an audience of academics and postgraduates and, as their focus is typically narrow, they may be of limited use to undergraduate students. However, monographs are generally excellent for a thorough exploration of a topic.

Grey literature. The term 'grey literature' refers to published and unpublished research and reports not controlled by commercial publishing groups. Grey literature is produced by governments, commercial and public organisations and private individuals and can be in print or electronic format. Significant sources of grey literature in the area of social problems are government documents and research reports produced by public organisations such as the Joseph Rowntree Foundation.

Conference papers and proceedings. Conference papers are produced by researchers from, amongst others, university research institutes, advocacy groups and professional organisations and detail the findings of specific research carried out by that researcher or group. At conferences, researchers present papers detailing their research findings and these may then be published either as individual papers in journals or in volumes. The volumes of collected papers are called *conference proceedings* and may be available on the website of the producing organisation. Conference papers may be published in journals or written up as monographs.

News media. Newspapers and other news media can be very useful but are not academic literature. The advantages of using newspapers for information when researching social problems are many; for example, you could compare how different types of newspapers (tabloid and broadsheet or those considered right wing or left wing) report on issues such as single mothers, poverty or youth crime. You may notice a sometimes subtle, sometimes blatant, difference between the positions taken on these topics by different newspapers. Also, newspapers can provide a good historical overview of a particular issue. Most universities provide access to news databases, such as NexisUK, which can be searched for articles in a topic area.

Journals. These are a key resource for students and researchers, and learning how to locate and use articles from journals in your subject area is a skill best learned early in your studies. From experience, I am aware that many students find journals difficult to understand, to find and to use. The prominence given to journals in this chapter reflects this. The advantages of using journal articles in your research are the following.

> They contain up-to-date information and debate on current topics in your subject area.
> They contain specialised information that may not be available elsewhere.
> They describe research by experts in your subject area.
> Many academic journal articles are peer-reviewed before publication. This means that the articles in them have a guarantee of quality, as they have been scrutinised and approved by other experts in the subject area.
> The works cited in articles are a useful source of further relevant information.

3.4 How journals are organised

A journal, also referred to as a periodical or serial, is a publication produced on a continuing basis. New issues may be published monthly,

researching social problems

quarterly or bi-annually. The non-academic equivalent to a journal is a magazine, such as *The New Statesman*. The titles of journals, for example *Critical Social Policy*, usually give a good indication of the general focus of the subject matter to be found in the articles within. As they are published on a regular basis, journals have volume and issue numbers to help identify and locate them. The *Volume* number usually covers a specific year (e.g., 2008 may be Volume 45) and the *Issue* number refers to a specific instalment of the journal within that volume – i.e. Issue 1 or 2 or 3 etc., depending on how many times per year the journal is published. Sometimes the month of publication is used instead of an issue number. This information is key to locating specific articles.

There are two main types of journal.

Academic journals (also called scholarly journals) usually contain research articles written by subject specialists, scholarly commentary and critical evaluation of issues by experts, articles written in academic style. Most academic articles are peer reviewed, which means they have been evaluated by independent subject experts. Examples: *Critical Social Policy* or *Sociology: a Journal of the British Sociological Association*.

Trade or professional journals these usually contain news articles and commentary on current issues. Articles are written in everyday language; they have practical information and often a 'jobs' section. Example: *Sociology Review, Children and Young People Now*.

Each issue of a journal contains several articles, written by subject experts or researchers or practitioners within the subject area. The title 'British Journal of Sociology', for example, indicates that this journal contains articles relating to all aspects of sociology. The title '*British Journal of Sociology of Education*' indicates that this journal contains articles within the sub-topic of education in sociology. Not all journals, as you can see from the example above, have the word *journal* in the title.

There are three main types of article.

Commentary/debate: an author perhaps describing or evaluating a piece of legislation relating to a specific social group or critically examining and commenting on several pieces of previous research.

Primary (or empirical) research: the author/s have carried out first-hand research, for example interviewing a group of young men about gang membership, and are presenting, describing, evaluating and drawing conclusions from their research.

Review articles: the author summarises, synthesises and draws conclusions from the published works of other authors.

The typical layout of a journal article reporting research looks something like the example below, but not all are laid out in this exact way.

Title: indicating/describing the subject covered in the article.

Author/s: name/s and, often, their credentials/qualifications and place of work/affiliation.

Abstract: a summary of the article describing the article's purpose, research method (where relevant), findings and conclusions.

Keywords: words used to describe the main topics within the article. These are used for various reasons, e.g. when scanning for relevance of the article to your own studies or to help retrieve the article from an online database.

Introduction: sets the scene; describes what the article is about, what problem/issue is being addressed in the article.

Section heading: detailed statement of the problem/issue being addressed. The title of the heading should indicate the specific sub-topic being described in that section.

Literature review: this section details literature related to the issue being addressed and how it informs the current work. Not all articles have a separate literature review section, but most research articles do.

Research methodology and/or method: (if the article is describing research) this section describes the methodology and/or method applied to the research. It may also highlight key theories (such as feminism, multiculturalism) that are used in the paper.

Findings: if the article is describing research, this section details the results of the research.

Conclusion/discussion/recommendations: this section summarises the conclusions drawn from the research (if a research article), it discusses the implications of the research findings for the topic area and may recommend further research.

References: an alphabetical list, by author, of the sources (e.g. books, journal articles, reports and statistics) referred to (cited) in the article.

3.5 Evaluating journal articles

This is a guide to a basic critical evaluation of a journal article. When evaluating an article, the main questions are as follows.

Is the article relevant to the topic you are researching?
Is the content of the article reliable?

To answer these questions, examine the article, asking the following questions:

What is the main issue being discussed? Is this issue significant/relevant to the topic you are researching? The abstract and/or keywords will usually provide enough evidence to help you decide.

Is the article related to the UK (geographical context)? This is of significance to many courses in the social sciences, as government policy and practice issues are country specific. However, if you are doing a comparison between the UK and another country you will obviously need articles relating to that country. The abstract, keywords or references made in the main content of the article will indicate the geographical context.

Does the author provide their credentials (authority)? Do these credentials indicate that this author has the expertise or experience to write on this topic? This can be established either alongside the author's name, under the title of the article, or in the main content of the article.

What are the major concepts discussed in the article? Is the article dealing in depth with issues relating to the topic you are researching? Also, you may need to establish the theoretical standpoint or approach of the author, such as critical, feminist, Marxist – or a combination of theoretical standpoints. Sometimes the author will state her/his theoretical standpoint, but often this is implicit in the text.

What are the important facts presented in the article? To quickly establish this, look at the conclusion, as this is where the facts and findings are summarised.

Can you verify the facts presented by the author in the article? A scholarly/academic article will have citations within the text, used to provide evidence of claims made, and a reference list providing full details of the sources of these citations.

What conclusion does the author come to about the main issue? Do these conclusions match your own (or other authors' works you have read) views on the issue? If not, are the arguments good enough to make you reconsider your own views? If not, can you find evidence from other articles or sources to support your views? Do they make a more persuasive argument and, if so, why?

What are the arguments presented as evidence of, or supporting, the conclusions drawn at the end of the article? Do the facts presented by the author support the arguments? A good scholarly article will present the evidence in a clear, systematic manner, laying out each issue and describing exactly how the evidence proves the claim the author is making in the conclusion. Sometimes the author's conclusion is that the research has not provided clear evidence to support an issue and recommends that further research is necessary.

Does the author use emotional words or phrases or is the article written in a neutral manner? A good academic/scholarly article should not use emotional terminology or words in order to influence the reader into accepting the author's views. An argument written in a neutral, emotionless manner, presenting evidence for claims made, is a key element of a good academic article.

3.6 How to recognise a journal article reference (Harvard referencing style)

Figure 3.1 is an example of a journal article reference. It is important that you recognise the journal title, as this is what you will need in order to search your library catalogue.

Journal article references can be easily distinguished from book references, as book references do not have a Volume and Issue number. There is no place of publication or name of publisher in a journal article reference, as there is in a book reference.

For comparison, Figure 3.2 is a book reference.

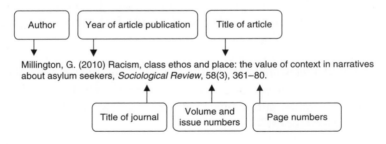

Millington, G. (2010) Racism, class ethos and place: the value of context in narratives about asylum seekers, *Sociological Review*, 58(3), 361–80.

Figure 3.1 Journal article reference.

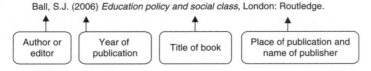

Ball, S.J. (2006) *Education policy and social class*, London: Routledge.

Figure 3.2 Book reference.

researching social problems

Finding a journal article via a library catalogue

The key to finding a journal article is to first locate the journal title. The process is similar to finding a chapter in a book: when you need to find a particular chapter in a book, you search for the book's title first, not the chapter. First search for the journal title. When you have located that, then find year when the article was published, then the volume number, then the issue number, then the page numbers. When you have familiarised yourself with how a journal reference is laid out (see above), finding an article is easy. Most online library catalogues have a specific area for journal searches.

Most journals are available online, usually accessible via your library catalogue with a username and password. Databases in this context are searchable collections of journal articles: enter keywords or phrases into the database search boxes to retrieve articles related to your topic. Some databases are subject specific; *PsyARTICLES*, for example, is a database of scholarly literature in the field of psychology. Some databases are multidisciplinary; *Academic Search Complete*, for example, is a database of scholarly literature in the social sciences, humanities and sciences. Databases are searched using keywords or phrases, rather than sentences. Extract the keywords and phrases from your topic and use these to retrieve articles from a variety of journals. No single database will have the full text of every article published on a topic. Some databases, such as IBSS (International Bibliography of the Social Sciences) may provide no full-text access but are invaluable for locating information about published articles. These are known as indexing and abstracting databases or services.

3.7 Government documents: Green Papers, White Papers, Bills and Acts of Parliament

Government documents are a key resource in the study of social problems and most are available online, on government websites. When researching homelessness in the UK, for example, it is important to be familiar with legislation related to statutory homelessness, such as the 1996 Housing Act and the Homelessness Act 2002. The text of these documents and all other UK legislation is available on the legislation.gov.uk website. During the process of enacting an Act of Parliament, Green Papers, White Papers and Bills are produced by the government. Green Papers are the first step, setting out the government's objectives in a particular area, and the public are invited to comment on these. *Quality and Choice: Decent Homes for All* (2000) is an example of a Green Paper. The next step is the White Paper, a more detailed document, which incorporates comments and further research. *Building Britain's Recovery: Achieving Full*

Employment (2009) is an example of a White Paper detailing the UK government's plan to tackle unemployment. The next step is the Bill. Bills are discussed in the House of Lords and the House of Commons and a vote is taken on whether to pass these. When a Bill is passed it becomes an Act of Parliament. In the Queen's Speech of 2013 several new Bills were announced, these included the Immigration Bill, the Offender Rehabilitation Bill and the Anti-social Behaviour: Crime and Policing Bill.

3.8 Statistical data

Statistical data are a key resource in the study and research of social problems. The ONS (Office for National Statistics) is the main source of data relating to the population of the UK in areas such as health, education, ethnicity, housing, families, household spending and unemployment. A census is carried out in the UK every ten years (the last one was in 2011), during which every home receives a questionnaire; the responses are collated by the ONS and the results are published online. In addition to census data, the ONS publish statistics on crime, business and the economy, transport and more. This data is used to inform policy making at a national and local level. Use the data available on the ONS website to support your arguments in essays and other coursework. When using statistics, ensure that you understand exactly what is being examined and what claims are being made in relation to the data.

3.9 Primary and secondary sources

Primary sources are contemporaneous accounts of events, written by people who witnessed the events. Some examples of primary sources are diaries, interviews, speeches, personal journals, photographs, film recordings and biographies. Secondary sources are less easy to define than primary sources: essentially, secondary sources make use of existing data and many books and journal articles are often interpretations of primary data. The data has been collected by somebody other than the author, who assembles and interprets the data for his or her own purpose. Some examples of secondary sources are textbooks, journal articles, encyclopaedias, histories and reviews.

3.10 Reading at university

The main tasks for you as a student at university are reading, researching and writing. Writing critically about a topic requires an understanding of the topic, which does not come from lectures or seminars alone. A report on research carried out at the University of Huddersfield (Stone, Pattern and Ramsden 2012) showed that students who borrowed most books and accessed most online resources got higher grades. Of course it isn't enough to just borrow a book or log in to an online journal or e-book: the literature has to be read critically in order to be useful. Reading at university is an acquired skill and there are many good books and websites available to help students to develop their reading skills. Most universities provide study skills guides and classes or workshops. Check out your university website or ask your librarian for information on these. Though the amount of reading at university can seem daunting, learning reading techniques will make the task much more manageable and maybe even allow some time for a social life.

3.11 Researching social problems: planning and carrying out a literature search

The task of researching for essays or other coursework can be approached in a systematic manner, whatever the subject or scope.

Developing a search strategy is arguably the most important part of any literature search. A well-considered search strategy saves time and returns the best available results. Keep the question 'what do I need to know?' in mind when planning and reading, and review your search strategy regularly. Ask yourself what the key themes are and note down the answers. If you are unsure of any aspect of an assessment, ask your tutor. As you progress through your research it is easy to lose focus and thus get diverted from your original goals. Review your progress regularly and return to your themes when reviewing any literature you find in your research. Ask yourself if the literature helps to answer the question and serve as evidence to support an argument you want to make.

The first task in a good literature search is to carry out a thorough analysis of your topic.

> Extract the keywords and/or phrases and consider alternative words or phrases (synonyms) associated with these. You will use these words and phrases, rather than sentences, when doing your literature search.
> Next, consider whether any of these words or phrases needs a specific definition. For example, the topics of homelessness or poverty are not clear-cut issues. Are you researching rough sleeping, those who live in hostels, those who sofa-surf etc.? How will you define poverty?
> Are you focusing on a particular age range in the population?
> What geographical area are you focusing on? Do you want to find literature relating to the whole of the UK, to England only, to a city such as London only, or to a borough within the city?

Table 3.1 Planning a search strategy: resources

Library resources	Web resources
Books/E-books: List relevant books here.	Google Advanced Search: for reports from organisations, government documents etc. Use site/domain search to limit results to specific websites.

Databases: to find several journal articles on your topic, from various academic journals, for example:
    Academic Search Complete
    IBSS
    Sociological Research Online
	Google Scholar: for summaries of journal articles and books. Also possible to set up links to your university library collections and get direct access to full text, where available.

Individual journals in your subject area, such as:
    Journal of Social Policy
    Race and Class
    British Journal of Sociology
    Critical Social Policy
	Office for National Statistics: for national or regional statistics. Neighbourhood Statistics section is useful for local data.
	
	Zanran Numerical Data: for reports and other documents containing numerical data in your topic area.

Are you looking for particular methodological and theoretical stand-points or approaches? For example, social construction, functionalism, communitarianism, cosmopolitanism.

What do you already know about this topic? Did you attend a lecture or seminar on the topic? Have you got notes from these? Have you got a recommended reading list from your tutor?

When you have completed your initial topic definition you should then turn your attention to a consideration of the resources you will use in your research. It is helpful to consider these in the manner laid out in Table 3.1, with resources available via your library in one column and web resources in the other.

Search techniques

Using search techniques can save time and ensure that searches retrieve relevant results.

Phrase search. This is a useful technique when you want to retrieve literature containing a specific phrase. Using quotation marks at the beginning and end of the phrase, such as 'hidden homeless' or 'social problems'

researching social problems

ensures that the words are retrieved adjacent to each other, exactly as you entered them.

Boolean searching: using AND, OR, NOT. You can broaden or narrow a search using the Boolean operators, AND, OR and NOT. For example, if you are searching for literature on the topic 'homelessness amongst young people in England', but want to limit your results to literature relating to the 'hidden homeless', Boolean searching can help to retrieve more relevant results.

> *AND*: using this limits the search; results will have both phrases.
> Example: 'young people' AND 'hidden homeless'
>
> *OR*: using this expands the search.
> Example: 'young people' AND 'hidden homeless' OR 'sofa surfing'

This search will retrieve literature related to surfing, and therefore more results.

> *NOT*: this allows you to eliminate results that you are not interested in.
> Example: 'young people' AND 'sofa surfing' NOT 'rough sleeping'.

Truncation. Using a symbol at the end of a word stem will retrieve all variants of the word. Example: **educat*** will retrieve the words educate, *education, educational, educator* and other derivatives.

Wildcard. This is similar to truncation but only one letter is replaced. The most common symbol used in truncation is **?** but **!** is also used. Example: organi**?**ation will retrieve examples of both spellings of this word, *organization* and *organisation*.

Nesting. This is an effective way to limit results by using brackets (parentheses). Example: (hidden homeless OR sofa surfing) AND 'young people'

The phrases in brackets will be searched for first and the Boolean OR is generally used.

3.12 Using search engines and reliable websites for research

A search engine is a piece of software used to search the World Wide Web (www). Google is the most popular search engine but is not the only one.

Other examples are Bing, Alta Vista, Yahoo (Directory Search). Meta-search engines bring together the top results from other search engines. Some examples of these are WebCrawler, MetaCrawler and Dogpile. Google has some very useful features for students, such as Google Scholar, Google Advanced Search and Google Books.

Google Scholar can be a good way to begin your research, to find journal articles, books and other academic literature in your topic area. It does not usually provide full-text articles, just abstracts or summaries of articles. However, it may be possible to set up links to your university library collections and get direct access to full text, where available. If not, when you find a journal article abstract that looks relevant, search your university's library catalogue for the journal. If the library subscribes to it you may be able to access the whole article. The same applies to books found on Google Scholar and Google Books.

Google Books searches only for books and often provides a preview of sections of these. Use the search techniques listed above to refine searches.

Google Advanced Search allows for more refined searching of the web. This is crucial as not all websites provide reliable information. One of the most useful functions on Google Advanced Search is the site or domain search, which searches specific sites only. When looking for government documents, which can be difficult, searching the domain *.gov.uk* limits results to UK government websites only. Similarly, use *.nhs.uk* for health information or, if you want to find documents from a local authority, for example the London Borough of Tower Hamlets, use *towerhamlets.gov.uk*. Advanced Search also has the ability to limit searches to specific date ranges, countries, reading level and file types.

Using the main Google search can also be useful for research, but be aware that not all websites are reliable or relevant to university-level studies. Tutors take a dim view of student work that references random websites. Instead of randomly searching Google for information on a topic, get to know the reliable subject websites and use these. Often your tutors will list these along with the recommended reading for a subject.

3.13 Managing the literature search

When undertaking a literature search it is a good idea to keep records of searches undertaken from the outset. Use a table or worksheet similar to that in Table 3.2, listing the keywords and phrases you have used and the resources (databases, journals, books etc.) you have searched. This will save time and help you to stay focused on the search topic.

It is a good idea to begin taking note of references as soon as you identify the relevant literature. It is easy to lose this vital information and this may result in charges of plagiarism if you paraphrase or quote directly from

Table 3.2 Managing the literature search

Date	Keywords/ phrases	Academic search complete	Socio-logical research online	IBSS	Dawsonera e-book	Critical social policy	Google scholar
21 March 2013	'Youth crime' AND 'gangs'			X	X		X
23 March 2013	'youth justice' AND 'inequalities' OR 'discri-mination'	X	X		X	X	

the literature without attribution. There are many ways of doing this, ranging from using reference management software such as *End Note* or *Ref-Works* to simply noting the details in a Word document. Check with your tutor or librarian for information about the software available to you. When saving downloaded articles or reports, organise these in folders and files, perhaps a separate file for each section of an essay. Additionally, always use the same naming format when saving downloaded items: use author's name and date, for example. Organising your literature in this way will ensure that you can find things easily when writing up your work and you won't waste time saving duplicate copies.

3.14 Plagiarism and referencing

Many students new to university are concerned that their tutors will not approve of using citations and references in their coursework as it looks like they have no original ideas. This is not the case. Citing the work of authors, and using these as evidence to strengthen your own arguments, is considered the best practice for students and researchers. Read a journal article or a subject handbook for evidence of how citations and references are abundantly used in the work of scholarly authors. Authors do this to acknowledge the work of others, work that has helped to inform their own work.

By not referring to the literature you have used, and not using citations when you have quoted or paraphrased from the literature, you are committing plagiarism. Plagiarism can be avoided by learning how to reference and cite correctly in written coursework.

Plagiarism is commonly defined as deliberately or accidentally taking someone else's work or ideas and passing them off as your own. Plagiarism is taken very seriously by academic institutions and penalties for those who plagiarise range, depending on the seriousness of the offence, from expulsion to being required to re-submit assessed work. Plagiarism takes many forms and some common examples are:

copying the work of another student
copying and pasting from websites
paraphrasing from a source without providing a citation
incorrect information in references
not using quotation marks when quoting from a source
changing some words from the work of another and presenting the result as your own work.

3.15 Collusion

Collusion is the unauthorised presentation of the work of another student, in whole or in part, for formal assessment. Students are very often required to work together in small groups, frequently to prepare presentations for assessment. These are authorised collaborative assessments and, as such, are not collusion. However, when students work together on a piece of individual coursework and then submit identical work, in whole or in part, then they are considered guilty of collusion. Working with other students, such as in study groups, is a very effective way to learn but formally assessed coursework submitted must be the work of the individual student. Deliberately submitting somebody else's work, or allowing somebody else to submit your work, is collusion and penalties for this are usually the same as penalties for plagiarism.

3.16 What is referencing and citation?

Referencing is the practice of acknowledging the sources you have referred to in your coursework. There are several different styles of referencing, but the Harvard system of referencing is generally used in the social sciences, with the exception of psychology. In the UK most universities have their own referencing guides. If you are unsure about which specific guide is recommended, check with your course leader. Harvard referencing has two parts: the reference list and in-text citations.

Citations are abbreviated details of sources you have used in your essay and are used within the text of the essay. If you have quoted, paraphrased or referred to the work of another person in your written work, you must cite the work you have referred to. Full details of the work are then placed in your *Reference* list at the end of your work. Your recommended referencing guide should have details of the exact format required for in-text citations.

Many students new to university find referencing confusing and begin to wonder if they should reference almost every sentence they write in essays. Obviously this doesn't make sense as a certain amount of every essay will comprise what is known as common knowledge. Common knowledge could be described as facts known to a large number of people, facts that are easily accessible. To help clarify whether what you are writing is common knowledge or not, ask yourself if you were aware of the fact/s before you started your studies. For example, the fact that Britain is a welfare state does not need to be referenced in an essay, as this is a generally known fact. If, however, a student writes in detail about the foundations of the British welfare state, the student would have had to carry out some research relating to this era. Details about it such as the reforms put in place by the Liberal Party in the early 1900s, and descriptions of some of the Acts of Parliament from this era, such as the Children Act 1908, would therefore come from literature the student had read and this literature would need to be referenced.

3.17 Your academic librarian

Almost all UK universities have subject specialist librarians whose role is to support students with their information and research needs. Wise students get to know their librarian early in their studies. Your subject librarian will support your studies by recommending resources for your essay topics and show you how to search library resources such as the library catalogue, databases and journals. They can advise on referencing issues, and on devising search strategies for literature searches. As well as offering individual support to students, teaching classes in the use of library resources and purchasing the books and journals on your reading lists, academic librarians create online guides for students in their subject areas. These subject guides are usually available on the library web pages and list key library and web resources in various subject areas.

3.18 Digital literacy and information literacy

Both digital literacy and information literacy are essential attributes for study, research, work and lifelong learning. Information literacy involves knowing how to find, evaluate, use, manage and communicate information. Digital literacy involves finding, organising, managing and communicating information by means of digital technology. This chapter has outlined the skills and knowledge necessary to become information literate and these skills can be transferred and used to plan any essay or other task requiring information gathering. Digital literacy encompasses the attributes of information literacy and also the ability use digital communication tools and to carry out tasks in a digital environment. It is important to learn how to effectively use all of the ICT tools you come across in your studies, including your VLE (virtual learning environment), to be aware of how you are representing yourself on social media sites and to communicate effectively and appropriately using digital technology.

References

Stone, G., Pattern, D. and Ramsden, B., 'Library impact data project', *SCONUL Focus 54*, 25–28, 2012. Available from: http://www.sconul.ac.uk/sites/default/files/documents/8_0.pdf [Accessed 7 June 2013]

Further reading

Bryman, A., *Social Research Methods* (4th edn), Oxford: Oxford University Press, 2012

Burns, T. and Sinfield, S., *Essential Study Skills: the complete guide to success at university* (3rd edn), London: Sage, 2012

Cottrell, S., *The Study Skills Handbook* (4th edn), Basingstoke: Palgrave Macmillan, 2013

Cottrell, S., *Critical Thinking Skills: developing effective analysis and argument* (2nd edn), Basingstoke: Palgrave Macmillan, 2011

Gilbert, N. (ed.), *Researching Social Life* (3rd edn), London: Sage, 2008

Grix, J. and Watkins, G., *Information Skills: finding and using the right resources*, Basingstoke: Palgrave Macmillan, 2010

Pears, R., *Cite Them Right: the essential referencing guide* (8th edn), Basingstoke: Palgrave Macmillan, 2010

Punch, K.F., *Introduction to Social Research: quantitative and qualitative approaches*, London: Sage, 2005

Solomon, A., Wilson, G. and Taylor, T., *100% Information Literacy Success*, Boston, MA: Wadsworth, 2012

Some useful websites for studying and researching social problems in the UK

British Youth Council, http://www.byc.org.uk/

Child Poverty Action Group, http://www.cpag.org.uk/

Centre for Research in Social Policy, Loughborough University, http://www.lboro.ac.uk/research/crsp/

Shelter, http://www.shelter.org.uk/
Joseph Rowntree Foundation, http://www.jrf.org.uk/
Office for National Statistics, http://www.ons.gov.uk/ons/index.html
Refugee Council, http://www.refugeecouncil.org.uk/
Zanran Numerical Data Search, http://www.zanran.com

Some useful websites for study and research skills

Learn Higher: Resources for students, http://learnhigher.ac.uk/home.html
Safari: The Open University, http://www.open.ac.uk/safari/
Social Research Methods, http://www.socialresearchmethods.net/

chapter 4

Poverty

Stuart Isaacs

4.1 Introduction

The poor, it is often said, will always be with us. In a purely empirical sense this is true. In a market economy there will be income gaps between people according to their earnings. If we use household income to measure poverty, then there will always be a percentage of people at the bottom of the economic scale, those earning less than average. In the late nineteenth century, when socially concerned individuals became interested in trying to map poverty in Britain, this was the measure that they used. It is perhaps the most obvious, 'common sense' approach. But, as we shall see, it isn't the only way of measuring and defining poverty. In many ways it is also quite limited. However, considering household income is a good starting place. Seebohm Rowntree was among the most well-known of the late nineteenth-century social surveyors who first sought to systematically measure poverty. He used the idea of a poverty line.

Key thinker: Seebohm Benjamin Rowntree (1871–1954)

In 1899 Rowntree conducted his famous study on the conditions of working people in York. He argued that there ought to be a basic minimum level of income provided by the state that allowed for subsistence living. This he initially took to be what people needed to provide themselves with food and shelter in order to survive. However, in his later, interwar studies of poverty he revised this to include a broader range of consumer goods and emphasised the idea of an 'acceptable standard of living'. Beveridge used a calculation of subsistence level to set social security income in the 1940s. But he was criticised for not taking account of the need to give people support beyond Rowntree's earlier, very basic measure.

This is a level of income below which a household ought not to fall. If a family fell below the pounds, shillings and pence required for subsistence living, then it was considered to be below the poverty line and, therefore, poor. The poverty line was meant to provide a clear indicator to government about where state support was required. The early social surveyors believed that the idea of the poverty line would be a powerful weapon to provoke action from the state. They wanted to show that the use of empirical social scientific methods could highlight urgent social problems and point government in the right policy directions.

The notion of a poverty line, based on what is judged to be an adequate budget for people to live on, is a measure that government still uses extensively. The Household Below Average Income (HBAI) is the standard measure that the Department of Work and Pensions (DWP) employs for all social security payments. The poverty line is set at 60 per cent of the median average income. In other words, to qualify for most of the income-related benefits that people receive from the state, households have to be at least 40 per cent below average income. This is a very tidy, transparent way for government to measure and define poverty. By looking at these figures we can also get a general idea of who is poor in the UK today. For example, in 2010/11 the DWP's figures showed that 27 per cent of children in the UK, 3.6 million, were in HBAI households, after housing costs are taken into account. There are many other demographic indicators that we can find out about by using the HBAI measure. We can see whether the poor are married/cohabiting or single people, or lone-parent families, or from particular minority ethnic groups and so on. This helps to build up a useful understanding of the social groups that might most often fall into income poverty. Yet, although it is a useful tool for social scientists, and even more so for government, who like clear, standardised measures, this does not give us the whole picture. Simply drawing upon quantitative data to analyse poverty is not enough. We would always need more and more data to fill the gaps. For example, the figures given above do not indicate whether there have been increases in income for those above or well above average earnings. We would need further statistics to inform us whether the gap between rich and poor has been growing or shrinking. Furthermore, as the HBAI is based on average income, if household incomes for the country as a whole fall, the poverty line will be set at a lower income amount too. That would artificially remove some households from being officially poor, even though their incomes would not have changed. In the end, however thorough our research, collecting statistics and data will never give us the social insight into poverty that we seek.

4.2 The social construction of poverty

The solely empirical and 'common sense' approach to defining and measuring poverty, based around income, is narrow and limited. To get a fuller understanding of poverty in the UK using quantitative methods would require a wide range of indicators, including historical shifts, the gap between rich and poor (and indeed across various occupational levels) and the cost of living. Even then, quantitative evidence alone could not capture the social and cultural dimension of poverty: what has been understood as relative poverty in the past and, more recently, what we take to be social exclusion. But before looking at UK poverty in this more qualitative manner, there is another aspect of poverty not captured by the poverty line approach. That is, of course, the social construction of poverty.

Perceptions, assumptions and normative judgements about the poor have always permeated debates about poverty. Public discussions around issues that affect the poor, in particular those concerning social security benefits, are intertwined with discourses that seek to determine the characteristics of poor families in specific ways. Many of these are moral critiques of the poor: that they are lazy, work-shy welfare dependents, happy to sponge off the taxes of 'decent hard-working families'. This is a construction of the poor that can be traced back at least to the Victorian Poor Laws. The Victorian state's response to poverty, and one that has been common ever since, was to offer those prepared to work a small, means-tested *relief* of poverty, rather than a sustained wage or income. While the Victorian Poor Laws provided some cash relief to poor families, the centrepiece was the quintessential self-help institution, the workhouse. The social message from the state was clear. Poverty was the responsibility of the individual. If someone was not prepared to work, even for the most rudimentary subsistence relief, they did not deserve help.

The workhouses may be long gone but the values that they represent still remain. There is a still a strongly held view that if the state provides a basic minimum relief of poverty individuals have to show a willingness to work. The linking of poverty, welfare and work is a discourse which is reinforced in government policy. The well-known quote below is a good summary of this position.

'I have a problem, I'll get a grant.' 'I'm homeless, the government must house me.' They're casting their problem on society. And you know, there is no such thing as society. There are individual men and women, and there are families. And no government can do anything except through people, and people must look to themselves first.

(Margaret Thatcher, 31 October 1987,
Woman's Own magazine interview)

This type of construction of the poor as taking 'something for nothing' and being a drain on society's resources is a moralised and individualised approach to poverty. Often such statements are tied to a view of our society which maintains that there is no longer poverty in the UK. Go to any large social housing estate and you will find HD TVs, it is argued. People have Sky and Virgin cable packages. And those on benefits are carrying around smartphones and tablets. This sort of moralised individualist approach to poverty feeds off people's limited personal experiences and anecdotal evidence. It focuses on the emotive, sensational issues that are the stuff of newspaper headlines and TV reports designed to create newsworthy stories. It is not based on social research or sociological analysis. It ignores the underlying social institutions and structures that give rise to inequalities that are the causes of poverty. These are particular and diverse: a range of factors that come together to limit people's opportunities and life chances. It might be poor housing which undermines educational achievement; racist attitudes; assumptions about children on free school meals; lack of awareness of disability; local or national economies that have failed, causing long-term high unemployment; poor neighbourhoods where gang and anti-social behaviour have become alternative sub-cultures. All these institutional and structural issues as well as many other social problems identified in this book might underlie poverty.

In order to say something meaningful about the diverse group whom we may consider to be poor we need to act as social scientists, investigate the social research, look at the arguments put by authors who have studied these problems and try to set aside common-sense opinions based on limited experience.

One of the first things that the social research tells us is that poor people tend to work harder than anyone else. Polly Toynbee (2003) documents this well in her turn-of-the-millennium study, *Hard Work*. In this book she presents quantitative and qualitative evidence to suggest that the poor work longer and harder now than they did forty years ago. Comparing the wages of some of the lowest-paid workers, she illustrates how the poor have seen their wages rise more slowly than the rest of the population. For example, hospital porters (a typical minimum wage occupation) have seen their wages drop in real terms since the 1970s. Not only incomes but working conditions have also got worse. This includes many thousands of low-paid workers in the public sector. This is particularly true for those working for privatised or contracted-out agencies that provide welfare services. According to Toynbee, people working in these jobs have very little in the way of security or rights. Many people on the lowest incomes (a disproportionate number of whom are from minority ethnic communities) have to put together two or even three jobs in one day to generate enough money to live. This is particularly true for women, including women who are lone parents. They have to juggle childcare with jobs that have unsocial hours, no career prospects and give them little sense of self-worth. Toynbee concludes that, far from being lazy or work shy, the poor work longer and in tougher working conditions than most.

Toynbee's study does not stand alone. There is a substantive body of social research that you can investigate that indicates that the social construction of the poor as work shy does not match up to the social experience of many. O'Hara (2014) shows this in her study of poverty in Britain since the Coalition government came to power in 2010.

Another way to think about this is to look at income maintenance. Alongside the view that the poor are lazy often sits the related argument that the poor are usually unemployed people who live a life of comfort on benefit payments. Indeed the very language that is deployed suggests that 'welfare' or 'benefits' in themselves are give-aways by the state to the 'undeserving poor'. Some readers might have noticed that I have previously been using the term 'social security'. This is how cash-based income support has also been understood, as a form of social protection that is needed by those who qualify for it. However, increasingly the use of the terms 'benefit' and 'welfare' have come to replace 'social security' and 'social protection'. This language is ideologically loaded. Whereas security and protection sound like claims that social citizens might reasonably make on the state, claiming 'cash benefits' or 'welfare' implies using other people's taxes for you own unearned income. Increasingly, those reliant upon the state for additional income to live face being seen as welfare spongers. As well as having to cope with poverty they also have to take the blame for their poverty. The idea that there ought to be some form of social security to protect vulnerable people from the risks of the market economy and the insecurities of the labour market seems to be withering away. There is, then, a construction of the poor as welfare dependents and the architects of their own circumstances through their unwillingness to work. However, despite these views being common currency, the way that income maintenance has developed since the 1980s would suggest that this is unlikely to be universally true. From the New Right Conservatives under Margaret Thatcher, through New Labour to the Coalition, there has been a policy trend to ensure that the vast majority of people receiving social security benefits are actually working. Even government figures show this. Only 3 per cent of households on benefit are completely workless. Furthermore, fewer than 1 per cent of benefits are claimed illegally, suggesting that the system is not open to wide abuse.

If the social construction of the poor as lazy and not wanting to work is so easily dismissed by social research, why then is it so prevalent? One of the reasons might be the invisibility of the poor. Cheap clothes stores, new and second hand, as well as cheap technology, might disguise the visible sense of poverty that was so discernible in the Victorian age. The poor are not in rags or sleeping in large numbers on the streets of our cities. The poor on the whole may not be starving, although according to the Child Poverty Action Group a sizable minority do go hungry.

The poor look like you and me. Except that when they go home they may live in sub-standard housing or temporary, insecure accommodation. They may struggle to pay for public transport or for nutritious fresh food or a mobile phone to communicate with people. The poor today, many of whom are elderly, will be scared to put the heating on in case it costs too much. They count every penny. This is how around 20 per cent of the population of the UK live.

Another reason why the poor might be constructed negatively may have something to do with politics and ideology. Ha-Joon Chang (2010) suggests that since the early 1980s the neo-liberal, free-market discourse has dominated the way that we think about poverty. He argues that reflecting upon social problems begins with the assumption that individuals have total control over their own lives and destinies, regardless of their personal circumstances and background. Celebrities, successful business people, sports stars, Hollywood actors and so on deserve their wealth because they have worked for it. The implication is that the poor are poor because they haven't. This takes away from structural inequalities such as historically deprived neighbourhoods where many have inappropriate, insecure housing, lack of localised investment in jobs and people, educational underachievement because of insufficient household resources or knowledge, as well as disadvantages because of discrimination, based on ethnicity, gender, sexuality or disability. In a way, Chang points to a remarkable turnaround in the way that the rich and the poor are perceived in our society. To return to the nineteenth century, even though the poor were constituted in many respects as undeserving, there was also a similar view of the very rich. They were often portrayed in newspapers and satirical pamphlets as greedy individuals feeding off the hard work of others. Yet the term 'the idle rich' has almost disappeared from popular discussions about the distribution of wealth in the UK. In a consumer society where material wealth is often prized as a mark of success in itself – regardless of the achievement – the poor have suffered just as the very wealthy have benefited. For example, although the UK recessions from 2010 were the consequence of decisions and policies made by the global financial industries, under weakly regulated structures, it was the poor who got the blame and welfare spending that was cut.

As we have seen, blaming the poor for being poor ignores the underlying causes of poverty, which are institutional and structural. Individual circumstances will be particular and may indeed involve responsibility on the part of that person. But, thinking through the issues as social scientists, looking at the research, the evidence and the arguments, it is wrong to suggest that the poor are work shy and undeserving. In order to understand further how we might best articulate the circumstances of poverty in the UK the next section of this chapter will look at poverty in the context of social exclusion. This theoretical approach suits our social construction methodology. It also offers an alternative to the useful but limited income-based, poverty line tradition as a way of defining and measuring poverty.

4.3 Social exclusion

If we situate our understanding of poverty within the context of social exclusion we are able to compile a set of broad issues that affect the poor. Unlike the poverty line tradition, using a theory of social exclusion enables us to think about circumstances beyond the distribution of wealth and income. The theory of social exclusion also shares many of the characteristics of the social construction methodological framework we are trying to develop. When we apply social exclusion to poverty we are drawing upon quantitative evidence, but also making judgements about the kinds of people we might argue are in this category. In other words, determining how social exclusion affects those on low incomes involves 'making a case', articulating our values about social justice as to why a social group (understood as an 'ideal type', see Chapter 2.4) deserves to be the focus for policy solutions. Social scientists disagree about the definition and use of this theory; there is a large body of literature concerned with the theoretical debates alone. Nevertheless, it is possible to work through a basic understanding.

One way of explaining the social exclusion perspective is to see it as originating in the debate about relative poverty. In 1979 Peter Townsend (1980) published a landmark study entitled *Poverty in the UK*. In this text he argued that poverty ought to be understood in terms of relative deprivation, rather than just in terms of income. To cut a very long study short, Townsend argued that there is a social–cultural dimension to poverty. In order to understand the real impact of poverty on people's lives a methodology was needed that took account of changing living standards, affluence and people's expectations. With an army of researchers, Townsend set about asking a large sample of the UK's population to list the sort of consumer goods as well as activities that they thought they ought to have access to in order to have a decent standard of living. This being the 1970s, people mentioned central heating, a TV, a home phone, a car, at least one holiday a year and so on. The methodological details of the study and its findings are complicated and can be read in Townsend's book. For our purposes the interest of this study is that it indicated that without access to three or more of the listed consumables or activities people could be deemed to be 'relatively poor'. In other words they fell (and possibly felt) outside of a social norm as defined by the majority of the population. They were not able to participate in what might be considered an average life-style. This may well have had its underlying cause in a lack of income but the effects of this were that people were 'excluded' from a perceived normal way of life. Although Townsend and his researchers would not have used the term 'social exclusion', his study was important in pushing us towards this idea.

The notion of relative poverty gets us some way to understanding the notion of social exclusion as a way of constructing poverty. But social exclusion as a concept goes further than Townsend's relative poverty model. In a strange way, it is the in the work of the American libertarian social scientist Charles Murray, whose perspective is directly opposite that of Townsend, that we find the next development. Murray is notorious for suggesting that intelligence and genetics underlie individual achievement. However, we must remember that he did also acknowledge that social factors had a part to play too. In his study of the underclass he maintained that as well as the poor being determined by their genetic heritage and IQ, there are also historical, social and cultural factors at play. Murray argued that people living in poverty become welfare dependents. Over the years this developed into a way of life, a norm that was passed on from generation to generation. Although his methodological assumptions construct an argument that individualises poverty and ignores many of the institutional and structural issues considered above, his conclusions are ones that also fuelled the development of the notion of social exclusion. Writing in the 1980s and 1990s, Murray argued that the key to removing these generations of poor families away from their poverty cycle is to empower them to take charge of their own lives. In other words, to integrate them into mainstream society so that they feel that they are socially included. This might most successfully be done, he suggested, through the education system and employment.

FAST FORWARD >>>>> 7.5

For an argument that the education system is not simply an institution that can be used for social progress, see this section.

By the 1990s, then, it can be seen that influential social scientists like Murray, from an individualist perspective, and Townsend, from an anti-inequalities viewpoint, were pushing at the same idea. To address poverty we need to consider the wider social and cultural dimension. Perhaps because of this intellectual atmosphere developing around the need to include people on low incomes in society, the idea of the poor being socially excluded became explicit in social research and government policy. Officially, the term 'social exclusion' was first used at the level of the European Union, around the development of the social charter and social chapter of the Maastricht Treaty. The concept soon became widely used and was to become especially important in the UK under New Labour, as we shall see.

Socially excluded now generally defines any individual who is disadvantaged in multiple ways so that they are excluded from a 'normal' course of life expectations, particularly in education and work. What 'normal' might mean is open to interpretation and debate. This is the part of the theory of social exclusion mentioned above that is the site of controversy. Furthermore, it is true to say that most academics who are sympathetic to the ideas of social exclusion tend to favour the strand of thinking that stems from Townsend's approach. Murray would not agree, but social exclusion is now most often associated with underlying social inequalities. This is because the types of social groups linked with social exclusion are also those that are most commonly found to suffer some form of discrimination. This includes low-income pensioners, people with a disability or impairment, lone parents, young adults, certain minority ethnic groups, the long-term unemployed and asylum seekers. In the case of these groups, they are socially excluded not only in relative terms but also because they have cumulative obstacles to overcome. That is, as well as low incomes there may be problems of poor education and training, lack of employment, inadequate housing, issues to do with healthy lifestyles and nutrition and difficulties accessing transport, as well as means of communication (such as the internet). These socially excluded groups and the social problems that they face were identified by New Labour. In government it sought to address issues of poverty, particularly child poverty, through policies designed to promote social inclusion. However, the persistence of common-sense constructions of the poor as work-shy welfare dependents and/or the cause of economic problems also affected the way that it went about implementing these policies. New Labour appeared contradictory in its approach. On the one hand, it had a thorough analysis of the way that poverty was linked to issues of social exclusion. But, on the other, it often implemented these policies within the context of loading individuals with responsibility and not addressing the structural aspects of inequality that underlay people's personal circumstances. In other words, unlike most social scientists, New Labour took as much from Charles Murray's individualist approach to poverty as it did from Peter Townsend's view.

4.4 New Labour and social exclusion

New Labour came to power in 1997 with the explicit aim of tackling social exclusion. One of the first things that it did in government was to establish the Social Exclusion Unit. This oversaw the introduction of policies designed to challenge social exclusion through every government department. It also regulated and monitored local authorities to do the same. Targets were set at national and local level to bring about a wholesale and fundamental programme to socially include groups identified as socially excluded. The centrepiece of these policies was to introduce a work-based training scheme known as the New Deal. This was Labour's welfare-to-work initiative, paid for by a windfall tax on the previously privatised utilities. Between 1997 and 1999, £5.2 billion was raised in this way and spent on the New Deal in its early phases. New Deals were targeted at social groups that consisted of a disproportionate number of people likely to face the difficulties associated with social exclusion. So there was a New Deal for Young People, a New Deal for Lone Parents, the over-50s, the disabled, and even for musicians! The sole aim of the New Deal was to get people into work. Most of the jobs were low paid. The argument was that any job was better than no job at all. This was because it provided a foundation that could lead to long-term employment opportunities. The assumption behind this was that people would become work shy if they remained on 'welfare'.

> ### FAST FORWARD >>>>> 5.3
>
> For a discussion about work and the work ethic as a strong ideological component of British society.

In this way New Labour both expressed a desire to aid those who were identified as socially excluded, and also reinforced the individualised perception of the poor as having developed a lifestyle in which the work ethic had been lost. During its time in office New Labour believed that paid employment was the golden route to social inclusion. If people had a job, then they would have a stake in society. There was an assumption here too that disregarded structural inequalities, a belief that the labour market functioned according to merit, regardless of age, gender, ethnicity, sexuality, disability or any other form of social identification. Finally, there was probably the most fundamental assumption of all underlying this strategy: jobs would always be available. It was simply up to individuals to take the responsibility to go and get one. Oddly then, New Labour displayed sensitivity to constructing poverty around the broad and sophisticated definition of social exclusion. Yet it did so within a market-led, individualist framework.

New Labour initiated other areas of state intervention designed to complement the New Deal. The introduction of the minimum wage and the tax credit system gave real cash benefits to people to make them better off in work. There was also help with childcare, for lone parents and low-income families, through tax credits, vouchers and increased state nursery places. There was help in education through Sure Start and Connexions. The Academy programme was also designed to help children in poor neighbourhoods have well-resourced state-of-the-art facilities at school. In this respect New Labour did try to address poverty by increasing cash benefits for the low-paid and removing some of the institutional and structural barriers to work, particularly for lone parents and women.

So, how successful were New Labour's rather ideologically mixed-up set of policies? Evaluations of the New Deal have indicated that there were initial moderate successes. Higher employment rates were achieved for most targeted groups through the New Deal. However, in the medium term the success was more limited. The economic downturn from 2009/10 played its part in undermining the New Deal. But so too did the poor quality of jobs on offer. This was particularly true of the New Deal for Young People (NDYP) (2002). The National Audit Office, reporting on the data of the NDYP in 2002, stated that a worrying aspect of the scheme was that 30 per cent of young people had dropped out of it. It claimed that the NDYP had actually bred a *resistance* to work among these young people. They had not only left their New Deal jobs but had actually dropped out of the benefit system altogether. Their destination was 'unknown'. It seems that although government may have assumed that low-paid jobs with few career prospects were better than no jobs at all, these young people disagreed and voted with their feet. This may well have been because the jobs that were created were perceived as 'dead-end'. The New Deal places were also often forced on young people, under the threat of having their benefits cut. The use of the 'stick' of sanctions as well as the 'carrot' of paid employment was a very crude way of implementing a policy around the notion of social exclusion. As is so often the case, central government policy designed around a 'one-size-fits-all' solution did not work. Evidence suggests that the over-50s were more receptive to New Deal opportunities and had a different attitude to work. But young people, we can speculate, were more sceptical about being exploited. In the end, by ignoring the needs and views of young people, the NDYP had unintended outcomes. New Labour hoped to induct young adults into a work ethic. It constructed the problem along the lines of a work-shy youth. However, the issue for young people was not being work shy but needing to feel as if the jobs they were being offered gave them genuine opportunities. Offering a low-paid job with little substantive training and no prospects was not enough to make them feel socially included. A programme such as the NDYP would have had to make a substantive, long-term and material difference to their lives in order to give them a sense of belonging.

New Labour used the language of social exclusion to address poverty. However, ultimately its policies were tied to an individualised construction of the poor as needing to be pushed into work, of whatever quality. Once given this 'opportunity' individuals had to take the responsibility to make the best of it. The emphasis on job creation relied not only upon the belief in the power of individuals to change their own lives, but also on the misguided view that paid employment was the key to alleviating poverty. A report in 2012 by the Institute of Fiscal Studies (IFS), sponsored by the Joseph Rowntree Foundation, concluded that improvements in education and employment under New Labour did little to prevent poverty in the long term. Although this might go against a 'common sense' approach – that would assume there was a link between being in paid employment and getting out of poverty – this is not what the social research indicates. The IFS study illustrated that insecure and low-paid jobs do not resolve issues of poverty. Employment remains sporadic in these cases and does not necessarily make a poor household better off.

To its credit, the gains that New Labour did make in combatting poverty came not with the New Deal or the social exclusion strategy but through the more direct, benefit-related redistributive policies around the issue of child poverty. New Labour targeted the reduction of child poverty by 50 per cent between 1998/99 and 2010/11. By the redistribution of wealth through the benefit and tax credit system, a third of households coming under this category were removed from poverty by 2002. By 2010/11, 1.1 million families were removed from poverty, a figure arrived at by using the HBAI measure (although that is *before* housing costs). This was 600,000 households short of New Labour's target. However, during its time in office, on average New Labour's benefit changes made children from poor families £77 per week better off. This was a significant increase in resources for those households, even though the gap between rich and poor expanded at the same time. The moderate success of these income-related policies seems to suggest that, although social exclusion as a definition and measure of poverty is more sophisticated than either a poverty line or relative poverty measure, in terms of what government can effectively do, good, old-fashioned redistribution of wealth has a more immediate effect. This is not to say we ought to dismiss theories of social exclusion as a way of understanding poverty. However, the New Labour period suggests that if this theory were to be applied in practical policy terms it would need a much more considered approach.

An important aspect of this would be more localised sets of policies that engaged with the views and needs of the people that were targeted, as the case of the NDYP showed. 'Top-down' policies set around national and universalist criteria have not proved to be effective. The other important lesson of the New Deal is that sustainable jobs with the potential for good career opportunities would have to be at the heart of any welfare-to-work programme. The prospect of policies designed to combat poverty being based around a theory of social exclusion that reflects the sophistication and nuance of that approach seems remote. The social construction of the poor as welfare dependents and work shy has continued since New Labour, under the Coalition government. The Coalition has scrapped the New Deal. More significantly, it has cut welfare benefits through the implementation of austerity measures such as Universal Credit. This means that any of the lessons learned or tiny steps forward made by New Labour will be set in reverse. This is despite the Coalition signing up to new targets to combat child poverty by 2020, set by the outgoing Labour government. Sadly, we have to agree with the IFS report that there is no realistic chance that the child poverty targets will be met under current policies.

4.5 Homelessness

One of the perennial social problems associated with poverty is homelessness. Just as it is said that the poor will always be with us, a similar pessimism pervades this issue. If you were asked to think of an image of the homeless you might find yourself remembering someone you have seen in the street: a dirty, smelly old bloke lying drunk on the pavement. Or a desperate-looking young person, sitting on a high street with a sad-looking dog next to them, begging for money. While many people may have experienced seeing these types of people, and have different reflections on the validity of their claims to be homeless, these experiences are far from the reality of what homelessness means to the vast majority who are actually in that position.

Rooflessness, or rough sleeping, is only a very small part of the social problem of homelessness. For example, estimates for the number of people who sleep rough in England are very sketchy. They range from 1600 to 3000. The figures vary because these are a very difficult group to keep track of. While some rough sleepers have regular places where they stay, most have erratic lifestyles. In addition, although those that sleep rough in a city might have a fairly ritualised and structured lifestyle, many rough sleepers live in rural areas and are harder to pin down. There are also particular personal problems that rough sleepers tend to suffer from that distinguish them from the majority of homeless people. Rough sleepers are often drug addicts or alcoholics. They may have mental health problems too. In a sense, the fact that rough sleepers are on the streets is not primarily a problem of not having a home, but it is a condition brought about by much more deeply rooted personal issues. For this reason it is more appropriate, in terms of looking at social problems, to focus this final section of the chapter on the majority who are homeless. In 2011 there were 1.8 million people who were officially recognised as homeless and on local authority waiting lists in the UK. This was a 14 per cent increase on the previous year, although the trend had been downwards over the previous few years. These people are officially recognised as homeless because they do not have a permanent, secure and appropriate home to live in. However, as we shall see, those that are 'officially homeless' in this way (qualifying for social housing under the terms of a local authority's rules of 'priority need') account for only some but not all those who fit this definition.

Poverty and social exclusion often underlie homelessness. But there are other causes that also need to be discussed. These may or may not have an association with poverty. The first of these is demographic changes. If we take London as an example, its population has grown by 20 per cent since the mid 1990s. This growth has been due to an increasing older population, internal domestic and external foreign migration to the capital, as well as increased fertility. Such trends put pressure on public services like hospitals and schools as well as housing. However, on their own these demographic trends are long-term changes that government can plan for. It is not unusual for a city to grow in this manner over the course of a few decades. London in particular has the scope to expand and absorb a larger population, given the right planning.

The political will to make provision, including for demographic change, is the link to the second main cause of homelessness. This is government policy. Since the 1980s there has been a sustained decline in the number of social houses being built. This affects people on low incomes, who subsequently struggle to afford a home. The Right-to-Buy policies from the era of Margaret Thatcher onwards are symbolic of this deliberately chosen policy direction.

Under the Conservative government of Margaret Thatcher people were encouraged to buy their own homes. Local authority housing was said to be of poor quality, badly managed and helped to sustain a 'nanny state', making people dependent on 'welfare'. It was therefore a political decision to decrease investment in social housing and sell off existing stock through the Right-to-Buy scheme. This allowed council house tenants to buy the property that they had rented from the council at hugely discounted rates. For families, some of them on low incomes, this gave them a chance to own their own home for the very first time. Or at least buy it and sell it on quickly at a very healthy profit. But although this may have given some families the chance to have the sort of investment that they could never have otherwise dreamed of, it took hundreds of thousands of state-subsidised homes permanently away from the public sector. This housing was never replaced.

The direction of government policy ever since has been to remove housing stock owned and controlled by local authorities into the private sector, largely to housing associations. The social housing that has been left under local authority control has largely been less desirable homes on large estates. At the same time as state-subsidised housing has diminished and been residualised, rents have gone up.

These policy decisions through successive governments have led to the death of council housing in the UK. Their legacy is a housing shortage that seems almost impossible to ever see being manageable. As a result of social housing being in short supply, the private rented sector has also seen prices rise. This again affects the poor, who are more likely to be without secure, permanent and appropriate housing. In other words, many families and single people living on low incomes may have a roof over their heads but they can still be classified as homeless.

The final cause of homelessness to think about is actually a number of individual circumstances that can be grouped together. These include personal circumstances such as no longer being able to stay with family or friends. This could be due to emotional tensions, or simply changing circumstances, such as the friend moving away. Relationship breakdown is another common cause of homelessness. So too are mortgage arrears and loss of tenancy. These latter two may relate to particular individual circumstances, but they are likely to also have a general, underlying social cause. In fact, potentially, all of these individual factors that social scientists have consistently recorded as significant could have a relationship to poverty. For example, one of the most common reasons for relationship breakdowns is problems over household finances. Demographic change, government policy and individual circumstances can all be said to be causes of homelessness. However, as we have seen, although individuals will have particular personal issues there often are structural factors affecting these. The most common is to do with low income. This is borne out by the fact that those groups which are identified as officially poor (HBAI) or have been targeted as more likely to be socially excluded are also the most vulnerable to homelessness. Increasingly, the homeless population is made up of elderly people on low incomes, young people who have struggled to find jobs, as well as victims (mostly women) of domestic violence and harassment. Asylum seekers are also increasingly homeless, often ending up as rough sleepers, as they have no familial support or friendship networks.

FAST FORWARD >>>>> 6.1 and 6.5

Far from being the recipients of generous benefits and cheap housing, former asylum seekers are among the poorest in our society.

Of the causes given above, it is government policy that might be said to be the factor that we have most control over. It may come as a surprise, then, that attention to homelessness as an issue of welfare came very late in the day. Given that the modern Beveridge welfare state was established in the mid-1940s, it wasn't until 1977 that we had the first attempt at a coherent national strategy to deal with homelessness. If we situate home-lessness as an aspect of government housing policy, then it is not hard to see why this might be. Except for exceptional periods after the First and Second World Wars, all governments have been reluctant to engage in costly, state-led house-building programmes. Rather, UK governments have prioritised home ownership. A private and privatised model of hous-ing is the cultural and political tradition in the UK. Given the preference of political decision makers to prioritise homeownership, it is no wonder that the homeless were off the mainstream welfare radar for so long.

It wasn't until the 1960s that pressure really built up, external to govern-ment, for something to be done about homelessness. The 1960s were a boom time in Britain. This period has often been labelled 'the affluent society'. There was full employment, good wages and a growing economy. Young people had money in their pockets for the first time and a youth culture developed around their styles and music. This was the time of 'swinging London' and the Beatles and a sense that the class barriers were down. Everyone had money. Britain was becoming a truly modern, merito-cratic society. Part of this affluence was the affordability of consumer goods, particularly TVs. This brought entertainment into people's living rooms. But it also brought facts that they had perhaps previously not known. One evening in November 1966, millions of people sat down to watch a programme called *Cathy Come Home*. It told the story of a young woman living with her family who is let down by the welfare state and in the end loses her husband, her child and her home. Thousands of people rang the BBC to offer the now homeless Cathy a place to stay. They were touched by how easy it seemed for an ordinary young woman to become homeless. But this wasn't a documentary, it was a drama. The awareness that this was a fictionalised account, that was symbolically telling the story of what was happening to thousands of people in the UK's affluent society, made the issue even more pressing. The programme provoked debates in parliament and huge support for the newly set up homeless charities of Crisis and Shelter. It was the momentum from this TV programme that just over ten years later finally saw the first statutory provisions for the homeless.

The Housing (Homeless Persons) Act 1977 introduced criteria that meant that all local authorities had a duty to house people who came under a new category of 'priority need'. On the one hand, this was a step forward in the recognition that people on low incomes were struggling to find secure, permanent, affordable homes. However, at the same time it set clear limits on those that local authorities could help. This is understandable, given the huge demand for state-subsidised housing. There had to be boundaries. However, 'priority need' constructed categories of the 'deserving poor' and 'undeserving poor' in a way that we have seen is part of the discourse of poverty in the UK.

The main people who were deemed to be 'deserving' were homeless women with children, or women who were pregnant; people who were vulnerable due to age, mental illness or disability; as well as those that had lost their homes due to natural disasters. It was single people, particularly men, who were excluded from 'priority need'. They were deemed 'undeserving', following the British tradition that able-bodied individuals ought to take responsibility for their lives and find work. It was not until 1996 that an amendment was made to the 1977 Act to include victims of domestic violence under 'priority need', thereby making them 'deserving'. New Labour's Homeless Act 2002 also extended this category to care-leavers under 21 and 16/17-year olds. Unfortunately, no extra resources were put in place for local authorities to cope with these newly discovered 'deserving' groups.

The use of 'priority need' is understandable as a pragmatic solution to manage high demand. Yet it also has an ideological and political aspect. In a rudimentary way it makes it possible for government to lower the homelessness figures by sticking to the official statistics based on those accepted by local authorities. Perhaps more importantly, it has also constituted an artificial difference among the homeless between those accepted as 'priority need' and those who are not. Campaigning organisations have tried to address this by constructing the idea of the 'hidden homeless'. These are the people that are not officially recognised as homeless but are no less homeless for all that. They are made up of single people as well as those who are deemed to have made themselves 'intentionally homeless'. It also includes, according to Shelter, over one million children who are living in poverty. These children might be living in conditions that are not considered to come under the legislation and qualify them for a place on the housing waiting list, but their circumstances are still such that they do not have a secure, affordable and appropriate home. For example, families living in over-crowded conditions. This might seem a trivial issue, but for many people, estimated at around half a million, it is a serious problem. It might mean school children not having a space for homework or study, which undermines their education; or teenagers not able to have any privacy; or young children having to sleep with their parents.

Sofa surfing is another predicament of the 'hidden homeless'. This is an increasingly common experience for many young people. Unable to remain with parents, perhaps because of arguments or over-crowding, they skip from one friend's sofa to another. Single people on low incomes who may not have work or who experience sporadic employment have very little chance of securing a permanent affordable home. Private rents have increased as social housing has declined. And house prices are way out of reach.

The lack of resources given to local authorities by central government means that even for those that they do accept, they do not have enough social housing to place them in. These families in all likelihood will be forced to live in unsuitable bed-and-breakfast accommodation, sometimes with waits of many years before they secure a permanent home. The lack of sufficient funding means that local authorities have to implement 'strict eligibility' rules. In other words, if you turn up at a housing office to register as homeless it will attempt to get rid of you. In particular, it will try to find out if you have become intentionally homeless. Intentionality can be broadly interpreted under the legislation. So if you have not been able to afford your rent and are being evicted, perhaps because you lost your job through no fault of your own, this is generally classified as you making yourself intentionally homeless! This reflects the situation that social housing in the UK has now become a minimal provision.

4.6 Summary

We began the chapter by looking at the poverty line as a way of defining and measuring poverty. This approach, developed by the early social surveyors, uses quantitative data to highlight statistical and demographic information. This is a useful tool for relating general trends and telling us which social groups are most affected by having low incomes. However, it is a limited measure, as it does not highlight other aspects of poverty, namely its social construction and the broader context of social exclusion. That said, for governments, the use of a base-line measure of average household income is very useful. It allows the state to apply a universal measure to legitimate claims for income maintenance. It also facilitates national policy making under the assumption that the circumstances of the poor are similar. The introduction of Universal Credit by the Coalition government is a good example of this.

The social construction of poverty was the next aspect of poverty that was explored. It was argued that poverty is not a neutral, value-free social condition that is capable of being captured by statistics. This is because there are moralising discourses that have developed that construct how we think of the poor in particular value-laden ways. One of the most powerful social constructions of poverty has at its centre the view that the poor are lazy, work-shy individuals who are happy to live off the luxury of state benefits, paid for by the taxes of 'decent hard-working families'. In this way the problem of poverty is not understood as a social problem, with underlying institutional and structural causes, but, rather, a moral lack of responsibility on the part of individuals. Such a perception can symbolically be traced back to the ethos of the workhouse, which distinguished between the 'deserving poor' (who were willing to work) and the 'undeserving poor' (who were unwilling to accept low pay conditions). The individualised, moral construction of the poor in this manner ignores the structural issues that may have led to poverty. These might include issues of discrimination around ethnicity, disability, gender or class. As well as a lack of educational opportunity, poor housing, unemployment, issues to do with adult- or child-care and ill-health. Furthermore, in the work of Polly Toynbee we saw that, in fact, the poor are hard at work. Most households that rely on benefits have at least one person in work. The poor often work longer hours and in worse conditions than most people.

The social research that has been looked at reflects a view of poverty that has little relation to the notion of the poor as lazy and work-shy welfare dependents. It was maintained that the reason why this perception remains a powerful one is because of the ideological dominance of neo-liberal, free market ideas. That is, the view accepted by the major political parties that private sector-led enterprises will always be the best means of distributing wealth. The state's role is merely as a regulator of market conditions. This is where the idea springs from that if an individual works hard they will 'get on'. But, as we have seen, the poor do work hard but remain tied to low-income jobs.

A theory of social exclusion was investigated as an alternative means of defining, measuring and constructing poverty. The development of this idea was traced from Townsend's socio-cultural argument about relative poverty, to Charles Murray's analysis of the underclass. Using the broader notion of social exclusion, issues of poverty were deemed to go beyond matters of income, and even further than the comparative cultural dimension of relative poverty measures. Rather, social exclusion highlights some of the underlying institutional and structural factors associated with poverty. These include educational underachievement, a lack of job-relevant training and skills, disadvantages around communication and transport, as well as possible issues of poor housing and health. It can be seen that these issues correspond with the types of social problems and structural issues indicated in the social research. This becomes even clearer when considering the social groups revealed by studies of social exclusion: lone parents, young people, people with a disability, the elderly with low incomes and black and minority ethnic groups.

New Labour's application of social exclusion when in government was examined to see at how it was applied in practice. It was argued that New Labour narrowed its commitment to social inclusion around paid employment. This was because it did not move away from the discourse of the poor that constituted them as lazy and work shy. New Labour's acceptance of neo-liberal assumptions about the role of the free market and enterprise undermined its social exclusion strategies. These involved rather punitive measures against those who did not accept a welfare-to-work place. The New Deal for Young People was analysed in this respect. This highlighted that by not taking account of the views of the socially excluded groups that were being targeted, New Labour failed to appreciate how its welfare-to-work scheme would be received. For many young people it was coercive, a way of getting them to work in no-hope jobs for very little wages. Consequently, the policy had the opposite effect to the one that was intended, by creating a resistance to low-paid work.

The area of policy where New Labour did make a difference to poverty was through increasing cash benefits to poor families. This saw their incomes rise in real terms. It was maintained that this wasn't evidence that social exclusion as a theory could not be applied in practice but, rather, that it would not work in a universalist manner or by being imposed from the top down, without a genuine engagement with its intended target groups. Furthermore, unless the individualistic, moralising discourse about the poor was disregarded, policy would never begin to approach the institutional structural issues underlying poverty.

Homelessness was given as a final example of the long-lasting legacy of this discourse. Not only did emphasis on homelessness by government develop rather late in the twentieth century, but when it did become a concern of the state there was yet another construction of the 'deserving' and 'undeserving' poor embedded into it. Seen in the context of UK housing policy, homelessness and the need for affordable, state-subsidised social housing have been undermined by the privileging of home ownership. It was argued that this was particularly promoted by political decisions made from the 1980s, notably the Right-to-Buy. The emphasis on home ownership has resulted in the decline of social housing. Thought about another way, there is nothing inevitable about wide-scale homelessness. It is the result of political decisions that have kept people in poverty rather than alleviated it.

Revision notes

Defining poverty by using only a measure of household income is limited. To understand poverty fully we need to have a method that incorporates statistical and demographic trends, an analysis of normative debates and allows for the examination of the structural causes of poverty. Investigating the social construction of poverty and looking at the broader features associated with social exclusion equips us to do this.

Poverty in the UK is often constructed as an individual issue, not a social problem. Political discourse and successive government policy decisions situate poverty as the responsibility of the individual. If a person is poor they are deemed to have not taken their educational opportunities or not been willing to work. This is a morally loaded constitution of the poor as lazy and work shy. It is often associated with the view that the benefit system perpetuates a lack of moral responsibility. Welfare is understood not as necessary social security for vulnerable people, but as an easy ride of cash benefits that encourages a workless lifestyle. This perspective is often tied to an underlying ideology that takes the free market as an equitable and meritocratic distributor of wealth and life chances.

Social research continually indicates that the poor work hard and that cash-based social security is essential to tackling poverty. All the main official and academic statistical indicators available highlight the fact that the poor want to work and that most of them do work. The vast majority of benefits are given to the 'in work' poor. There is no social research to suggest that any group identified as socially excluded are unwilling to work. These people just want to be able to access jobs that can give them meaningful occupations and the potential to improve their social circumstances. Welfare initiatives by New Labour that increased cash payments to those in child poverty made a real impact on the lives of these families. Conversely, the introduction of Universal Credit is likely to take away the gains that many low-incomes families saw during the early part of this century.

Social exclusion in theory and its application in practice were very different. There is a wide and complex academic debate about the meaning and application of social exclusion. Discussions centre on the need for consultation, voluntary participation by targeted groups, as well as on social justice. However, when New Labour attempted to apply social exclusion to policy it did so in an authoritarian and reductionist manner. Work was taken as the main route to social inclusion. The jobs created under the New Deal were predominantly low paid, without any career prospects. This led to a large degree of resistance, especially among young people.

Homelessness is a feature of poverty that successive governments have ignored. If we are looking for an example of the way that individualised moral discourses and the orthodoxy of neo-liberal ideas have affected policy decisions, then the issue of homelessness is a prime one. There has been a continual reluctance by governments to fully fund state-subsidised housing, to the extent that the state has all but removed itself from this area of collective welfare responsibility. Homelessness is in large part the result of political decisions. Political leaders have failed to seriously address one of the most important welfare issues associated with poverty.

Seminar tasks

Poverty

1 Issue:

We can see from the discussion above that there are different social constructions of the poor. One of the most prominent is that poverty is an individual problem. It maintains that individuals must take responsibility for removing themselves from these circumstances. Everyone has the same educational opportunities. It is up to parents to make sure their children study, and school pupils to do their work. Similarly, in the labour market there are low-paid jobs that people can take and then gradually improve their occupational status and their income.

EXAMPLE:

The language deployed by politicians and social commentators reinforces the idea that the poor are unwilling to work. Discourses are constituted that attempt to blame the poor for their poverty. This is often done by constructing a language of 'them' and 'us'. 'Decent hard-working families' are set against 'welfare dependents' to create a sense that there are a large number of people who are abusing the benefit system and are not willing to work. A 'something for nothing society' is opposed to a 'big society' or 'one nation' to embed the same idea that the tax-paying majority are paying for a welfare-scrounging minority.

EXERCISE:

In small groups write a list of features associated with the individualist perspective of poverty. Then write another that takes the perspective that poverty is largely caused by underlying problems to do with social institutions and structures. Discuss to what extent members of your group agree with the individualist view. And to what extent do they share the views of the social structural perspective. This discussion should take account of the sort of ideologically loaded language given in the example above.

2 Issue:

In 2013 there were nearly 2 million people waiting for housing on local authority registers. These are the 'officially homeless'. The number of 'hidden homeless' could be three times as much. In 2011 homelessness went up, some due to repossessions but also because of people being unable to pay private rents or unable to stay with relatives and friends. Despite what can only be described as a housing crisis, these issues rarely make the headlines. Yet the social problem of affordable permanent housing for families on low incomes is an urgent one.

Successive governments have looked for cheap, short-term solutions to homelessness. The 'bedroom tax', introduced in April 2013, is an example of this. People who receive housing benefit will have their homes assessed. If they are deemed to have too many rooms for their needs they will face a benefit cut. They will have to find the extra money or move out. The government argues that this is a way of freeing up larger properties for families that need them. Campaigning organisations like Shelter argue that this could affect the elderly, the disabled and those that have had their roots in a particular neighbourhood for many years.

EXERCISE:
Which homeless groups would you consider to be a 'priority need'? And why?
And/Or
Is it possible that one day all homeless people, official and hidden, could have their housing needs met? Should this be a welfare priority?

Coursework questions

Is social exclusion a useful way of measuring, defining and understanding poverty?

Can a notion of social exclusion work in policy practice?

To what extent is poverty an issue of individual responsibility? To what extent is it a consequence of social institutions (like the welfare system and government policies) and/or social structures (like social class divisions)?

What are the main social problems associated with homelessness?

References

Chang, H.-J., 23 Things They Don't Tell You about Capitalism, London: Penguin, 2010

Cribb, J., Joyce, R., and Phillip, D., Living Standards, Poverty and Inequality in the UK, IFS Commentary C124, London: Institute for Fiscal Studies, 2012

Murray, C., The Emerging British Underclass, London: Institute of Economic Affairs, 1990

O'Hara, K., Austerity Bites: a journey to the sharp end of cuts in Britain, Bristol: Policy Press, 2014

Townsend, P., Poverty in the United Kingdom: a survey of household resources and standards of living, London: Penguin, 1980

Toynbee, P., Hard Work, London: Bloomsbury, 2003

The New Deal for Young People, *The New Deal for Young People*, National Audit Office report, HC 639, 28 February 2002

Child Poverty Action Group n.d. *Child Poverty Action Group*, http://www.cpag.org.uk/

Crisis, n.d. *The National Charity for Single Homeless People*, http://www.crisis.org.uk/pages/rough-sleeping.html

Shelter, *The Housing and Homelessness Charity*, http://england.shelter.org.uk/

Further reading

Alcock, P., *Understanding Poverty* (3rd edn), Basingstoke: Palgrave Macmillan, 2006

Gordon, D., Levitas, R. and Pantatazis, C., *Poverty and Social Exclusion in Britain: the millenium survey*, London: Policy Press, 2006

Lund, B., *Understanding Housing Policy* (2nd edn), Bristol: Policy Press, 2011

O'Hara, K., *Austerity Bites: a journey to the sharp end of cuts in Britain*, Bristol: Policy Press, 2014

chapter 5

Work and unemployment

Brian McDonough

5.1 Introduction

Work is among the most important social activities within industrial capitalist societies. It is, of course, the most common way to acquire sufficient income to satisfy needs and wants, although the distinction between these may not always be clear. For most people work occupies a larger part of their lives than all other activities in the public sphere. The vast majority of us must work to earn a living, or rely on pensions and other benefits that are often a redistribution of taxes collected from other people's employed work. Work also provides a measure of social worth and status. We are often categorised, assessed, ranked and rewarded on the basis of our position at work. Our income from paid employment might dictate the sort of area we can afford to live in, whether we are in social housing, the kind of house or flat we have, what sort of car we own, should we have one, and determine other sorts of goods we are able to afford. Our job and work status not only largely dictates our income and possessions but also impacts upon our broad way of life. It influences the sorts of people we meet, the friends we have and the social activities we engage in, many of which continue over the whole course of our lives.

For most of us, work is also bound up with our social identity. This is why, for example, when people are asked about 'what they do' they take it to mean what they do for a living. Our work, therefore, can tell others a lot about who we are. This association between work and identity is nothing new. Historically, people have associated their occupation with who they are, for example naming themselves after their work. Consider the surnames

Mason, Butcher and Baker, which all began as descriptions of occupations people once did. Work has been, and still is, of crucial importance to the way we live our lives. And so it is not surprising to find that work raises some fundamental social problems and is related to a range of social issues.

This chapter discusses a number of these questions. One of the main problems addressed in this chapter is the way in which work is socially constructed in our society. We shall discuss the underlying discourses which illuminate our understandings of work and the 'work ethic' and offer alternative ways of viewing 'work'. Following on from this discussion, we shall look at unemployment as a social problem, this time highlighting the way in which unemployment is socially constructed. We shall consider different 'constructs' of unemployment from a range of perspectives, but first it will be useful to discuss the issue of work in more detail, not least because our understandings of what work is can determine the meaning of work and non-work, and the varying definitions of unemployment.

5.2 Defining work

If we intend to investigate work activities, then we must first decide what we mean by work. One way of understanding work is to define it in terms of task-based activities for which people are paid by an employer, client or customer. However, this definition fails to recognise work which is unpaid but still contributes significantly to the functioning of society. For example, voluntary work contributes to the functioning of the UK in a variety of ways. Unpaid charity fundraisers, community workers and those who altruistically give up their time to help others are rendered invisible when a narrow definition of work is used. So too are youth work-experience 'employees' who may not be paid, even though they are carrying out the same work as formal members of staff. This definition of work as 'paid employment' is made even more problematic if we consider that many of the activities people do within employment are also carried out by people who are technically not employed. Care workers employed by the healthcare service and private care homes are paid and recognised as 'real' workers because they have a contract of employment, but those people in the UK who work as carers for their elderly or impaired parents or partners do not get the same recognition. The Office for National Statistics (ONS) reported that there were approximately 5.8 million people providing unpaid care in England and Wales in 2011. These people are often not seen as workers, despite the fact that the activities in which they are engaged are the same as those provided by full-time paid employees.

As feminist sociologists have pointed out, domestic chores like washing, ironing, cooking, child minding and many other tasks all exist both as paid and as unpaid labour. Yet within political discourses the former is more usually considered as 'real' work and so is more valued than unpaid labour (Grint 2005). Women's work in the home, in particular, is often made invisible in this way; as Oakley (1966) and others have argued, domestic work and childcare come to be seen as lacking in value and are unrecognised when considering work only as paid employment. Feminists since the 1970s have challenged the traditional conceptual boundaries of work and non-work when criticising the taken-for-granted assumption that work undertaken in the private sphere of the home is not real work. Yet without the enormous volume of domestic labour carried out by women, the formal economy of wages and salaries would cease to function. Feminists have argued that the historical allocation of domestic labour to women, along with responsibilities for sustaining the social network of the family, are aspects of the ways in which power is organised and deployed in society so that the 'relations of ruling' (Smith 1987) are organised in the interests of men.

Since the 1990s the proportion of households headed by single parents has increased. Turning to the ONS once more, its research estimates that there were nearly 2 million lone parents with dependent children in the UK in 2012. This figure has grown steadily and significantly from 1.6 million in 1996. The majority of these parents are women, although some are men. For single parents who wish to attend courses and join work-experience schemes or take part-time or full-time paid employment the difficulties of juggling economic activity with childcare responsibilities can be particularly severe.

From a 'common sense' viewpoint the term 'work' appears easy to define. But when we consider the specific ways in which 'work' is constructed the picture is more complex. What counts as work depends upon the specific social circumstances under which activities are undertaken and, importantly, upon how these circumstances and activities are interpreted by those involved (Grint 2005). This problem with defining work has called for a re-evaluation of what is meant by the term.

Glucksmann (2006) argues for an understanding of work as the 'total social organisation of labour'. This definition is more inclusive, and recognises the labour carried out which is unpaid but of value and importance to the UK economy and society overall. But, whilst this alternative definition of work may be more sociologically appropriate we still may need to recognise that the ways in which work is commonly defined within political discourse reflect in part the relations of power within society as it is. So, for example, if domestic work or childcare is regarded as 'real work' or, alternatively, 'leisure', then it is because we are constructing our activities through a particular sort of viewpoint, or discourse (Grint 2005).

As Grint (2005) states, the discourse of work is constituted by symbolic representations through which meanings and social interests are constructed, mediated and deployed. To put it simply, what is meant by 'work'

work and unemployment

is a matter of competing ideological discourses that are embedded in particular power relations in society.

5.3 Work and the 'work ethic'

As we have seen there are several contending discourses that constitute the way in which people think about work. Levitas (2005) argues that work has been central to a discourse of inclusion, where participation in paid work is seen as the main way of combating social exclusion. She maintains that social policy in the UK has been preoccupied with the idea of inclusion in the labour market and that the importance of paid employment has dominated UK politics for many years, in conjunction with the important conception of the 'work ethic'. As the nineteenth-century sociologist Max Weber (1864–1920) showed, the idea that work in itself constitutes a value has its historical origin in particular parts of Europe following the period of the Reformation and extending into the eighteenth century. The consequence is that in our culture we polarise a notion of the 'work ethic' with, on the other hand, laziness, which we condemn.

This discourse of social inclusion as participation in paid work was evident in the thinking behind New Labour Chancellor of the Exchequer Gordon Brown's New Deal Scheme (introduced in 1998, and renamed the Flexible New Deal in 2009), with its emphasis upon 'making work pay' (Levitas 2005). The New Deal was aimed at increasing labour market participation among specific groups, including the young, the long-term unemployed, people with disabilities and lone parents, and with amending the benefits system so that people could not be better off on benefits than in paid work. This aspiration continued in the Conservative-Liberal Coalition government. The introduction of Universal Credit, developed in 2013 by Work and Pensions Secretary Iain Duncan Smith, is based on the idea that everyone of working age should be in paid work, rather than dependent on the state. These policies aimed at getting people into work have been accompanied by an emphasis on the 'work ethic' and the moral importance of paid work. Because of the focus on paid work, *working* families are seen as morally more worthy than others.

REWIND <<<<< 4.4

For a further discussion about government policy and inclusion in the labour market see New Labour and social exclusion.

There are many strains and contradictions in these policies. In political discourse there is often an emphasis on the importance of parenting and of community, but these can be in some tension with an overriding emphasis on paid work. In fact both of these aspects of society depend on unpaid labour. If, for example, two lone parents look after their own young children they are deemed not to be working, but if they register as child minders and swap children for 35 hours a week they will be defined as working.

Feminists have challenged the terms in which we think about the value and productivity of domestic labour. In the case of Smith (1987), the author argues that the unpaid work which women undertake in the private sphere of the home ensures the functioning of the public sphere of paid work. A Marxist tradition has also provided the theoretical context to develop a critique of the concept of 'work' in capitalism. For Marxists, the ways in which work is defined within political discourse, as well as the symbolic significance of the 'work ethic', can be grasped only if we locate our analysis in the context of the class relations of capitalism. For Marx himself the key contradiction in capitalist society lay in the class conflict between a ruling class, the bourgeoisie, and a class whose labour is exploited by them, the proletariat. In his early writings, such as the *Economic and Philosophical Manuscripts* of 1844, Marx developed the concept of alienation to characterise the damage done to people forced to work within the constraints of a capitalist economy. He argued that in capitalist societies workers were distanced from the product of their labour as well as their own creativity, and from other workers. In this sense people were alienated from their full human potential.

The critical traditions which are the inheritors of Marx's analysis have continued to emphasise that capitalism is an economic and social system which distances people from truly fulfilling activities. This is because under capitalism work is limited to an activity that is necessary in order to survive. Capitalism is organised to pursue and accumulate profit rather than to benefit the mass of members of society. Writers such as Gorz (1999) have sought to apply aspects of this analysis to contemporary capitalist societies.

 Key thinker: Andre Gorz (1923–2007)

Gorz is a key thinker in debates about the future of work. Influenced by Jean-Paul Sartre's existentialist approach to Marxism, Gorz became associated with the New Left movement of the 1960s and 1970s. Some of the main themes he addresses are wage labour issues and the idea of a guaranteed basic income for all. His work includes *Critique of Economic Reason* (1989), *Farewell to the Working Class* (1983), *Paths to Paradise* (1985) and *Reclaiming Work: Beyond the Wage-Based Society* (1999). The ideas that Gorz presents in his work are important for rethinking our conceptions of work and the ways in which work is socially defined in capitalist societies.

work and unemployment

In a critique of work relations within capitalism, *Reclaiming Work: Beyond a Wage-Based Society*, Andre Gorz (1999) argues that capitalism has socially constructed the idea of work and what it represents. Under a capitalist social and economic system there is a discourse which sees work only as paid employment, and does not recognise the 'real work' that many people carry out. Gorz argues that we must learn to see work differently: no longer as something we have or do not have, but as what *we do*. Drawing on Rifkin's (1995) book, *The End of Work*, Gorz (1999) argues for an end to work which is peculiar to industrial capitalism: 'the work we are referring to when we say "she doesn't work" of a woman who devotes her time to bringing up her own children, but "she works" of one who gives even some small part of her time to bringing up other people's children in a play group or nursery school' (Gorz 1999: 2).

According to Gorz, a conception of 'real work' ought to encompass the broad creative scope of human activity and not be limited to what we do when 'at work'. Rather, socially we must move beyond the constraints and exploitation of the wage relation and beyond the wage-based society in order to achieve a system in which there is a decent livelihood for all.

Like many radical thinkers, Gorz argues for a Basic Income. Basic Income proposals vary considerably. Gorz stresses that he is not talking about a minimum income, which permits mere subsistence, nor a participation income, which (as the Commission on Social Justice in 1994 suggested) would depend on 'approved' activity such as involvement in some form of education, work or caring. For Gorz, such an income must be both unconditional and adequate for a decent existence in the society in question. Only on this basis can discontinuous labour market activity be made consistent with continuous income, and discontinuity be flexibility *for* rather than *of* workers. Only on this basis could there be effective validation of, and adequate recompense for, caring, voluntary and non-market activities. A combination of basic income, decent public services and ecologically sustainable urban regeneration would make 'inclusion' a more meaningful term – partly because it would entail greater equality. Gorz's argument is that it is not simply a matter of reinstating and extending the redistributive policies favoured by old-style social democracy, nor even of rethinking what constitutes work, but of abandoning the work ethic itself.

Gorz has a radical vision which points to a society beyond capitalism. For him, it has to be recognised that 'neither the right to an income, nor full citizenship, nor everyone's sense of identity and self-fulfilment can any longer be centred on and depend on occupying a job' (Gorz 1999: 54). Critics argue that this is simply unachievable and often point to the dystopic results of attempts through the twentieth century to create non-capitalist societies, such as the Union of Socialist Soviet Republics. However, Gorz's utopian thinking can make us reflect upon the social construction of work, the ideological assumptions underpinning the 'work ethic' and the sometimes debilitating consequences of the ways in which work is made central to our ways of thinking.

The importance placed on being in paid employment makes unemployment all the more of a problem for those experiencing it. As we have seen, our understanding of what it means to be 'in work' or 'out of work' is crucial for determining the nature of the 'problem', and if indeed it is a problem at all. In the next section of this chapter we shall examine more closely what 'being out of work' involves. We shall see that defining and measuring unemployment is as difficult as our attempt to define the nature of work.

5.4 Defining and measuring unemployment

It is extremely difficult to compare rates of unemployment over time in any one country or between countries. This is because governments frequently alter the way unemployment is measured, often for political reasons. For example, between 1979 and 1989, Conservative governments in the UK changed the way unemployment was measured 30 times and virtually every one of these had the effect of reducing unemployment figures (Edgell 2012). Today, most countries are adopting a definition of unemployment held by the International Labour Organisation (ILO), a specialist UN agency. It classifies people as unemployed if they are without a job, actively seeking employment and are available to work. But some governments define unemployment by those who are registered as unemployed and in receipt of unemployment-related state benefits. It is not surprising, then, that these two rates of unemployment are very different, given that they measure different things. The ILO measure 'typically produces a higher level of unemployment rates than the "claimant count"' (Edgell 2012: 175).

These differing measures of unemployment tell us that the unemployment rate is a product of the decisions taken in relation to how to define unemployment. In other words, what is measured is not unproblematic but is a phenomenon constructed through social and political decisions about definitions. For example, in November 1982, those who were not eligible for benefits were excluded from the unemployment figures in Britain. And in March 1983, men over the age of 60 who were claiming long-term supplementary benefit (now called income support) were no longer required to sign on and so were no longer recorded as unemployed.

Although as sociologists we will want to attend to official statistics relating to employment rates, we will need to bear in mind that these figures do need to be treated with great caution. As a student of the social sciences you will become familiar with the manner in which statistics are put together in particular ways and for particular purposes (indeed the argument that statistics are socially constructed is a theme that runs throughout this book).

work and unemployment

FAST FORWARD >>>>> 8.3 and 8.4

Illustrate how statistics are socially constructed in relation to organised crime.

Debates about unemployment are often intensely political. For example, in the 1980s, when unemployment was at its peak in the UK, Lord Young, the then Employment Secretary, and Jeffrey Archer, the novelist and former vice-chair of the Conservative Party, claimed publicly that up to one million people were included in the unemployment statistics who should not be because they were working and claiming benefits illegally or were not genuinely looking for work. This view was decisively rejected by politicians of the Left who saw this claim as an attempt to justify a Conservative strategy to use unemployment as a tool to deal with an economic crisis. Sociologists usually argue that official unemployment statistics have under-estimated the amount of unemployment rather than exaggerated it. However, the main point to take from this section is this: unemployment is something that is measured in particular ways, by particular groups of people and for particular reasons – often politically motivated. No unemployment statistic can be taken as a purely 'objective' figure, but must always be understood in relation to the way it has been produced and, arguably, the purposes it may serve.

5.5 The social construction of unemployment

There has recently been intensification in the discourse which depicts the unemployed as lazy or idle individuals who are disinclined to work. A particular public discourse presented by the media tells us that the 'unemployed' are welfare dependents sponging off the state, using the taxes of others to pay for their widescreen TVs and mobile smartphones. Tabloid newspapers, such as the *Sun*, have consistently reported on 'the benefit scroungers' of Britain, calling for them to be stopped. This is a construction of the unemployed which typifies them as 'scroungers' who have become a drain on society. They take from society but they give nothing back. This perception of the unemployed is sensationalised by tabloid newspapers, consistently discussed in public and political debate and used as clear justification by political parties for reducing welfare benefits. For example, Prime Minister David Cameron declared in 2013 that the benefits bill was 'sky-rocketing' while 'generations languish on the dole and dependency'. In the same year, the Chancellor, George Osborne, also added: 'where is the fairness...for the shift-worker, leaving home in the dark hours of the early morning, who looks up at the closed blinds of their next-door neighbour sleeping off a life on benefits?' (Ian Mulheirn, *New Statesman*, 15 March 2013).

The question raised by Osborne is imbued with a number of assumptions. One is that the population can be divided between those who work and those who receive benefits. Another is that people on benefits are parasitic. However, many people who receive benefits are in fact also legally employed. Also of interest is some research which was carried out by the Department for Work and Pensions (March 2013) looking at the benefit histories of dole recipients. Their findings undermine the view that our welfare system is full of people taking advantage of a 'something for nothing' deal. The analysis looks at the benefit-claims history of people who made a claim for unemployment benefit in 2010–11, going back four years prior to their latest claim. For a sample group of 32- to 33-year-olds who claimed Jobseeker's Allowance (JSA) in 2010–11, 40 per cent had not made a claim before in that period; 63 per cent had spent no more than six months of the previous four years on JSA; and almost four out of five claimants had spent at least three-quarters of the past four years off the 'dole'. On the basis of this data, the idea that claimants are universally 'trapped' in a 'dependency culture' is hard to defend.

The assertion that the unemployed are 'sleeping off a life on benefits' also implies that life 'on the dole' is enjoyable or even luxurious. But for those living below the poverty line life is often anything but enjoyable. In practice, it's difficult to find families in which no member has ever worked, let alone generations of people on the 'dole'.

REWIND <<<<< 4.2

For more of a discussion that links poverty and unemployment.

There is, therefore, a particular social construction of the unemployed that often structures common-sense perceptions and has been used as a political cover for policies aimed at cuts in welfare benefits. It could be argued that this social construction operates as an ideology in a Marxist sense – that is, that it obscures the economic and social relations which give rise to high rates of unemployment by blaming the unemployed themselves. The conclusion which can be taken from the research findings of the Department of Work and Pensions pulls in a different direction: most people who claim unemployment benefit each year spend at least three-quarters of their time in work. And for 40 per cent of claimants, the claiming of JSA is not part of a lifestyle choice, since they have no recent history of having done so before. Only a minority of adults, 11 per cent of claimants in 2010–11, had a history of spending more than half of recent years on the dole.

work and unemployment

Another contemporary issue around unemployment is that there has been a shift in the sorts of work contracts available to people as employees. Full-time jobs with permanent contracts and strong pension arrangements have become less available. More people are self-employed or employed on the basis of short-term contracts which do not offer the same job security as was available to people employed in earlier generations. The Labour Force Survey in 2012 reported that more than 250,000 people were on zero-hours contracts (0.8 per cent of the total workforce) – contracts which do not offer a guarantee of any hours or times for work, but under the terms of which would-be employees commit to being available or 'on call' to work for organisations as and when required. However, the reported figures for zero-hour contracts are probably understated, given that many respondents in the survey may be unaware of their contractual arrangements or may not recognise the term 'zero-hours contract' at all. These shifting work relations feed into, and serve to decrease, unemployment statistics. Changing patterns of work and work contracts – which also involve a restructuring of the economy so that many newly created jobs are actually part-time jobs often paying only the legal minimum wage – have led some sociologists to refer to a portion of the workforce as the 'precariat' – a section of the workforce whose employment is characterised by its insecurity in terms of skills, lack of protection and casualisation (Fitzgibbon 2013). This argument is most developed in G. Standings' (2011) text, *The Precariat: The New Dangerous Class*. The depiction of the unemployed as lazy and unwilling to work sits uneasily with this reconfiguration of work relations.

For those relatively small groups of people who are long-term unemployed there are a number of structural issues as well as many other social problems identified in this book which might underlie why certain groups remain unemployed. For example, it may be that the local or national economies have failed and caused long-term high unemployment; or factors relating to disadvantages in the education system or neighbourhoods where gang and anti-social behaviour have become alternative sub-cultures. All these structural and cultural issues play a part in people's lives and can constrain the opportunity for some people to find employment. Some of these structural issues are examined more closely in the following section.

5.6 Structural issues: gender, ethnicity and social class

As we have seen, there is a common perception that unemployment is a problem which stems from the choices made by individuals. Some of us are keen to find jobs and work, whilst others are lazy, work shy and/or incapable of finding work. But if unemployment depended upon the free will and independent choices of individuals, then we would not expect to find social patterns among groups in the population based on such things as gender, ethnicity and social class.

In relation to gender, for example, official figures show consistently higher rates of unemployment for men than for women, with the unemployment rate for men sometimes two and a half times that of women. In explaining these figures we need, however, to recognise that married women are sometimes ineligible for benefits and do not show up as being registered unemployed (refer back to Section 5.4 on measuring unemployment). In fact, where partners are cohabiting, entitlements to state support are often affected. Despite rates of unemployment being higher for men than for women, it must be noted also that women are more likely than men to occupy part-time employment, and many of these jobs are low-paid and low-status work (Edgell 2012). Also note that this impacts on the gender pay gap, with men earning on average significantly more than women in nearly all sectors of work. Nevertheless, these differences in unemployment rates between men and women are gendered differences and therefore structural, not simply a matter of an individual's personal decision to work.

Another structural factor that impacts on unemployment is social class. The conception of class within sociology is complex, but here we will take it to refer broadly to occupation. As we have seen in the section above, the occupations available to people and the contracts which govern them change over time. Research shows that 'lower' social classes are generally more likely to experience unemployment than other social classes. Table 5.1 shows figures for unemployment by occupation for May 2013.

If you place your finger on the table and shift it across from left to right, you will notice a range of different figures for different occupational groups. Those occupations starting from the left tend to be those occupied by the 'higher' social classes (managers and senior officials, professionals and those with jobs requiring technical skills). These are followed by the middle sections (administrative and secretarial and skilled occupations). Those on the right (sales and customer services, machine operatives and elementary occupations) tend to have occupations typically defined predominantly as working class. If you run your finger downwards in any one occupational type group, you will see a consistency with the level of unemployment. This in itself shows that different sectors are subject to certain levels of unemployment. Let's take two occupational groups and compare them. For those in 'Professional Occupations' the Labour Force Survey counted 101,000 unemployed. But for those who occupy 'Elementary Occupations' the number is nearly five times as many, with 489,000 unemployed. Given the consistency of these figures over several years, we can say that those who occupy 'Professional Occupations' are far less likely to suffer the effects of unemployment than those who occupy the 'Elementary Occupations'. What is apparent and most important is this: the differences in unemployment are structural differences to do with

work and unemployment

Table 5.1 Unemployed by occupation of last job (May 2013)

Unemployed by occupation of last job (Standard Occupational Classification SOC 2000)

	Managers & senior officials	Professional occupations	Associate professional & technical	Admin & secretarial	Skilled trades	Personal services	Sales & customer services	Process, plant & machine operatives	Elementary occupations
Persons									
Jan-Mar 2011	149	93	148	172	189	118	216	174	440
Jan-Mar 2012	156	113	166	183	196	139	276	170	473
Apr-Jun 2012	162	96	147	183	183	126	257	149	465
Jul-Sep 2012	148	105	162	167	180	148	216	159	460
Oct-Dec 2012	142	106	164	152	183	151	217	128	439
Jan-Mar 2013	137	101	148	154	191	161	249	150	489
Change on year	−19	−12	−18	−29	−5	22	−26	−20	16
Change %	−12.3	−10.2	−10.8	−16.1	−2.6	15.8	−9.5	−11.9	3.5

Source: Labour Force Survey (May 2013) Office for National Statistics.

societal factors that impact upon the opportunities for certain groups of people (in this case certain occupational groups/social classes) to be employed and cannot be simply a matter of choices made by individuals.

Evidence concerning ethnicity and unemployment also shows clear variations, with ethnic minority groups suffering from much higher rates of unemployment than those of the ethnic majority. The Labour Force Survey carried out in 2013 found that just 7 per cent of white people were unemployed, as compared with over 17 per cent of Pakistanis, 19 per cent of Bangladeshis and 18 per cent of black people. The unemployment rate for other minority ethnic groups also exceeds the national average, although the rate for Indians remains closest to the rate for white people.

Ethnic minorities can find employment particularly difficult when faced with racist prejudice before they even enter the workplace. In 2013 there was an employment tribunal over race discrimination. A man claimed that Virgin Atlantic had discriminated against him on the grounds of race when it rejected his job application, allegedly because of his African name. The man was a British citizen with a degree in international relations and was shocked to find he had not been interviewed for a job in a Swansea call centre working for Virgin's organisation. Suspicious that it could be due to his foreign-sounding name, he reapplied with a typically British name and was invited several times to attend an interview. 'There was an enormous difference in the way I was treated when I used a British name,' he said (*The Guardian*, 11 April 2013).

This experience is not unprecedented. Stories from applicants and recruiters suggest that prejudice and discrimination are still commonplace. Racist attitudes towards job seekers, serve only to worsen unemployment for ethnic minority groups.

5.7 The consequences of unemployment

There are a number of consequences of being unemployed. Some unemployed people miss out on a number of opportunities, not least because they are not earning a wage or salary. For example, long-term unemployed people are often unable to sustain friendships, social contacts and networks, they have less control than the employed over their social environment to achieve external goals, lack financial security and can suffer from low self-esteem and social status. The consequences of unemployment are different depending on social and cultural aspects of those unemployed. In this section we shall take a look at the consequences of unemployment by way of age, gender and social class.

For younger people about to enter the labour market, their financial needs are very different from those of prime-age males and females who may have families to support. Young people and school leavers are a social group who suffer considerably from unemployment. They are more unlikely to find a job during a recession and do not always qualify for unemployment

work and unemployment

benefits, which are typically based on being in work for a given period of time (Edgell 2012). To make matters worse, long spells of unemployment for young people can result in permanent scars on their curriculum vitae and future employers are unlikely to give jobs to young people with histories of long-term unemployment.

Unemployment for the middle-aged can also cause severe health and social problems, and people in their fifties can find it difficult to be redeployed, since employers are typically reluctant to recruit older workers (Edgell 2012). This happens despite the recent Employment Equality Regulations (2006), which make it illegal for employers to discriminate on the basis of age (ageism). On top of this, long-term unemployment can result in low self-esteem, poor health and depression (Edgell 2012). Unemployment also relates to marital status, with single men more likely to be unemployed than married men (Grint 2005). This, however, is probably related to a number of interrelated factors: married men with families to support are probably more inclined to retain their employment status, and women are arguably more likely to seek marital relationships with men who have a 'steady' and secure employment history. Also, employers may prefer married men because they are deemed to be more constrained by domestic commitments. When a married man becomes unemployed, however, this can result in marital discord – minor quarrels between married couples can increase in situations of deprivation and be intensified by unemployment (Edgell 2012). All in all, however, marriage appears to stabilise employment for men (Grint 2005).

Unemployment can affect various social classes differently. The working class are said to suffer more from the financial consequences and the lack of financial savings of unemployment and are more likely to take the next job on offer, than are those of the middle class. And for many of the working classes in areas of high unemployment, the problem is exacerbated by the fact that unemployment becomes more of a social condition than an individual problem. Despite the mass numbers and mass experience of unemployment, the problem is still experienced individually – people blame themselves for not being able to find work.

REWIND <<<<< 2.2

Earlier in this book we discussed C. Wright Mills and his book *The Sociological Imagination* (2000). Revisit this chapter for a discussion of the relationship between individual and social issues.

This individualising of what is fundamentally a social problem is what Wright-Mills (2000) brought attention to in his book *The Sociological Imagination*. He argued that the public issue of social structure becomes perceived as the personal troubles of a milieu (Wright-Mills 2000). Social problems are experienced as personal problems and the 'issue is drawn off from the social structure and relocated within the apparent personal failings of an individual' (Grint 2005: 39). Where unemployment is caused by redundancy, there is still widespread belief among future employers that those individuals may have lost their jobs because of their work records, and so employer hostility increases the longer the person remains unemployed. And despite some arguing that the unemployed should lower their demands and seek work of any kind, few employers are prepared to take on unemployed workers who do this because they assume that the person must be desperate and therefore have no real interest in the job (Grint 2005).

5.8 Unemployment, social problems and crime

One of the many social problems associated with unemployment is crime. Emile Durkheim (1858–1917), one of the founding fathers of sociology, argued that actually, from the point of view of sociology, crime is normal. Not only is it a characteristic of all societies, in the sense that all societies impose boundaries on permissible behaviour and negatively sanction behaviour which is deviant from the norm, but also in doing so societies reaffirm their own moral substance. Durkheim also developed the concept of *anomie* to refer to the idea that in modern societies traditional norms and values become undermined: there is a disjunction between societal organisation and societal morality. Anomie exists when there are no clear standards to guide behaviour in particular aspects of social life, particularly when the norms and values in society break down due to the rapid pace of social change. In Durkheim's time he saw a problem in that a morality based on a taken-for-granted traditional social hierarchy was out of kilter with occupational developments related to the complex division of labour in industrial society, which called for a more meritocratic morality.

 Key thinker: Emile Durkheim (1858–1917)

Durkheim, a French sociologist, was one of the pioneers of social science. His work includes *The Division of Labour in Society* (1893), in which he first introduced the concept of 'anomie'. He also wrote several other key texts, including *The Rules of Sociological Method* (1895), *Suicide: A Study in Sociology* (1897) and *The Elementary Forms of the Religious Life* (1912). Durkheim's work showed how external constraints operated at the level of the social, both limiting and opening up opportunities to think and act in certain ways. Durkheim's studies have built a foundation for contemporary social sciences.

In the twentieth century Robert Merton developed a useful perspective for understanding the relationship between unemployment and crime in his 'strain theory'.

FAST FORWARD >>>>> 9.4

For a discussion of how Merton's ideas have contributed to debates about how gangs are formed.

Merton (1957) developed his ideas by drawing on Durkheim's conception of anomie. He argued that in American society not everyone can realise the dominant dream of material success. When legitimate opportunities to achieve success are blocked, some people – whom Merton called 'innovators' – develop illegitimate means to acquire societally approved goals such as nice houses and big cars. People may engage in illegal activity, such as buying stolen goods, or taking something which does not belong to them. Or they might avoid paying taxes from cash-in-hand work carried out. Or even tell lies to government agencies to maximise state benefits. Significantly, people may also engage in black-market economic activity such as drug or people trafficking. Merton also identifies a category of 'rebels' who both reject the socially approved means and ends and seek to overthrow the capitalist system itself, developing a vision of a society that transcends capitalism and the goals it deploys.

Merton thereby explained that it is possible for culturally prescribed goals to overcome and completely dominate consideration of culturally prescribed means. In his words, 'there may develop a very heavy, at times virtually exclusive, stress upon the value of particular goals, involving comparatively little concern with the institutionally prescribed means of striving toward these goals' (Merton 1957: 132). According to Merton, society and social institutions place a greater emphasis on cultural goals than upon institutional or legitimate means to achieve them. When these goals (i.e. 'making money') are so emphasised that they get far more attention than the institutionalised means (i.e. going to work) to achieve them, the result is anomie and criminality. The unavailability of work and rising unemployment levels can, therefore, lead to various criminal activities.

One example we can examine here is the London Riots of 2011. The media tended to report the unrest in terms of an irrational, meaningless kind of deviance. The Home Secretary, Theresa May, talked about 'sheer criminality'. However, as social scientists we would want to consider whether the concepts that Durkheim and Merton have developed can be of use here. Whilst there was much speculation in the media that the rioting was caused by 'gangs', data collected at the time suggested that gangs were not the main source of the rioting. It may be, however, that the riots expressed both the problem of anomie as developed by Durkheim – a problem of lack of moral consensus rooted in the disjunction between society's values and the recent economic crisis – or that they could in part be explained through Merton's conception of 'innovation', where people employ illegitimate means to acquire goods they could not otherwise have. The phenomenon of the riots is complex, in part because people gave a variety of accounts for their motivations and experiences of involvement.

5.9 Summary

We began the chapter by looking at work and the various ways in which work could be defined. We said that the definition of work, as paid employment, is problematic because large numbers of people in the UK carry out work which is unpaid. Yet this activity is still valuable to the functioning and economic stability of British society. Charity workers, carers and those who look after children or carry out domestic duties all carry out 'real' work, whether this is paid or not. What counts as work, it was argued, depends upon the specific social circumstances under which such activities are undertaken and, importantly, how these circumstances and activities are interpreted by those involved. Grint (1998) argues that there is a discourse of work provided by symbolic representations through which meanings and social interests are constructed, mediated and deployed. Some types of activities take on those characteristics appropriated by the given discourse (such as making food in a café), whilst others do not (such as cooking at home).

Next we discussed work and the 'work ethic'. We said that the work ethic was part of a particular discourse which has dominated British politics for many years. We looked at the work of Levitas (2005), who argues that social policy in Britain has been preoccupied with the idea of inclusion in the labour market. Politicians have created policies which are directed at getting people into employment. But we saw that this preoccupation with paid work inherently puts a higher value on working families, and assumes that they are morally more worthy than others. Gorz (1999) argues that in order to rescue and sustain 'real work' we must recognise that work is no longer what we do when 'at work'. For Gorz (1999), capitalism has socially constructed the idea of work and what it represents. It has created a discourse which sees work as paid employment, and not the 'real work' that many people carry out. Following this, Gorz (1999) emphasises the point that, as our understandings of work are socially constructed and not fixed, what we take to be work has the possibility to be changed.

The rest of this chapter looked at unemployment. Just as the definition and organisation of work are socially constructed, so too unemployment can be seen as a product of particular ways in which it is defined and measured. We showed evidence of this by the unevenly dispersed rates of unemployment between different social groups, such as middle class and working class, ethnic minorities and the majority white ethnic population, and different age groups.

We said that measuring unemployment is difficult, because it is extremely hard to compare rates of unemployment over time in any one country or between countries. It was argued that this was because government frequently altered the way unemployment is measured, often for political reasons. Because of this, rates of employment can be very different over time.

It was also argued in this chapter that there has been a recent underlying discourse which depicts the unemployed as lazy individuals who are disinclined to work. We discussed a particular public discourse presented by the media that tells us that the 'unemployed' are welfare dependents sponging off the state, using the taxes of others to pay for their widescreen TVs and mobile smartphones. We said that this is a construction of the unemployed which typifies them as 'scroungers' who have become a drain on society. This perception of the unemployed has permeated common-sense knowledge. It is fed into public and political debate, often sensationalised by tabloid newspapers, and can be deployed by political parties as justification for reducing welfare benefits. But we gave a perspective on this which avoided common-sense assumptions and the sensationalism of tabloid newspapers. Instead, we looked at research that showed that the so-called 'dependency culture' of welfare recipients is a myth.

We also paid attention to the changing patterns of work and work contracts. Many newly created jobs are part time and often paying only the legal minimum wage. This has led some sociologists to refer to a portion of the workforce as the 'precariat' – a section of the workforce whose employment is insecure, casualised and has poor promotion and career-development opportunities. The idea of the unemployed as lazy and unwilling to work sits uneasily with this reconfiguration of work relations.

Overall, this chapter has tried to show that certain social categories in the working-age population are over-represented among the unemployed, and this in itself tells us a great deal about the character of unemployment. Unemployment is not a social problem that arises from individual decision making, but is related to structural factors in our society: social factors related to gender, ethnicity or age, poverty, crime and a whole other host of social problems which we explore in this textbook.

Revision notes

Defining work. This is problematic, as we cannot define work as merely paid employment. For example, people who look after elderly relatives might carry out the exact same work as paid carers working within a nursing home. Similarly, employed cleaners get paid for work, yet women who look after their children and carry out domestic responsibilities are said to be 'out of work'. This has called for a reconsideration of work, and to consider the total social organisation of work.

The 'work ethic'. There is a discourse of inclusion in the labour market. This discourse provides us with assumptions and expectations that everybody in society should work (with the exception of the very young, old or ill). Those of us who participate in paid work are 'working', whilst those of us who are not in paid employment are deemed to be 'out of work'. The 'work ethic' is tied into social policy in Britain – e.g. benefits or allowances which encourage people to enter paid employment. But the 'work ethic' is focused on paid work, and not on all other work that is of equal importance to the smooth running of society.

Measuring unemployment. There is great difficulty in comparing rates of unemployment over time in any one country or between countries. This is because unemployment is measured differently by different people, often for political reasons. For example, the ILO measure 'typically produces a higher level of unemployment rates than the so called "claimant count"' (Edgell 2012: 175). These differing measures of unemployment tell us that unemployment is a product of the social because it is both defined and measured by it.

The social construction of unemployment. Political and public discourse views unemployment as a social problem stemming from lazy and work-shy individuals. A particular public discourse presented by the media discloses the 'unemployed' as idle, lazy individuals who 'sponge' off the state. They are welfare dependents using the taxes of others to pay for their widescreen TVs and mobile smartphones. This is a construction of the unemployed which typifies them as 'scroungers' who have become a drain on society.

Unemployment in the UK is often constructed as an individual issue, not a social problem. Public discourse views unemployment as the responsibility of the individual. If a person cannot get a job they are deemed to have not taken up all opportunities available to them. But unemployment is intrinsically related to social structures which operate outside of any individual's

work and unemployment

decision to get a job or not. Structural factors include: age, ethnicity, social class, gender, as well the economic conditions (such as available jobs) and locations in which people are born.

Consequences of unemployment. Unemployment can have diverse consequences for different social groups. Young people can suffer considerably from unemployment, because they lack experience and may not necessarily have the right skills for the jobs currently available. Employers are unlikely to give jobs to young people who have suffered from long spells of unemployment. The middle-aged can find it impossible to be redeployed after short or long-term unemployment, since employers are typically reluctant to recruit older workers to their organisation. Overall, there are many consequences of unemployment that relate to various other social problems discussed in this book.

Seminar tasks

Work and unemployment

1 Issue:
We saw from the discussion in the early part of this chapter how difficult it is to define work. The difficulty with this definition is to do with the conflicting perspectives about what constitutes 'real' work. Some argue that work is paid employment, but this is perhaps a narrow and naïve definition of work. Others use a much broader view of work incorporating the activities people do (e.g. looking after children, or domestic duties) outside of paid employment. In recent years in the UK the government has been preoccupied with getting people into paid employment. But it is debatable as to how important this is.

EXAMPLE:
Many elderly people who are in nursing homes receive 24-hour care from paid nurses, managers and care workers. Workers in nursing homes receive a paid salary to carry out their jobs. However, many elderly people living at home receive care from family members in the same way, only these family members do not receive the same income or work benefits (like holidays) as those looking after elderly people in nursing homes.

EXERCISE:
Does the work carried out by family carers constitute 'real' work? Should they receive a salary in the same way as nurses, managers and care workers do?

2 Issue:

We can see from the discussion above that unemployment in the UK is often constructed as an individual issue rather than a social problem. If a person does not work and cannot find employment, then the responsibility is placed on them as an individual to keep looking and eventually get a job. This idea assumes, however, that there are enough jobs for everybody, and that those applying for jobs have the necessary skills required for the specific post. It also fails to recognise the fact that unemployment is related to social structures which operate outside of any individual's choice to find a job or not.

EXAMPLE:

A 50-year-old black male mechanic called George is made redundant from the company where he has worked for over 30 years. He tries his best to find another job, but is unsuccessful. Ideally he wants to find employment in garages or car manufacturing companies but this is extremely difficult. Because of the economic recession car garages are systematically reducing labour costs by employing cheaper labour – this usually involves recruiting apprentices and other less experienced mechanics. George is happy to work elsewhere, but because of his lack of experience in other industries he finds it impossible to get another job.

EXERCISE:

In small groups identify at least three structural factors that might be preventing George from finding new employment. Put these factors in rank order, starting with what your group thinks is the most important. To what extent do these factors determine the chances of George finding new employment?

Coursework questions

Is the 'claimant count' a useful way of measuring unemployment?

The welfare 'dependency culture' is a myth. Discuss.

To what extent is unemployment an individual issue and to what extent is it a consequence of structural inequalities?

What are the main social problems associated with unemployment?

References

Department for Work and Pensions, *Annual Report and Accounts 2013*, 2013, https://www.gov.uk

Edgell, S., *The Sociology of Work: continuity and change in paid and unpaid work*, London: Sage, 2012

Fitzgibbon, W., 'Riots and Probation: governing the precariat', *Criminal Justice Matters*, 93(1): 18–19, 2013

Glucksmann, M., 'Shifting Boundaries and Interconnections: extending the total social organisation of "labour"', *The Sociological Review,* 53 (s2): 19–36, 2006

Gorz, A., *Reclaiming Work*, Cambridge: Polity Press, 1999

Grint, K., *The Sociology of Work*, Cambridge: Polity Press, 1998

—, *The Sociology of Work*, Cambridge: Polity Press, 2005

Levitas, R., *The Inclusive Society? Social exclusion and new labour*, Basingstoke: Palgrave Macmillan, 2005

—, *Social Theory and Social Structure*, New York: The Free Press, 1957

Mulheirn, I., *New Statesman*, 15 March 2013

Oakley, A., *Sex, Gender and Society*, London: Temple Smith, 1966

Rifkin, J., *The End of Work: the decline of the global labor force and the dawn of the post-market era*, New York: Putnam Publishing Group, 1995

Smith, D.E., *The Everyday World as Problematic: Feminist Sociology*, Milton Keynes: Open University Press, 1987

Standings, G., *The Precariat: the new dangerous class*, London: Bloomsbury, 2011

The Guardian, Can Anonymous CVs Help Beat Recruitment Discrimination? 11 April 2013, www.theguardian.com/money/work-blog/2013/apr/11/can-anonymous-cvs-help-beat-job-discrimination

Wright-Mills, C., *The Sociological Imagination*, Oxford: Oxford University Press, 2000

Further reading

Edgell, S., *The Sociology of Work: continuity and change in paid and unpaid work*, London: Sage, 2012

Sennett, R., *The Culture of the New Capitalism*, New Haven, CT: Yale University Press, 2006

Sennett, R., *The Corrosion of Character: the personal consequences of work in the new capitalism*, London: W.W. Norton, 1998

91

chapter 6

Migration

Norman Ginsburg

6.1 Introduction

Immigration has been an issue which has come dramatically to the fore at several moments in contemporary British history (Panayi 2010). In the 1960s hostility to postcolonial economic migrants from the Caribbean and the Asian subcontinent led to a series of Immigration Acts, installing racialised immigration controls. In the 1970s a vocal white minority pressed for repatriation of non-whites of immigrant origin, whilst the leader of the Opposition, Margaret Thatcher, railed against immigrants 'swamping' British culture. Yet, in the 1980s Britain finally became reasonably comfortable with the reality of being a multi-ethnic, multicultural society. In the 1990s and early 2000s, hostility to political migrants demonised the 'asylum seeker', generating another round of exclusionary legislation from both the Conservative and New Labour governments. In the 2000s the economic boom generated a wave of economic migration, particularly from the new EU member states in central Europe, accompanied by New Labour's efforts at 'managed migration'. Since the economic bubble burst in 2008, another crescendo of hostility to immigration has built, this time led by the UK Independence Party (UKIP) and powerfully linked with deep-seated opposition to the EU, whose support for 'free movement' of workers is portrayed as a prominent example of Britain's loss of sovereignty to Brussels. Not surprisingly, perhaps, immigration has never been a popular cause – economic immigration driven by employment has been tolerated and even quietly encouraged in reluctant, hushed tones by governments, particularly in the boom decades of the 1950s and 2000s. Political migration of refugees has been accepted grudgingly as international human rights obligations have been pressed on governments by non-governmental organisations, jurists and other receiving countries.

6.2 The construction of immigration as a social problem

The social construction of immigration is obviously a much-contested discourse. On the one hand, there is the construction of immigration as a major social problem which can be resolved only by creating more of a fortress, ending both economic and political immigration. On the other hand, there is the construction of immigration as a necessary, even welcome feature of Britain's embrace of economic and political globalisation. It is impossible to deal with these conflicted constructions in an unbiased, neutral way. This chapter is more sympathetic to the pro-immigration perspective, while attempting to analyse the anti-immigration view as honestly as possible.

Framing the issue in such a simple, bipolar way is useful, though in reality, of course, there are many shades of opinion in between. Here we will explore, briefly, the dimensions of each pole, starting with the construction of immigration as a major social problem. In economic terms, immigrants are conceived as a drain on public resources and the welfare state and a threat to the livelihoods and employment prospects of the indigenous population. Immigration is portrayed as a demographic problem, making Britain too overcrowded and worsening environmental degradation. Sociologically, the presence of immigrants is seen as a threat to social cohesion and national solidarity, weakening the ties that maintain a sense of national and local community. This is linked with the notion of a cultural threat – the swamping of long-established British cultural heritage by alien elements.

Case Example 1

Migration as a major social problem

A.N. Wilson (2012), a columnist in the *Daily Mail* suggests that '...the effect of the huge increase in immigration in the past decade or so has left millions of us feeling a little shell-shocked. We no longer recognise the country we grew up in. We are increasingly aware that a uniting British culture that evolved over centuries is fragmenting. It is not racist to suggest that our social infrastructure, our schools, hospitals and housing stock cannot cope with such enormous numbers of migrants so quickly. The numbers of foreigners settling in this country must be reduced. And one thing which could and should be done immediately is for the Government to ban the use of any language other than English in schools. Until we all speak the same language, there is small hope that we could ever come together and cohere as the new society of the future.'

Case example 1, deserves a little deconstruction. First, who are the 'we' referred to? Rightly or wrongly, it is assumed that the reader is part of a majority who feel alien in their own land. Second, there is an assumption that there is a clearly defined, unifying British culture, which, third, cannot be ascribed to by newcomers. Understandably perhaps, the author himself recognises that these opening assumptions could be construed as racist; however, this issue is left hanging in the air.

Of course the text is correct in identifying the significant increase in immigration (see below), but it is surely an exaggeration to say that the country is unrecognisable as a result. The strength and nature of a fixed 'uniting British culture' is seriously contestable. The point about pressure on public resources is more plausible, but most new immigrants are taxpayers and relatively youthful. It is certainly not beyond the scope of government to devise a rational managed migration policy that can include investment in public services to meet new needs. The argument about language in schools is spurious, and a complete language ban would be draconian. Furthermore, there is little, if any, school teaching in anything but English. Certainly there is a pressing need to improve the English-language skills of migrant communities, as there is in various other social groups we might think of too.

The many shades of the anti-immigration view are represented widely within the political mainstream, mostly on the Right, but also within the centre-Left.

 Key concept: the left–right political spectrum

In political theory a traditional way of generalising about the ideological position of a political party, pressure group, think-tank or any other organisation is to set it somewhere along an imaginary straight line. Those on the left would be associated with state intervention, some degree of redistributive welfare and taxation and a belief in social equality. On the right there would be collected more conservative elements that stress law and order, patriotism, the 'natural' differences in individuals abilities and the belief in the traditional family. The centre of this imaginary line is sometimes characterised as 'liberal', taking aspects of both left and right ideologies usually tied to a belief in the free market as well as social justice. That said, in a contemporary context it is not so easy to use these divisions so readily. For example, New Labour, from the traditional left, accepted many of the ideas of the Right and was itself, largely economically, liberal.

The mass-circulation print media, particularly the *Daily Mail*, wage an incessant campaign against immigration, exemplified in the *Mail*'s reaction

migration

to the publication of initial findings from the 2011 Census on 11 December 2012. Over the following three days, headlines read 'Migrants will push house prices up an extra 10 per cent', 'Immigration on this scale and at this speed is too much to cope with', 'Immigration: Labour's unforgivable betrayal of the British people', 'I no longer recognize the Britain I grew up in', the latter heading the A.N. Wilson article quoted above. Such perspectives are backed up by a number of think-tanks and pressure groups. The most prominent is MigrationWatch, which is a bit of both. To operate within the mainstream, this organisation cannot be completely anti-immigration, but it argues for a very restrictive and strongly managed immigration policy which would reduce net migration to zero (i.e. equal numbers of emigrants and immigrants). MigrationWatch is linked with a cross-party parliamentary group called Balanced Migration, co-chaired by the former Labour minister Frank Field MP. The fundamental position of MigrationWatch and Balanced Migration is rooted in concern about population growth – the overcrowded island problematic. But behind that is the issue of social cohesion, and the construction of ethnic diversity/multiculturalism as a social problem leading to political and cultural conflict.

The perspective which constructs immigration as a major social problem has recently been articulated persuasively by the 'left-liberal' writer David Goodhart (2013). He asserts that immigration undermines the national community, which underpins the welfare state and restrains rampant individualism: 'sustained mass immigration, without appropriate integration, damages the internal solidarity of rich countries'. He makes direct links between contemporary immigration and the settled postcolonial ethnic communities, revisiting some familiar assertions from the 2000s about Muslims.

Case Example 2

The 'liberal-Left' construction of migration as a major social problem

'...multiculturalism, particularly in the more separatist form that emerged in the 1980s, has allowed "parallel lives" to grow up in some places and made it harder for ordinary Britons to think of some minorities, and especially Muslims, as part of the same "imagined community" with common experiences and interests. Race and identity politics has too often turned minority Britons into a sectional interest with their own "demands"...And too often the demands of minority leaders have been for a separate slice of power and resources rather than for the means to create a common life.' (Goodhart 2013)

Goodhart conflates 'immigrant' status with 'ethnic minority' status in being alarmed by the loosely framed predictions that 'in several European countries the immigrant and ethnic minority population is rising to 15 or 20 per cent in the next few years' and that 'many large towns are already around 40 per cent minority'. There is a thinly veiled hostility to long-settled minorities as well as immigrants here. Goodhart is sceptical about the economic benefits of immigration, suggesting that, at best, the net effects on the labour market and the economy are neutral. He argues that the asylum system is too liberal in giving refuge to people whose 'lives or personal security are not at serious risk'.

Anti-immigrationists like Goodhart, Field and the supporters of MigrationWatch are looking at the issue through the lens of the 'native' British, or at least a substantial swathe thereof. It is essentially a national communitarian view which seems to strike an intuitive, 'common sense' chord with many of the public. They would argue, nevertheless, that the pro-immigration position became dominant by default in the 1950s and again in the 1990s and 2000s.

There is no equivalent of MigrationWatch or Goodhart arguing a pro-immigration stance specifically for Britain. Instead there are a diversity of perspectives supporting different aspects of immigration, essentially looking at the issue either in terms of the benefits accruing to the economy and employers, or from the point of view of migrants and potential migrants. Pro-immigration social constructions are based in various interpretations of 'liberalism' – the free movement of workers, the freedom of employers to recruit, the human rights of migrants and potential migrants. On the biggest canvas, writers such as Legrain (2007) and Goldin et al. (2011) see immigration as an inevitable and beneficial feature of globalisation for the West and for migrants. If globalisation embraces the transnational flow of goods, services and capital, then it must also include the free flow of human beings, whether they are investment bankers, fruit pickers or fleeing persecution.

The most important player of all in the construction of immigration as a 'problem' is the government itself, in the form of legislation and policy, and also in shaping political and media discourse. In terms of transnational migration, this goes back at least to the beginning of the twentieth century, when controls on the entry of Jewish refugees from Central Europe were introduced. In the mid twentieth century, government was directly if furtively involved in recruitment of migrant workers from the former colonies, and then in closing the door to them from the mid 1960s. Labour and Conservative governments from the 1960s to the 1990s endorsed and strengthened the notion of immigration as a major social problem. There was little or no attempt to promote the benefits which migrants could bring to the economy, nor much support for the notion of human rights obligations to the world's refugees. In the 1970s, refugees from authoritarian regimes in Chile and Vietnam, for example, were accepted in small numbers, and supported almost in secret by sympathetic local authorities and charities. In the 1990s, governments' anti-immigration stance shifted somewhat, under pressure from the international human rights movement for refugees and from employers for migrant workers, particularly as the economy entered its boom phase. With the advent of New Labour in 1997, immigration policy became more explicit. Popular and successful efforts were made to deter asylum seekers from reaching Britain, while economic migration was acknowledged as an important element in the enthusiastic embracing of economic globalisation. For the first time, government offered a positive construction on the migration of some workers. Hence, in 2000 the Immigration Minister announced that Britain was in competition with other nations for the 'best and brightest talents' in the world and that 'economically driven migration can bring substantial overall benefits both for growth and the economy' (Spencer 2011: 88). This signalled the development of a 'managed migration' policy, which from 2008 took the form of five entry channels or tiers, respectively for 'highly skilled workers', 'skilled workers', 'low-skilled workers', students and temporary workers. Tier 3 ('low-skilled workers') has never been used – it was assumed that these needs would be filled by British or EU citizens. This 'system' constructs professional, managerial and skilled migrant workers as relatively unproblematic, with the implication that low-skilled/temporary migrant workers are problematic and cannot be allowed to settle. Only the first two tiers have the possibility of long-term settlement. So New Labour tried to deconstruct the holistic category of migrant into the 'good', the brightest and the best, and the 'bad', the problematic, not least, those who take jobs which allegedly could be done by indigenous people, not least, those languishing on benefits. From 2010 the Coalition government has laid much more emphasis on the latter construction, so that migration in general (apart from the wealthy and highly skilled) is once more portrayed as overwhelmingly problematic rather than beneficial.

The most significant pro-immigration pressures come from within the 'labour market', which is in reality a myriad of different labour markets and different types of employer, from large transnational corporations seeking skilled professionals to fruit and vegetable farmers needing workers, to families seeking a home carer for an elderly relative. The nearest thing to a pro-immigration lobby group, equivalent to Balanced Migration, is the Migration Matters Trust (MMT), a cross-party parliamentary group formed in 2013, voicing the 'positives of migration' for employers, universities and the economy. It is endorsed by the Mayor of London and the City of London Corporation. MMT argues that if net migration ended, the national debt would increase to catastrophic levels. There are also a range of interest groups and voluntary organisations representing and supporting migrants, which cannot be construed as pro-immigration but are 'pro-immigrant' in the sense of defending and advocating the needs of both political and economic migrants. These include the Joint Council for the Welfare of Immigrants (JCWI), the Refugee Council, Refugee Action and the Migrants' Rights Network (MRN).

Standing back from the political and media noise about immigrants and immigration, it is worth considering what kinds of social constructions are involved in conceiving the difference between migrants and citizens. This distinction is not simply a hard and fast legal or bureaucratic one. The migrant is an outsider, a non-member of the national community, but the notion of the outsider, the stranger, often involves a normative, moral, cultural (almost certainly racialised) judgement or categorisation. The definition of 'migrant' is made in contrast with the definition of 'citizen', and how one is defined affects the definition of the other. Yet we should also be wary of a simple binary distinction: there are many grey areas across the spectrum of ideas of what constitutes a migrant and a citizen. Even so, 'the exclusion of migrants helps define the privileges and the limitations of citizenship' (Anderson 2013: 2). As Anderson explains, 'failed' citizens, the undeserving benefit scrounger and the criminal, for example, may be constructed as forfeiting some of the status of citizen as much as, and in a parallel process with, the migrant, particularly the undocumented migrant. So 'part of being an outsider is not sharing the same values – which easily becomes not having the "right" values' (Anderson 2013: 4). In the 2000s the descriptor 'asylum seeker' became widely constructed as synonymous with being undeserving, furtive and alien. The words associated with immigration are concepts which are drenched in meaning according to context and user.

> **REWIND <<<<< 4.2 and 4.5**
>
> The notion of the 'undeserving poor', of which asylum seekers are a part, is discussed in the chapter on poverty.

6.3 International migrants to Britain

Pinpointing the scale of international migration is not as straightforward as it might seem. 'When counting migrants and analysing the consequences of migration, who counts as a migrant is of crucial importance. Yet there is no consensus on a single definition of a "migrant"' (Anderson and Blinder, 2012: 3). Criteria such as country of birth, nationality, length of abode are all relevant; different government sources use different data. The population census yields data on two parameters – people resident for more than a year ('usual residents') and born outside the UK, and people resident for more than a year with a non-UK passport. Both have obvious limitations. Some people born abroad and some people with non-UK passports have been resident for many years. Data from the population censuses in 2001 and 2011 suggests that,

in 2011, 13 per cent (7.5 million) of usual residents of England and Wales were born outside the UK. In 2001 this was 9 per cent (4.6 million). There were 4.8 million non-UK passports held in 2011, accounting for 9 per cent of the resident population. Of these, 2.3 million were EU (non-UK) passports.

(ONS 2012: 1)

Such census data unquestionably captures the significant increase in inward migration over the decade 2001 to 2011. In 2011 the top ten countries of origin for non-UK born residents were (in descending order) India, Poland, Pakistan, Irish Republic, Germany, Bangladesh, Nigeria, South Africa, United States and Jamaica. Among these, comparing 2011 with 2001, Poland and Nigeria showed the largest increases; the Irish Republic was the only one to register a decrease. The global diversity reflected in this list is striking, particularly the continued importance of postcolonial migration. Germany and Poland are obviously the only two countries not to have been a British colony – although it was some time ago in the case of the US! In this top ten Poland is the only country among the ten Central/Eastern European countries which joined the EU in 2004–7, albeit by far the most populous.

While the census gives two snapshots, providing a picture of changes over a decade, the annual immigration statistics show a significant increase since 1993 in the number of those arriving and intending to stay for more than a year, maintaining a steady level of just under 600,000 a year from 2004 to 2011, and falling to 500,000 in 2012. In 2012, 55 per cent of immigrants were non-EU citizens, 16 per cent were British, 11 per cent were citizens of the countries that joined the EU in 2004 and 16 per cent were from the rest of the EU. The top five countries of origin were India (12 per cent), China (8 per cent), Pakistan (8 per cent), Poland (6 per cent) and Australia (5 per cent). There has been a significant recent increase in migrants from China, but when comparing the countries of origin with the census data it has to be borne in mind that the immigration data includes students, most of whom stay only for the length of their degree course.

So why do migrants come to Britain? This is not at all an easy question to answer, as the particular motivations and situations of individuals are almost always complex and diverse. The principal 'motivations' are to engage in formal paid employment, to engage in 'irregular work' (e.g. as a slave, trafficked, indentured or otherwise unpaid worker), to study, to join other family members and/or to seek refuge from persecution. These may well overlap and generate different perceptions of both sympathy and deservingness. Here we look at five of the common categories: 'economic migration'; 'political migration'; students; family migration; irregular migration.

6.4 Economic migration

In terms of numbers of people, the largest category is made up of 'economic migrants' – those who are in the formal labour market, conventionally measured as the percentage of working-age people who are foreign born – which has risen steadily from 8 per cent in 1996 to almost 15 per cent in 2012, with a blip in 2009–10. Foreign-born workers are widely distributed across the occupational structure and are certainly not predominantly confined to precarious or low-paid occupations. In fact, 'the skill composition of immigrants to the UK is biased towards skilled workers' (CEP 2012: 4). Nevertheless, 'the growth in employment shares of foreign-born workers in recent years has been fastest among lower-skilled occupations' (Rienzo 2012: 4), particularly food processing and preparation, cleaning, packing, 'unskilled' factory work. In the Great Recession since 2008 unemployment rates for the foreign-born and the UK-born have been similar and have risen together.

A 'common sense' view might suggest that migrant workers bring negative outcomes for indigenous workers. Thus it might seem that if an employer recruits a migrant worker this removes an employment opportunity for a British person. It might also seem that migrants are prepared to work for lower wages, with poorer employment rights and working conditions. Such negative common-sense perceptions inform much of the popular perspective on migration, reflected in political and media discussion. For example, newspaper headlines such as 'Migration is killing off jobs' (*Daily Mail*, 11 January 2012) and the notorious political slogan 'British jobs for British workers'. This latter was voiced by Prime Minister Gordon Brown in 2007 and reiterated in 2009 during a dispute over the use of EU workers in the reconstruction of the Lindsey oil refinery in Lincolnshire.

The reality is that such common-sense views are misconceived – the labour market is much more complex and more stratified than it may first appear. There is no such thing as an indigenous pool of workers willing and able to fill vacancies. This is known as the 'lump of labour' thesis, which conceives supply and demand in the labour market in a holistic way. It is widely recognised by economists as fallacious. In taking jobs for which there are no appropriate British candidates, migrant workers contribute to the expansion of British businesses, thereby creating the likelihood of further job creation, a ripple (or multiplier) effect benefiting indigenous workers too. Research on the British labour market suggests that 'it is hard to find evidence of much displacement of incumbent workers or lower wages on average' (Wadsworth 2010: R42) as a consequence of the heightened immigration of recent years. Nevertheless, the prominence of foreign workers in some occupations throws into sharp relief the difficulties faced by British-born unemployed people – the mismatch between their capabilities and availability and the needs of employers.

To illustrate the complexities, it is worth considering, briefly, a particular example – the use of migrant workers in the long-term care of elderly people. A survey in 2007 suggested that 'migrant workers account for 19 per cent of care workers and 35 per cent of nurses employed in the care of older people in the UK...in London 60 per cent of all care workers are foreign born' (Cangiano et al. 2009: 3). These figures cover formal services provided by the NHS, local authorities and registered private organisations. They do not include people providing live-in care, privately organised and funded by users, where migrants are likely to be much more strongly represented. Cangiano et al. (2009: 3–4) found that 'most foreign born care workers are recruited *after* they are already in the UK', countering the stereotype of migrants as recruited from abroad. The immigration status of foreign-born care workers is very diverse; many are British nationals or permanent UK residents, some have work permits; others are students and spouses with more restrictive visas. It is very difficult to verify whether more of these jobs in long-term care could be taken up by British-born workers. Many unemployed people would probably be unwilling or unable to do these jobs in terms of remuneration, capability and/or availability.

Here we have just dipped into some issues and examples around economic migration. Debates continue to rage about its impact on economic growth, business profitability, labour markets, wages, employment rights, working conditions and unemployment. Arguments and evidence suggesting that economic migration is beneficial to the economy have increased in strength and prominence in recent decades, particularly during the boom up to 2008.

REWIND <<<<< 2.1

To the very beginning of this book, where trying to draw a distinction between economic problems and social problems is discussed.

6.5 Political migration

People who migrate to escape political oppression are officially constructed as asylum seekers or refugees and seen as temporary visitors who are not entering the labour market. Indeed they may well be prevented from seeking a job. In practice, of course, such a distinction is often not so clear.

Someone escaping long-term unemployment, ethnic discrimination or the effects of climate change may be severely oppressed economically and politically, though such infringements of human rights are not internationally recognised as constituting a 'well founded fear of persecution', which is the criterion for refugee status. Roma people, escaping severe unemployment and discrimination in Central Europe have sought refuge in Western Europe as both economic and political migrants.

People of Somalian origin are often regarded as Britain's largest 'refugee community'. Somalis have lived in Britain for over a century, but most trace their origins to the flight from the collapse of Somali civil society in the late 1990s and early 2000s. Ordinary Somalis were 'the targets of violence, looting, banditry and rape', with 'mass displacement of populations, lack of property rights, gross violations of human rights and a war economy... organised and controlled through violence' (Aspinall and Mitton 2010: 16). So almost any Somali might very reasonably claim a well-founded and long-established fear of persecution. In the 2011 Census 101,370 people in England and Wales declared that they were born in Somalia. The Somali 'community' as a whole may well number as many as 350,000. There are substantial Somali communities across London, and also in Leicester, Bristol and Sheffield. In the 2000s and 2010s there has been a significant migration to England of Somalis from Denmark, Sweden and the Netherlands. Compared with other refugee and minority groups, Somalis in Britain have experienced quite severe economic deprivation, i.e. poverty and unemployment, linked to poor English-language skills and educational underachievement. There have been relatively high levels of lone motherhood, low levels of female participation in paid employment, and unemployed men sometimes resorting to chewing khat, a mild stimulant leaf, which has now been banned by the government on health grounds. It is all too easy to stereotype them as a Muslim community which is failing to integrate. In reality the past decade has seen much productive effort by Somali people to improve their situation, not least as the hope of returning home has receded and permanent settlement has been accepted. Many more young women are getting into paid employment and going to college and university, cultivating a 'modern' Muslim identity (Phoenix 2011). More Somali small businesses are starting up, despite very considerable challenges in terms of finance and social capital (Jones et al. 2010). The community has fought back against negative stereotypes and Islamophobia, developing a political presence and cultural and business organisations (Muir 2012).

The number of people seeking asylum in the UK has generally been much less than the number of economic migrants, but in 1991 and 1996 annual applications jumped to over 40,000, and in the early 2000s to over 80,000. By the late 2000s this had fallen back to around 25,000, not least because of popular hostility whipped up by conservative newspapers and by government measures to deter and prevent the phenomenon. The mid 1990s through to the mid 2000s witnessed a virulent wave of anti-asylum-seeker sentiment, bolstered by and reflected in repressive government policies. Asylum seekers seemed to be public enemy number one in the early 2000s. In the House of Commons Home Affairs Select Committee on 18 September 2002, Home Secretary David Blunkett was asked about rules which stopped asylum seekers working during their first six months in the UK, and responded thus:

> If these people are dynamic and well-qualified, and I don't dispute that they are, they should get back home and recreate their countries that we freed from tyranny, whether it be Kosovo or now Afghanistan... We are freeing countries of different religions and cultural backgrounds and making it possible for them to get back home and rebuild their countries...I have no sympathy whatsoever with young people in their 20s who do not get back home and rebuild their country and their families.

The media hysteria reached its peak at around the same time, with xenophobic, inaccurate headlines such as: 'Now there's one asylum claim every six minutes (*Daily Mail*, 9 December 2002); 'Britain "has more than share of EU refugees"' (*Daily Telegraph*, 9 December 2002); 'How "soft touch" Britain tops the asylum league' (*Daily Mail*, 31 December 2002); 'Asylum flood – immigration up fivefold in 10 years' (*Daily Express*, 31 January 2003); '110,000 asylum seekers slipped in unnoticed' (*Daily Telegraph*, 6 January 2003); 'The school where the pupils speak 33 languages' (*Daily Mail*, 28 January 2003); and '200 asylum seekers vanish every day – 329,000 now live here illegally' (*Sun*, 10 February 2003), as cited by Dean (2013: 224–5).

These forms of public discourse encouraged the New Labour government in its successful mission to prevent asylum seekers from using public services and benefits, to incarcerate them in detention centres and to collaborate with other governments and international agencies in stopping them reaching Europe altogether. Social scientists and journalists produced much solid research documenting and exposing the role of the media in constructing the anti-asylum-seeker, anti-migrant sentiment of the early 2000s, usefully summarised by Dean (2013: 231–9). A study by the human rights charity Article 19 (2004) showed that anti-asylum-seeker discourse was not only prominent in many newspapers, but was also to be found in television news and documentaries across the main networks. In another study Greenslade (2005: 28–9) concluded that:

> Prejudices amongst some sections of the public towards all incomers to Britain, normally held discreetly, have been aroused...There was no public

outcry against asylum seekers prior to a press campaign of vilification which had the effect of legitimising public hostility...If the only information provided to readers is hostile, one-sided and often wildly inaccurate, how can they be expected to see through the distorted media narrative?

Case Example 3

Pregnant women seeking asylum

By the early 2000s governments had successfully excluded asylum seekers from access to benefits and public services, with the explicit intention of deterring people from seeking asylum in Britain. Destitute asylum seekers can seek limited support in cash or cashless form but, as a condition, they are likely to be 'dispersed' to hard-to-let accommodation outside London and the South-East, where many refugee communities live. The consequences for pregnant women are particularly distressing. The pressure group Maternity Action (2013) interviewed 20 women who had been dispersed and/or relocated during their pregnancy, sometimes more than once. Their physical and mental health was adversely affected and their antenatal care was interrupted. Eight had no birth companion and there were no interpreters available. The postnatal situation was even worse, with some mothers isolated, in pain, in an upper-floor flat, with very little money.

The construction of political migration as a social problem has waxed and waned over recent decades. By the late 2000s the government had succeeded in reducing the numbers, but the human rights arguments in favour of a more liberal approach are as strong as ever, while the number of refugees globally continues to rise. The situation of many political migrants in the UK is often one of severe and deliberate social exclusion, which communities like the Somalis are working hard to overcome.

6.6 Students

To stretch the definition of 'migrant' to include young people who come to a UK university or college to study for a few years seems highly questionable. Students from the EU pay the same fees as domestic students, and international student mobility within the EU has been promoted since the 1980s. The great majority of international students leave after completing their studies. There has never been significant media or political concern about them; they have never been constructed as a 'social problem'. Far from it. Higher education for non-EU students was recognised as an important 'export'. However, in 2012 the Coalition government initiated

migration

a drive against allegedly bogus international students, after allegations by MigrationWatch that student status was being used as a backdoor immigration channel. MigrationWatch had alleged that around 50,000 non-EU students were either 'bogus' or over-staying, about 25 per cent of the total number. In fact only 6 per cent remain in the UK after five years. Nevertheless, the government got the Border Agency to investigate several colleges, culminating in the revocation of London Metropolitan University's licence to recruit Tier 4 students from August 2012 to May 2013. Suddenly all universities were thrust into the front line of implementing restrictive immigration policy, leading to a 23 per cent drop in the number of non-EU students coming to study in the UK in 2012, as compared to the previous year. So, because non-EU students are included in the net migration figures, the government used this 'easy' target to achieve a reduction in the headline figure. It has to be acknowledged that some smaller, private colleges have been more interested in 'selling immigration' rather than education, but the attack on international recruitment as a whole was a sledgehammer to crack a nut.

6.7 Family migration

The stereotype of the 'migrant' is of a single young adult, perhaps male, which is certainly at odds with the diversity of migrants in reality. 'Family migration' covers a number of processes – unification (bringing family members subsequent to first migration), marriage (bringing a spouse from abroad) and whole family migration (more common among refugees). The numbers involved in the 2000s were much smaller than those coming to work, but when the labour migration door is more firmly closed, as in earlier decades, this is a significant channel. It certainly signifies a path towards permanent settlement, i.e. long-term migration. So for anti-migrationists it is important to prevent it. For migrants and their supporters it is an essential feature of their right to family life. While upholding this latter principle, British governments have a long history of constructing family migration as a problem and, therefore, of trying to deter it. Notoriously in the 1970s, this extended to performing virginity tests on incoming spouses. Spencer (2011: 131–48) details the many and various ways in which the British government has exercised its considerable discretion to manage and restrict family migration. For example, in the first two years of a partnership an incoming spouse or civil partner can remain in the UK only if they are provided for by their family, which can leave them acutely exposed to abuse and domestic violence. Since 2010 the Coalition government has implemented new restrictions on family migration, including a stringent household means test (a minimum income requirement) for 'sponsoring' non-European family members, which has created significant hardship.

In 2013 the Migrants' Rights Network found that non-EU nationals from a wide range of countries, including Commonwealth and US citizens, had been unable to visit their British partner in the UK since restrictions were introduced in 2012, mostly because of the minimum income requirement (MRN 2013).

Case Example 4

Family separation

The consequences of harsh migration rules can sometimes evoke a sympathetic construction from the media, as in the case of a man separated from his wife and four children, despite living and working in the country for 12 years.

Edmond Danushi...cannot return here from his native Albania because his wife of ten years, Theresa [in London], does not have enough money in the bank...he used his temporary visa repeatedly until the Home Office advised him to return to Albania to collect paperwork for an application for indefinite leave to remain. However a change in immigration law meant that for someone to come to the UK to live, their partner needs savings of at least £18,600 [which they do not have]. Unaware of the change, Mr Danushi returned to Albania but now is not allowed to come back to his wife and children. (*London Evening Standard*, 23 August 2013)

The 'problem' in Case example 4 is bluntly one of class. The government is in effect trying to prevent the permanent settlement of families of modest means, despite the reality that they are clearly permanently settled in London. Family migration lies at the heart of the social construction of migration as a problem, because by trying to prevent it, government and society are actively hoping to deter permanent settlement, particularly of those with only modest economic resources. In effect, anti-family migration measures attempt to restore the guest worker model – the notion that migrant workers should stay for only a short period of time and then return to their country of origin.

6.8 Irregular migration

There are lots of phrases to describe migrants whose legal status is uncertain; 'irregular migration' is the term used by international agencies. In popular, political and media discourse the term 'illegal immigrant' is a widely used construction, with an aura of hostility and intolerance which has increased in volume and hysteria over the past two decades.

Illegal entrance is probably a relatively unusual means of becoming an illegal immigrant in the UK. Far more typical is entering legally on a visitor or student visa, for example, and staying longer than one has permission for ('overstaying'). Children that are born in the UK to people without legal status may be born into illegality without ever having crossed an international border (Anderson 2013: 122).

There is little hard and fast data on irregular migrants in the UK. It was estimated in 2007 that there were between 417,000 and 863,000 (including UK-born children), about two-thirds of whom were in London (Vollmer 2011: 4). Many will have been settled for several years, overstaying their original visa. Irregular migration is not simply the outcome of individuals' attempts to escape economic poverty, political oppression, climate change, family oppression or the judicial system elsewhere. It is also created by the complexity of the immigration rules and the high costs of getting legal status regularised. It is tacitly accepted too as a source of cheap and exploitable labour, whether for large firms, small businesses or private households employing carers.

There are also transnational businesses involved in the trafficking of workers. In the aftermath of the drowning of 23 Chinese cockle pickers in Morecambe Bay in 2004, some regulation of trafficking was introduced in the form of the Gangmasters Licensing Authority, but its remit and resources are limited. Trafficking is not exactly synonymous with forced labour, because trafficked workers are often 'voluntary' – they may have paid a considerable sum and been promised formal employment. They sometimes become illegal because gangmasters take their papers and fail to register them with the Home Office. There was something of a 'moral panic' about trafficking in the mid 2000s, which contributed to the demonisation of irregular migrants as a whole, 'diverting attention from the structural and systemic causes of abuse...and justifying increases in police powers and surveillance of migrant workers' (Spencer 2011: 170). In reality the situation of trafficked workers is not always that different from that of some other low-paid workers 'in legally tolerated employment contracts, or in abusive relationships in the sex trade or domestic work' Spencer (2011: 171).

Case Example 5

Summer 2013, the Home Office's Go Home vans

Public discourse on irregular migration was exposed as never before when, in July 2013, the Home Office piloted a concerted drive against illegal immigration involving spot identity checks on the streets and at stations, leaflets, posters and newspaper ads in six London boroughs. Most notoriously, the government deployed advertising vans emblazoned with the text: 'In the UK illegally? Go home or face arrest. Text HOME to 78070 for free advice, and help with travel documents. We can help you to return home voluntarily without fear of arrest or detention.' The Go Home vans were withdrawn after the threat of legal action and a barrage of criticism, but they succeeded in their aim of conveying the image of a government intent on hunting down illegal immigrants, whipping up anti-immigrant sentiment and blithely ignoring the complexities of defining illegality. Meanwhile the British government has sent out around 40,000 texts between May 2010 and October 2013 to alleged over-stayers with the message 'You are required to leave the UK as you no longer have the right to remain' (*The Guardian*, 18 October 2013).

Undercover journalist Hsiao-Hung Pai (2008) has suggested that as many as 200,000 undocumented Chinese people are working in the UK, particularly in factories, restaurants, takeaways, retail and the sex industry. Pai's contacts were not apparently 'trafficked', but had often fled severe rural poverty in China. Pai (2013) conveys vividly the plight of Britain's migrant sex workers. It has been estimated that, in 2008, 41 per cent of the 70,000 female sex workers in UK were born abroad, two-thirds in Central and East European countries (TAMPEP 2010: 290–91).

A common-sense perspective would suggest that irregular migration is the most obviously problematic feature of migration, not least the insecurity and exploitation faced by the individuals involved. Yet the phenomenon takes many different forms and evokes confused and contradictory responses. Efforts to regulate (e.g. the Gangmasters Licensing Authority) and to exclude (e.g. the Go Home vans) are clearly difficult and controversial. A report for the Greater London Authority (Gordon et al. 2009) argued for an 'earned regularisation scheme' for irregular migrants who had settled successfully for more than five years. The report suggested that this might contribute £3 billion a year to GDP. Such an 'amnesty' has been supported by the Mayor of London, but fiercely opposed by Migration-Watch and the conservative media.

6.9 Racialisation

Given the continual (if possibly receding) presence of direct and indirect institutional racism in Britain, it is inevitable that the construction of migrants as 'Other' involves a racial dimension. Racism lurks not too far from the surface of the social construction of migration as a social problem. The long and continuing histories of racialised immigration policy and of racialised media hostility to migrants are the two most prominent arenas in which this is played out. The great majority of migrants are almost by definition 'Others' in terms of ethnicity and often of 'race'. So in the 2000s and 2010s the 'problem' of migration quickly becomes associated in mainstream political and media discourses with the 'problem' of multiculturalism, defined as the alleged failure of minorities to integrate into British society (Rattansi 2011: 68–80).

Racialisation of migrants can be viewed through two lenses. Racialisation can be understood as embracing not only differentiation by skin colour or physiognomic features, but also differentiation by ethnicity and by 'culture' (first language, national origins, food, music etc.). Racialisation can also be applied to the category 'whiteness', which comes in 'shades' of Otherness. For example, Irish people migrating to Britain have experienced explicit, direct prejudice, while at the same time benefiting from comparatively privileged access to the British labour market. Using texts from the tabloid media and from government, Fox et al. (2012) explore the racialisation of recent migrants from Central and Eastern Europe. Their evidence suggests that Romanian migrants are often portrayed as 'dangerous criminals and social parasites' (Fox et al. 2012: 687), while such stereotypes are much less frequently applied to Hungarian and Polish migrants. Romanians (and Bulgarians) come from a much poorer society and are often inaccurately associated with Roma ethnicity, amplifying racialisation processes. The adverse racialisation of Romanian and Bulgarian migrants was also strengthened by government policy, which allowed only restricted entry to Britain after 2007, when the two countries joined the EU. This contrasted with unrestricted access for workers from the eight new Central European member states that joined in 2004, which was a deliberate move to address labour shortages using 'an accessible and mobile workforce'. As Fox et al. (2012: 684) suggest, official racism is here embedded in assumptions that 'when there is a need for foreign labour, it has often been white migrants from the [near] continent and Ireland who have been deemed the most desirable'. Nevertheless, a major interview study of Polish migrants to the UK by White (2011: 148–9) cites reports of anti-Polish racist incidents in local newspapers, though none affecting the actual project respondents.

6.10 The pervasive myth: the migrant as welfare scrounger

One of the most pernicious constructions of migration as a social problem is the notion that migrants, both economic and political, have come with the intention of claiming benefits and using public services, to live off the welfare state at the taxpayer's expense. This led in the 2000s to the passage of legislation to try to prevent asylum seekers using the welfare state, while at the same time preventing them from finding paid employment. The obvious intention was to make life very unpleasant for those in the country and to deter would-be asylum seekers outside the country. But the allegation of welfare 'abuse' is also extended to economic migrants, including people from other EU member states, who have been alleged to practise 'welfare tourism'.

A major research project commissioned by the European Commission ICF-GHK (2013) found very little evidence to support the notion that 'the main motivation of EU citizens to migrate and reside in a different Member State is benefit-related as opposed to work or family-related' ICF-GHK (2013: v). The project examined the use of public benefits and healthcare services by non-active (not employed) intra-EU migrants. Despite many requests, the British government has been unable to supply evidence of significant intra-EU welfare tourism to the European Commission.

Nonetheless, in a panic about the relaxation of restrictions on migrants from Romania and Bulgaria from January 2014, the government rushed through measures to deter all EU migrants' access to welfare benefits. They now have to wait for three months from their arrival before they can claim any out-of-work benefits. At the same time the government introduced a much tougher 'habitual residence test' for migrants making a home in the UK who might want to claim access to housing benefit, council tax benefit, pension credit or social housing. The test involves a hundred questions with supporting evidence required. The government would like to extend such tests to other areas of the welfare state, notably the NHS. The message is that EU migrants' access to the welfare state is unwelcome, paralleling the treatment of asylum seekers in the 1990s.

6.11 Summary

Migration or, more specifically, immigration to Britain has long been constructed as a social problem by large swathes of the media, the political class and the wider public. Most recently this has gathered force around the migration of EU citizens from Central and Eastern Europe. The most vocal discourse constructs the problem around alleged overcrowding, increased pressure on public services, reduced employment opportunities for British workers and so on. While many of these arguments do not stand up to critical scrutiny, perhaps the root of the 'problem' lies in the portrayal of migration as a threat to British culture or nationhood, which evokes a visceral, patriotic conservatism and hostility to strangers. Yet the reality on the ground is that the new migrants have often experienced a reasonably tolerant and friendly reception from locals (Griffiths 2013), as well as being welcomed by employers.

We have examined critically some of the most forthright constructions of 'the problem' by writers, researchers and journalists, suggesting that they exaggerate the negatives and underestimate the positive contribution of migration to the British economy and society. We did this by unpacking some of the discrete issues around particular types of migration – economic, political, students, family and irregular. In each case we observed that many of the stereotypical assumptions of the anti-migration cause do not stand up to critical scrutiny. Public discussion often embraces a stigmatising view of migrants as potential scroungers on the taxpayer and the welfare state, while the truth is the opposite – migrants are significant net contributors to the economy and to the welfare state. There is also a barely disguised racialisation of migrants, linked with xenophobic sentiments towards other white Europeans. This is much more difficult to challenge, but to the extent that Britons have become much more comfortable with Britain's multi-ethnic, multiracial identity, there has to be considerable hope that the various constructions of migration as a social problem will not prevail.

Revision notes

The anti-immigration construction is strongly represented in some newspapers, in vocal pressure group activity, by some mainstream commentators and, of course, on the far Right. It variously constructs migrants as a threat to the national culture, to social cohesion, to the welfare state and to employment for British citizens.

The pro-immigration perspective is a less strident, more muted discourse, which sees migration as essential to economic growth and job creation for everyone, which also enriches an increasingly cosmopolitan culture.

Economic migration generally does not involve displacement of British workers, while certainly highlighting the mismatch between employee capabilities and employer needs. Economic migrants are needed to do dirty and/or difficult jobs such as care work.

Political migration fulfils Britain's commitment to recognising global human rights and taking a fair share of the world's refugees. Increasingly restrictive and exclusionary asylum measures in the 2000s have developed in response to media hysteria about bogus, scrounging asylum seekers.

The panic over migrant numbers has failed to recognise that the figures include large numbers of genuine students who constitute an important and successful British export market. Family migration is also a humane and necessary complement to harmonious economic migration, which eases the marginalisation of lone migrants.

Migration:

1 What is a migrant?

Issue:

How a person is categorised as a migrant is a socially constructed process. The category has undefined and loose boundaries, yet most people take it for granted as a hard and fast distinction between 'migrant' and 'citizen'. Formal legal citizenship is certainly a simple definition, but there are many people who have settled in the UK as long-term, legal residents who choose not to take UK citizenship, perhaps because they cannot retain dual citizenship from their country of origin. Others such as refugees or trafficked workers may be in the UK involuntarily and temporarily. Overseas students and over-stayers may not see themselves as migrants or be considered by others to be migrants. A migrant is commonly defined as someone born outside the UK: what are the strengths and weaknesses of this definition?

EXAMPLE:

A middle-aged woman from the Philippines is working long hours as an informal carer for an elderly English widow; she has young children back home who are cared for by her family; she is sending as much money as possible back to them; her family has a very low income, and her money is critical to their welfare; she plans to go back to the Philippines after two years. She is an over-stayer on a tourist visa. Is she a migrant? Should her status be officially and positively recognised? Should she be deported?

EXERCISE:

Make a list of the different categories and types of migrant, and consider which are constructed as more 'deserving' and more welcome than others.

2 How do the newspapers present the issues surrounding immigration?

Issue:

There are widely contrasting constructions in the newspapers of the issues surrounding immigration; some papers have an anti-immigration bias, while others are neutral or even pro-immigration. The messages conveyed by the newspapers have some influence over public opinion, as well as reflecting it. There are several examples above of conservative newspapers railing against various aspects of immigration.

Coursework questions

1 Compare and contrast the pro- and anti-immigration discourses.
2 Describe and discuss the changing ethnic composition of migrants to Britain in recent decades.
3 To what extent is migration 'killing off jobs'?
4 What role have centre-Right newspapers played in the British migration discourse?
5 Describe and discuss the different ways in which migrants are categorised by the state and by social scientists.

References

Anderson, B., *Us and Them? The dangerous politics of immigration control*, Oxford: Oxford University Press, 2013

Anderson, B. and Blinder, S., *Briefing – Who Counts as a Migrant? Definitions and their consequences*, Oxford: Migration Observatory, COMPAS, 2012, www.migrationobservatory.ox.ac.uk

Article 19, *What's The Story: results from research into media coverage of refugees and asylum seekers in the UK*, London: Article 19, 2004, www.article19.org

Aspinall, P. and Mitton, L., *The Migration History, Demography and Socio-Economic Position of the Somali Community in Britain*, New York: Novinka, 2010

Cangiano, A., Shutes, I., Spencer, S. and Leeson, G., *Migrant Care Workers in Ageing Societies: research findings in the UK*, Oxford: Centre on Migration Policy and Society (COMPAS), 2009, www.compas.ox.ac.uk

CEP, *Immigration and the UK Labour Market: the latest evidence from economic research*, London: Centre for Economic Performance, London School of Economics, 2012, http://cep.lse.ac.uk

Dean, M., *Democracy Under Attack: how the media distort policy and politics*, Bristol: Policy Press, 2013

Fox, J., Moroşanu, L. and Szilassy, E., 'The Racialization of the New European Migration to the UK', *Sociology*, 46(4): 680–95, 2012

Goldin, I., Cameron, G., and Balajaran, M., *Exceptional People: how migration shaped our world and will define our future*, Princeton, NJ: Princeton University Press, 2011

Goodhart, D., *The British Dream: successes and failures of post-war immigration*, London: Atlantic Books, 2013, Kindle edition.

Gordon, I., Scanlon, K., Travers, T. and Whitehead, C., *Economic Impact on the London and UK Economy of an Earned Regularisation of Irregular Migrants to the UK*, London: Greater London Authority, 2009

Greenslade, R., *Seeking Scapegoats: the coverage of asylum in the UK*, London: Institute for Public Policy Research, 2005, www.ippr.org

Griffiths, C., 'Living with "aliens"', *Criminal Justice Matters*, 93(1): 26–7, 2013

ICF-GHK, *The impact on the Member States' social security systems of the entitlements of non-active intra-EU migrants to special non-contributory cash benefits and healthcare granted on the basis of residence*, Report for the European Commission, 2013, http://ec.europa.eu/employment_social/empl_portal/facebook/20131014%20GHK%20study%20web_EU%20migration.pdf

Jones, T., Ram, M. and Theodorakopoulos, N., 'Transnationalism as a Force for Ethnic Minority Enterprise? The case of Somalis in Leicester', *International Journal of Urban and Regional Research*, 34(3): 565–85, 2010

Legrain, P., *Immigrants: your country needs them*, Princeton, NJ: Princeton University Press, 2007

Maternity Action, *When Maternity Doesn't Matter: dispersing pregnant women seeking asylum*, London: Maternity Action and the Refugee Council, 2013, www.maternityaction.org.uk

MRN, *Family Visit Visas: the emerging crisis for Brits affected by the minimum income requirement*, London: Migrants' Rights Network, 2013, www.migrantsrights.org.uk

Muir, H., 'Somali Community Finds Its Voice in Britain', *The Guardian*, 21 February 2012

ONS, *International Migrants in England and Wales 2011*, London: Office for National Statistics, 2012, www.ons.gov.uk

Pai, H.-H., *Chinese Whispers: the true story behind Britain's hidden army of labour*, London: Penguin, 2008

—, *Invisible: Britain's migrant sex workers*, London: Westbourne Press, 2013

Panayi, P., *An Immigration History of Britain: multicultural racism since 1800*, Harlow: Pearson, 2010

Phoenix, A., 'Somali Young Women and Hierarchies of Belonging', *Young*, 19(3): 313–31, 2011

Rattansi, A., *Multiculturalism: a very short introduction*, Oxford: Oxford University Press, 2011

Rienzo, C., *Briefing – Migrants in the UK Labour Market*, Oxford: Migration Observatory, COMPAS, 2012, www.migrationobservatory.ox.ac.uk

Spencer, S., *The Migration Debate*, Bristol: Policy Press, 2011

TAMPEP, *National Mapping Reports*, Annex 4 to *Sex Work in Europe*, Amsterdam: European Network for HIV/STI Prevention and Health Promotion among Migrant Sex Workers, 2010, www.tampep.eu

Vollmer, B., *Briefing – Irregular Migration in the UK: definitions, pathways and scale*, Oxford: Migration Observatory, COMPAS, 2011, www.migration observatory.ox.ac.uk

Wadsworth, J., 'The UK Labour Market and Immigration', *National Institute Economic Review*, 213: R35–R42, 2010

White, A., *Polish Families and Migration since EU Accession*, Bristol: Policy Press, 2011

Wilson, A.N., 'I No Longer Recognize the Britain I Grew Up in', *Daily Mail*, 15 December 2012, www.dailymail.co.uk/news/article-2248365

Further reading

Finney, N. and Simpson, L., *Sleepwalking to Segregation? Challenging myths about race and migration*, Bristol: Policy Press, 2009. Calmly and critically deconstructs populist discourse about immigration numbers, failure to integrate, ghettoisation etc. using solid social science data and research.

Panayi, P., *An Immigration History of Britain: multicultural racism since 1800*, Harlow: Pearson, 2010. A thorough and up-to-date historical account which explores lucidly the links between racism, immigration discourse and migrant experiences

Ruhs, M. and Anderson, B. (eds), *Who Needs Migrant Workers? Labour shortages, immigration and public policy*, Oxford: Oxford University Press, 2010. A collection of articles solidly based on primary research, covering a wide range of economic sectors including healthcare, food, construction, financial services and social care.

Sales, R., *Understanding Immigration and Refugee Policy*, Bristol: Policy Press, 2007. An accessible yet detailed account of this central issue, giving appropriate attention to both explanations and experiences.

Spencer, S., *The Migration Debate*, Bristol: Policy Press, 2011. A definitive review covering each category of migrant in depth in an accessible and very well informed way.

Websites

www.migrantsrights.org.uk – The Migrants' Rights Network: campaigning NGO, monitoring and publicising the on-going struggle, particularly on family issues.

www.migrationobservatory.ox.ac.uk – The Migration Observatory: a great source of authoritative, evidence-based analysis of data on migration and migrants in Britain based on the best research.

chapter 7

Childhood and education

David Blundell

7.1 Introduction

No social group figures as consistently or frequently in the discussion of social problems as do children. This is not merely because external problems impact upon them and the quality of their childhood or even that children and young people are themselves often seen as problematic, it is also because children are uniquely hailed as a source of hope in the search for solutions to any number of society's problems. Furthermore, education and schools are presumed to provide the arena where many matters of social concern that may or may not directly concern children can be addressed. This is not only because education is implicitly considered to be about making things better, but also because of the practical fact that school is where children can be found for much of the time. These concerns range from questions surrounding how children's academic attainment can sustain economic viability, to remedying all manner of matters seen as challenging or damaging for social cohesion and the maintenance of order and well-being, including recent high-profile concerns about gangs, drugs and obesity.

FAST FORWARD >>>>> 9.6

For a discussion on the relationship between young people and gangs in the UK.

In this chapter we shall examine and appraise what are by common consent some of the problems of childhood, as well as the role that education and schools play in addressing these problems. However, we shall tackle this by asking a number of important questions that include: where our ideas about children and childhood come from; why we hold these ideas; and whether the ways we *think* about children contribute to some of the problems we identify. Furthermore, we shall ask why it is that children and childhood have become closely identified as means to solve society's problems and even as a hope for human salvation. I should say from the outset that our approach will be that of social construction. This proceeds from a view that, by questioning our taken-for-granted assumptions, even about things that seem to be certain and solid, we might be able to assess whether they are, indeed, so certain or solid and, therefore, unchangeable. This is done not merely as an academic exercise but because it may enable us to understand some of the knotted roots of the social problems that confront us and thereby help to find means of addressing them. But first it will be helpful to examine how the ways in which we think about children, childhood and education might contribute, for good or ill, to the way we construct these problems.

7.2 What do we mean by childhood?

Open the newspaper or catch the television news and there will be a story about childhood. The chances are that the report will express a suspicion either that all is not quite well with the nation's children or that the experience of childhood offered by various social institutions – including families, health and social care agencies, the media, youth and sport clubs and, not least, schools – is not as it should be. But can we assume that when people speak about 'childhood' they all mean the same thing? The vocabulary may be identical, but it may be that behind the words there are very different assumptions about what childhood is, what it should be like and what is meant by a 'good childhood'.

Examination of the many agencies catering for children and young people may help us to glean some sense of what people mean by childhood. We might look, for example, at nurseries, schools, colleges, Saturday morning clubs, Sunday schools, Islamic madrassahs, Jewish cheder, children's hospitals, drama schools, play centres and holiday play schemes. Social scientists describe all these places as *institutions of childhood*, and the long and diverse list is indicative of the place childhood occupies in the social structures of UK society.

Amidst this diversity, what will unite these institutions of childhood is that they all operate with 'working models' of what children and young people are like. This does not mean that they share the same working model or that each operates with a single model. But if we visited each one and asked key workers what they aimed to do, how they sought to achieve this and why they operated as they did, their replies would be shaped by the assumptions, beliefs, convictions and commitments that can be found in these working models for children and young people. Their sentences might start something like this: 'we do things this way because children need/deserve/have a right to...x, y or z'. The working models within which each institution will be operating can be understood as what Max Weber called 'ideal types'. These enable an institution to make sense of what it aims to achieve and determine how it should go about doing so as it establishes a language that workers, practitioners and users share and can use to direct, explain and justify the operations of the institution. In short, they will all be talking about the same thing.

REWIND <<<<< 2.4

For a discussion of Weber and 'ideal types'.

'Ideal types', which form the assumptions behind institutional or professional understandings of children, their needs and so on, are themselves informed by broader social discourses. I remember a discussion with my students about what children should and should not be expected to do around the house and it illustrates how working models for childhood can be informed by very different assumptions. One woman with young children argued forcefully that childhood is a short time and so she did not expect her children to do any chores, rather, they should be allowed to play and live in the moment. This was the cause of some consternation for another student, who was adamant that children should take up their share of housework, otherwise how would they learn to become responsible adults? Each of these mothers operated with different working models for the meaning and purposes of childhood and these provided important principles for how their families should operate. In this discussion, each student referred to 'children' and 'childhood', but it was clear that they were operating with very different meanings for the same words. For one, childhood was a time to enjoy *being* a child, but for the other, childhood was about *becoming* an adult. This basic difference in meaning for childhood, between *being* and *becoming*, is not trivial and has long been the subject of debate. They represent different discourses in our society about childhood and they have an importance in shaping our response to social problems in childhood, as we shall see.

Key concept: the idea of discourse

Differences in meaning are not simply matters of personal opinion but are shaped by culturally shared ways of seeing the world. Social scientists often refer to these shared ways of seeing as 'discourses' and find this a useful way to understand how our ideas about what is and is not normal are constructed. Discourses shape the meanings we share through language, but also inform pictures, films, adverts or the television news. Social scientists are very interested in how discourses inform our thinking and actions, and especially in how they support and maintain power in relationships between people. Think, for example, about differences in the way that men and women are frequently represented in adverts. Discourse is an important idea that you will encounter again and again as you learn more about social theory.

Another example of how differing discourses of childhood animate fierce debates comes from the New Labour government's attempts to ban the use of corporal punishment by parents. Advocates of a complete ban held that hitting a child was no different from common assault, but others drew a distinction between violent assault and what the Prime Minister himself described as an occasional 'tap on the legs'. On the one hand, was a discourse affirming children as people who should have the same rights as any other sorts of people and, on the other, a discourse stressing children's immaturity and distinctly different instincts and needs. The debate continues with little hope of a clear resolution between what are fundamentally opposed ways of seeing human nature.

Many social scientists and philosophers are unwilling to live with a situation like this where our views on such an important topic are split into what they would call a *dualism*. Indeed, they argue that the dualisms we frequently encounter when discussing social phenomena, including children and childhood, are not inevitable but are produced by the way in which we have been looking at those phenomena since a period in European intellectual history known as the Enlightenment.

 ## Key event: the European Enlightenment

This occurred between 350 and 250 years ago and it marks an important development in the emergence of modern European societies. Enlightenment thinkers argued that the power of reason and science would lead to the conquest of nature and the improvement of humankind. Critics have argued that in actuality reason and science have been used to impose European ideas and political power across the globe and gave birth to the Industrial Revolution, whose harmful environmental changes now threaten the very future of life on Earth.

childhood and education

Conventional Western approaches to understanding childhood and providing for children have their roots in the Enlightenment and rely heavily on scientific method and the rational search for truths about children's instinctual characteristics and the needs that accompany growth. The emphasis on instincts and needs suggests that childhood and children can be understood through what natural science tells us about their *nature*. In this account of childhood, children are shaped primarily by what nature provides and they grow and develop according to powerful and universal laws that cannot be changed and should not be transgressed if they are to become balanced, healthy and responsible adults. The most notable contributor to this way of thinking about childhood is undoubtedly Jean Piaget, whose theories propose that childhood is a natural phenomenon structured by scientifically observable and universal processes of development that bring physical and cognitive growth into broad alignment with one another and provide a vocabulary of 'stages', 'assimilation', 'accommodation', 'schemas' and 'readiness' that has widespread currency. This *developmentalist* view of childhood continues to inform and justify much institutional provision for children, especially for those in the early years of life, and its language and concepts have become such a commonplace discourse that it is difficult to speak of children in professional contexts without using the language it provides. It is the dominant 'working model' for childhood.

Recently, social scientists have questioned the claims of universality (that all children are the same) and naturalness (that there are clearly definable stages of child development) that are found in Piaget's work. Encounters with children living in very different societies to that of Western Europe and North America have challenged the claims that these developmentalist accounts embody universal laws or truths about childhood. Coming from a coalition of disciplinary backgrounds, including sociology, education studies, anthropology, women's studies, social psychology and cultural studies, many social scientists assert the need to reappraise how we think about children and have been leaders in the emergence of what is described as the New or Critical Childhood Studies. These academics do not deny the manifest differences between adults and children – most children are clearly physically, sexually and intellectually immature in comparison to adults; however, they argue that biology does not tell us what these differences mean or how we should respond to them. Rather, the ways in which biology is made meaningful are a matter of cultural interpretation. We know that many questions require us to make social, legal and moral judgements that draw on biological information but rely on cultural interpretation; for example, when does childhood end? Does childhood begin at birth? Or before? Or after? When are children morally responsible for their actions? When should child bearing begin? And seemingly less far-reaching matters, such as should infants learn fractions? Should children use mobile phones? Should television be censored for children? What sort of clothes should children wear and not wear? These are matters of cultural interpretation that cannot be answered by biological, natural science or developmentalist perspectives alone. It is necessary to have a social-scientific imagination in order to approach these questions and, arguably, the methodology of social construction is the best way to begin to answer them.

The anthropologist Alison James and sociologist Alan Prout have done much to challenge our existing ways of thinking about children and childhood: they have expressed the distinction between childhood as a given biological inheritance and the position of social construction in this way:

> The immaturity of children is a biological fact of life but the ways in which this immaturity is understood and made meaningful is a fact of culture. It is these 'facts of culture' which may vary and which may be said to make of childhood a social institution. It is in this sense, therefore, that one can talk of the social construction of childhood...
>
> (Prout and James 1997: 7)

Prout and James are redirecting our attention away from what they see as a fruitless search for essential truths about childhood – which, once captured, will resolve all our questions about how childhood should be – and towards an appraisal and understanding of what childhood means and the way that language, practices and institutions shape any number of childhoods as social realities. This also means that they are not attempting to present a better, improved or truer theory of childhood than that of Piaget and the developmentalists (or anyone else for that matter). But they are proposing that we look at the world very differently and turn our attention away from the search for essential truths and towards understanding the world as the product of socially constructed human meanings.

Feminists have also criticised Piaget's 'working model' of the child and childhood, suggesting that its claim to universality allows a male-centred account to dominate our thinking and excludes the female experience of growing up.

As can be seen, then, the social construction approach is alive to differences and diversity in human cultures and meanings and encourages us to question whether one particular, culturally located way of seeing childhood should dominate our thinking in the way it does.

Why is this important in a discussion of social problems in childhood? There may not be a neat answer here, but it is worth thinking about whether the social problems impacting on children's lives are linked to their social positioning *as children* or whether the quality of particular children's lives is

childhood and education

more meaningfully linked to their identities expressed in terms of social class, ethnicity, gender, disability or sexual orientation. Prout and James steer us away from a suggestion that the choice is clear cut; indeed, along with other scholars and academics in the New Childhood Studies they challenge the familiar assumption that this is a decision for us as adults alone to make. At the heart of the New Childhood Studies is a denial of the commonplace assumption that children represent a vulnerable, passive and incomplete form of human life in need of adult direction and guidance. Rather, it asserts children's capability and *agency* and, therefore, their entitlement to have their voice heard in matters that concern them – and even those that do not.

 Key concept: the idea of agency

This is an idea drawn from sociology and has been central to what Prout and James and other authors of the New Sociology of Childhood have to say. Their work challenges the idea that children are passive automatons driven by developmental and social forces beyond their control; rather, they assert that children are as keen to control and shape their lives as adults might be. These social scientists point to the resourcefulness and resilience shown by many children, not least when roles reverse and they become family carers. Furthermore, they propose that it is institutions, such as school, that seek to turn them into 'passive dopes', and construct agency as deviation. As Prout and James say, 'Children are and must be seen as active in the construction and determination of their own social lives, the lives of those around them and of the societies in which they live. Children are not just the passive subjects of social structures and processes' (Prout and James 1997: 8).

In educational terms this is vitally important, because as educators we should bear in mind that children and young people do not simply learn things in school as and when adults teach them, but are learning things about education and schooling all the time. Many of these things may not be what teachers intend. This may explain why it seems that the main lesson many young people seem to learn from school is that learning is too hard or too demeaning and doesn't suit who they consider themselves to be.

7.3 Education, schooling and the construction of modern childhood

We shall now turn to an examination of how education and schooling have become so closely bound up with most children's experience of childhood in western societies. We shall do this by looking at the historical circumstances that brought together children and their identification with schooling.

Along with the family, the most significant shaper of children's experience of their childhood in countries such as the UK is school. It is assumed by most of us that this is the place where they normally spend large chunks of their young lives. But we ought to be aware that the coupling of education and childhood comes out of a particular historical process. It emerges as part of the way of thinking about the world that changed across Europe during the period of the Enlightenment. This period of change saw the rise and privileging of science and scientific method, rational thought and the idea that humankind could conquer nature to transform and improve the world. The education of the young assumes central importance in this project to improve the world, and we see Renaissance luminaries such as Erasmus and Sir Thomas More writing at length in the early sixteenth century about the proper education of both boys and girls – although the actual opportunities for female education were few. Among the first thinkers to link children's education to questions of freedom and social progress was the Enlightenment philosopher Jean Jacques Rousseau, who in 1762 published two books: a discussion of the education of a young boy entitled *Emile, or on Education* and *The Social Contract* (see Blundell 2012 for a fuller discussion).

The growing importance attached to the education of children through the Enlightenment and Industrial Revolution led in 1870 to the passage of the Elementary Education Act by Gladstone's Liberal government. The 1870 Act was the first public Education Act to make mass education of the nation's young possible and was followed in 1880 by legislation that made school attendance compulsory. For the first time in history, legislation had been passed that installed a basic assumption that school was where children should be for much of the time. Thereby, our taken-for-granted assumption that childhood and school were fundamentally conjoined came into being in ways that had been unimaginable a generation before. Alongside the family, this development has proved the single greatest institutional influence on twentieth- and early twenty-first-century childhoods.

The sense that the nation's children were all in the same place at the same time was accompanied by a realisation that this particular group was reachable by government, largely *en masse*, as it sought to introduce any number of political, social and economic policies and measures. Thus, when in the early years of the twentieth century we see David Lloyd George's Liberal government confronted by concerns about the poor levels of fitness for battle of the British imperial army in the Boer Wars of 1899–1902, and the damning indictment of widespread poverty and malnutrition published by the philanthropist Joseph Rowntree in 1901, schools are conveniently placed to be a vehicle for social welfare interventions.

childhood and education

REWIND <<<<< 4.1

Where the social surveyors, like Rowntree, are discussed in relation to measuring poverty.

In response, Lloyd George set up an Interdepartmental Committee on Physical Deterioration, that proposed a raft of social welfare legislation, with schools as the vehicle for its implementation. This included: the Education (School Meals) Act of 1906; the unprepossessingly titled Education (Administrative Provisions) Act of 1907, which established the School Medical Service; and the Education (Choice of Employment) Act of 1910, which established careers guidance and advice as an entitlement. Schools and the education service thereby became uniquely charged not just with the inculcation of basic educational knowledge and skills, but also with being instrumental in improving the health and welfare of children and, hence, the nation (Foley 2001).

Schooling becomes a point where different and contradictory currents converge. Whilst it has the capacity to address the nation's pressing social problems, it seems unable to decide whether children are redeemers or in need of redemption. History suggests that it has frequently opted for a moral pessimism, expressing mistrust of children, parents and educators alike, believing that children must be reduced to 'pupils' who, like a counter in a board game, can be sequentially placed and ordered in pursuit of externally defined goals and targets. Some see this as one part of an emerging crisis of childhood in Britain, to which topic we now turn.

7.4 Is there a crisis of childhood, and what might it be?

There is evidence that people have always looked back on their lives and felt that the world has become a harder, harsher place than it used to be and yearn for the sort of golden age found in J.M. Barrie's Peter Pan – the boy who never grew up. However, over the last thirty years or so there has emerged a body of opinion suggesting that something has altered in the state of childhood and the quality of the lives we offer to our children; further, that this represents an objective shift and is not merely the product of nostalgic longing.

Among the early contributors to this discussion was the cultural commentator Neil Postman, who published *The Disappearance of Childhood* in 1983. Postman's conclusion is manifest in the book's title. He argues that television and new cultural media have broken down the distinction between the innocent worlds of childhood and the secrets of adulthood, much to the detriment of childhood. In his view, television side-stepped established ways to achieve social consensus about what were and were not appropriate experiences for children, and without much debate we have been presented with 'a broad social decision to allow young children to be present at wars and funerals, courtships and seductions, criminal plots and cocktail parties' (Postman 1983).

Postman's book catalysed an extensive and continuing debate about new media and the condition of childhood. For example, more recently Palmer has argued that the modern world is damaging our children as technology and new media constitute a 'toxic' youth (Palmer 2006). Similarly, Richard Louv, an American environmentalist, has found a receptive audience for his claim that a condition identified as Nature Deficit Disorder (NDD) is prevalent amongst urbanised children growing up without access to the affordances of wild spaces and places (Louv 2005). In the UK, the National Trust drew upon Louv's analysis as the basis for a report entitled *Natural Childhood* (Moss 2012). This report mourns the loss of children's engagement with natural environments and loosely correlates a number of statistical parameters showing a decline in children's fitness and well-being with the emergence of screen-based virtual cultures, on the one hand, and what Louv described as a parentally induced state of 'well-meaning, protective house arrest', on the other.

The report is grounded in the assumption that there is a thing called 'Natural Childhood' that flourishes when children engage with rather mystically conceived wilderness places. That said, much of the argument actually revolves around research showing that children spend more time indoors than they did in former times. This should encourage caution, for if the problem is being kept inside, rather than a denial of access to nature, it does not follow that children need a wilderness space or the sort of rural haven that is available to only a tiny minority of children as their play environment. Certainly, ways can be found to get children out more. As Joe Benjamin (1974), doyen of London's Adventure Play Movement in the 1950s and 1960s reminds us: 'The point is that the streets, the local service station, the housing estate stairway – indeed, anything our urban community offers, is part of the natural habitat of the child.'

We might suggest that what is deemed 'Natural Childhood' in these sorts of accounts represents a socially constructed ideal that is tied to a rather romantic discourse that privileges an unbounded freedom for children set in a rural lifestyle. This ideal seems to exert an extraordinary purchase on our imagination and slips into our thinking without much critical attention. But also, these arguments embody a series of uncritically accepted assumptions that childhood is somehow a condition that is independent of the social variables of class, ethnicity, disability and gender. This is exactly what Prout and James felt the need to challenge in their work, and we are

childhood and education

reminded that if we are to get beneath the surface of these arguments we need to examine their assumptions with the critical, discourse-spotter's eye of the social scientist.

So, do the grounds for a crisis in childhood, advanced by authors like Postman, Palmer and Louv, and captured in the report by the National Trust, constitute grounds to believe that this is a social problem? Furthermore, if there is a problem, does it lie with childhood and the condition of being an immature human being per se, or is it a problem linked to other sociological factors, such as class, ethnicity or gender?

The 'romantic' line of argument suggests that this is an example of childhood as a natural condition being compromised by the pernicious effects of contemporary society. Yet the idea that children represent a uniform social group seems to obscure more pressing issues of social justice. It may even mask a 'moral panic' in relation to how one powerful social group views another. Certainly, the National Trust's backlit photographs of white middle-class children romping through meadows and woodland have been selected to represent what it sees as the 'proper' condition for a natural childhood. We are led to infer that these children are immune to the epidemic of NDD. There is no expression in such a discourse of, say, the experience of exclusion that many people from black and minority ethnic backgrounds claim to encounter when entering rural green spaces beyond Britain's urban fringes. As social scientists, we should be alive to the ways in which the world and people are represented in this sort of material because they reveal the discourses through which we make sense of the world and what constitutes a 'normal' state of affairs.

The sociologist Chris Jenks (2005) has suggested that, far from holding a straightforward and unified view of children, our discourses are deeply ambiguous or dualistic and we frequently cannot decide whether we think of children as angels or demons. He identifies these opposing discourses with reference to the qualities and characteristics of the Greek gods Apollo and Dionysius. The 'apollonian child' is all things sweetness and light, the 'dionysian child' brings us chaos and disorder. Going back to Max Weber, we should note that these ways of seeing children are 'ideal types' that exert a powerful hold on our imagination and, thereby, on how we think about and provide for children. Consider what we mean when we use the very different ideas associated with being *childlike* and *childish* to describe adult behaviour; whereas one suggests endearing and appealing qualities, the other is distinctly unpleasant and unwelcome.

At first glance, the Natural Childhood arguments of Louv and the National Trust clearly buy heavily into the 'apollonian' discourse of the child as sweetness and light, but they also imply that 'dionysian' chaos and disorder are just around the corner if children are not handled with care. This dualistic way of thinking about children undoubtedly shapes educational responses to social problems. On the one hand, the 'apollonian' discourse encourages us to see children as the vanguard of a better, reinvented world so that education becomes a vehicle for change. But, on the other, the 'dionysian' discourse requires education to discipline the child and serve as a bulwark against moral and social chaos. This reminds us that these ideal types, the discourses that inform them and the childhood experiences they shape may be hugely prejudicial to children's well-being and life chances.

What might be seen as a more authoritative source of data on the condition of children and young people's lives in the UK and other countries of the economically developed world comes from a series of reports by the United Nations Children's Fund (UNICEF). In April 2013 UNICEF followed up an earlier examination of the quality of children's lives published in 2008 with a comparative overview entitled *Child Well-being in Rich Countries* (UNICEF 2008 and 2013). This report sought to assess the quality of childhood in 29 countries that are all members of the Organisation for Economic and Cultural Development (OECD). Twenty-seven of the countries were European, the remaining two were Canada and the United States. The evaluation was based in part on the following five statistically based dimensions: material well-being; health and safety; education; behaviours and risks; and housing and environment. Each of these five areas was given a score based on statistical data and then the countries were ranked, based on this score. In 2008 the UK propped up the league table of 21 nations; however, by 2013 it had risen to 16th place out of 29. The logic of the league table suggests that there might be grounds for some celebration here; however, a detailed appraisal counsels a more sober response, especially when we consider that we are thinking about children and their life-chances here, and not football league championships! That said, the continuing position of the Netherlands as an outlying league leader gives pause for thought about what might account for such a disparity in outcome between it and the UK, two ostensibly similar societies.

This disparity is confirmed by what children themselves had to say about their 'life satisfaction'. Once again, the UK finds itself in mid-table while the Netherlands occupies the top spot by some margin. At a finer level of detail, more than 80 per cent of children in the Netherlands seem to find relationships with peers and parents 'easy', whereas in the UK just two-thirds find both their classmates 'kind and helpful' and conversations with fathers easy. In terms of the five categories used by the report, there are concerns expressed about continuing high levels of pregnancy in the UK and of alcohol abuse amongst teenagers. However, education is the category where Britain performs least well, at 24th in the table. This reflects the lowest level of participation in education by young people between the ages 15 and 19, as well as high numbers who are also not in employment or training.

While UNICEF produced its reports on children's well-being, the Children's Society also undertook a research programme examining the meaning of and prospects for a 'Good Childhood' in the UK. The report, published in 2012, examined how children felt about their lives under the following ten headings: family; home; money and possessions; friendships; school; health; appearance; time use; choice and autonomy; and the future. Like UNICEF's this report presents worrying findings but also seeks to offer pointers for what might be characteristic of a good childhood and steps to achieve this. Overall, the Children's Society found that the majority (91 per cent) of 8- to 15-year-old children canvassed were happy with their lives, but stressed how statistics can obscure harsh realities, in that the remaining 9 per cent represented around half a million children who were not. Again, education does not come out particularly well; the fact that 80 per cent of children were clear that 'it was very important for them to do well in their school work' does not necessarily tell us that they enjoy school or find it rewarding. Furthermore, 'around 7% of children do not feel safe at school and three-fifths of these children are unhappy with their school life as a whole'. Apart from some 'small differences' in well-being between boys and girls and for differing types of household, the research does not find any clear-cut correlation between children's well-being and social factors. However, the UK's large population reminds us that these percentages mean that we could be dealing with around a quarter of a million children who are unhappy at school. Percentages may point the way, but statistics cannot tell us what it means and feels like to be unhappy at school (The Children's Society 2012). Furthermore, to register first as a social problem and then to identify solutions it needs to be established why these children are so unhappy, and so the report's finding should be a spur to further research.

In 2010 an educationally focused review of childhood and children's lives was published by academic and professional contributors to the Cambridge Primary Review. The Review's findings are more measured than some of the evidence we have examined. They are also interesting because the team recognised that social problems of childhood are constructed by discourses that underpin representations of 'ideal types' and are expressed through rhetorically deployed language. The report challenged the powerful influence of some of these unhelpful discourses, stating that children the researchers met conformed neither to the image of 'innocents in a dark and menacing world or as celebrity-obsessed couch-potatoes stirring themselves only to text their friends or invade the streets and terrorise their elders...' and went on to suggest that, based on the evidence, 'the "crisis" of modern childhood has been grossly overstated' (Alexander 2010: 487).

The report takes a relatively unfashionable and bold step by suggesting that children's lives and well-being are not being compromised and damaged by technology, being kept indoors or unhealthy lifestyles nearly as much as by social inequality and poverty. The report also maintains that schools frequently represent a vital point of anchorage in keeping children's and their families' lives together.

7.5 Educational responses to social problems of childhood – early childhood and child poverty

A central concern for the New Labour government that swept to power in 1997 under the leadership of Tony Blair was the disturbing evidence for the year-on-year increase in child poverty that had occurred since the early 1980s. It was asserted that in 1979 the percentage of children living in poverty in the UK had stood at 12 per cent; by 1997 this figure had doubled to 25 per cent and appeared to be rising.

> **REWIND <<<<< 4.4**
>
> For a full discussion on the assessment of poverty and policy responses.

The new government set itself the (now seemingly ambitious) target of reducing child poverty to three-quarters of the 1997 level by 2005 and halving it by 2010. As things turned out, despite a reduction of 16 per cent, the target was missed in 2005 and, thereafter, child poverty has actually increased.

Along with measures to reduce child poverty through monetary benefits there was concern to address identified problems in child welfare, both where it occurred in specific geographical areas and at key points in the life-course of children considered to be at risk. In particular, government policy makers were convinced by research demonstrating the merits of investing in social welfare measures targeted at the early years, because, as this author puts it, 'the weight of evidence suggests that a child's experiences in the early years are critical in shaping outcomes not just in health, but across education and welfare throughout that individual's lifespan' (Gidley 2007: 145).

Policy makers identified the need for what are termed 'upstream interventions', tackling the roots of deprivation, ill-health, poor educational outcomes and disadvantage before they imprint themselves on a child's future life chances. This contrasted with costly, so called 'heavy-end' provision that responded to the outcomes of the above, such as treating chronic illness or addressing the challenges of early pregnancy and criminality only once they had presented.

Sure Start was a specific policy response to these concerns and, as its name suggests, was targeted at deprivation in the early years. Consistent with New Labour's belief in holistic responses to regeneration and renewal in deprived areas and communities, Sure Start sought to tackle deprivation by working across institutional boundaries to form inter-agency collaborative partnerships. Early evaluation of the outcomes from Sure Start was difficult, given the long-term benefits expected over the life-span of the children that participated in this early-years learning scheme. However, the project itself provided a template for further development of a 'joined-up' agenda for children and their well-being.

Over and above research statistics, broad and diverse areas of social concern are frequently brought into sharp focus by quite specific and emblematic events. One such was the tragic death of Victoria Climbié at the hands of her supposed carers. The government's response to Victoria's death was to set up the committee of inquiry under Lord Laming. Whether this sad and quite specific event should have been the particular spur to action is a matter of controversy for some; however, the government's response to Victoria Climbié's death and the Laming Report transcended matters of child protection alone and led to the comprehensive 2004 Children Act, which expanded the Sure Start programme under the banner 'Every Child Matters'.

At the heart of the 2004 Act's provision was the rapid expansion and enhancement of a number of relatively new institutions and agencies for children and childhood, above all the children's centre. Not since the Elementary Education Act of 1870, which paved the way for mass schooling, had there been the development of a new institution for children in the UK on a comparable scale. The vision for an integrated, inter-agency approach to the education, care and well-being of young children (and also older ones) was focused on the children's centre as 'a one-stop shop' that, in the opinion of the National Foundation for Educational Research (NFER), represented a 'quiet social revolution'. A central, iconic figure in this is a holistic construction of the child, whose interests and well-being should not be split into separate fractions by structural agencies such as health, education and care that are external to it. Thus, key professionals are not merely housed together under the children's centre's roof, but they are required to collaborate in ways rarely seen. This aims to overcome the sort of fragmentation in service provision and failure so as to share information that was identified in the Climbié case. The spirit of partnership extends beyond the professional staff, with an expectation that management boards should contain representatives of parents and service users.

Although undoubtedly revolutionary in its reach and scope, the principle underlying the children's centre is actually not that new and in so many ways echoes the work of early pioneers who stressed the link between children's learning and well-being, such as the great Swiss educator Johann Pestalozzi and Maria Montessori, who began her work with children in the desperately impoverished slums of Rome. However, other examples are nearer to home, with the work of Rachel and Margaret MacMillan in South and East London around a century ago. An inspiration for the children's centre can be seen in the nursery schools, offering the children of the poor education combined with care, that were pioneered by the MacMillans. Indeed it can be argued that they represent a material bridge between the sisters' Christian Socialism and the vestiges of left-wing conviction found in the New Labour project. We might also reflect on how the discourse of the Natural Child and the need to obviate the fragmentary interest of society and its social institutions might be at work here (see Blundell 2012).

The children's centre is a response to the social problem of child poverty and the concern to arrest poor outcomes by early intervention. It is a socially constructed institution which operates within certain 'ideal types' in relation to views about children and childhood and their needs, as well as about parents and parenthood. Further, these ideal types are informed by discourses that shape and delineate both how it goes about making provision for children and also, more fundamentally, confirm what proper provision should be and who should rightly offer it. These discourses find a material form not only in the professional practices and language used within the children's centre but also the furniture, colour schemes, designs, layout and finishings and, furthermore, in the curricula of diploma and degree courses designed to prepare professionals to work in these institutions. All contribute to providing what is considered appropriate for the education and care of children, but also convey messages about what 'proper' childhood and, by implication, 'proper' parenting should be. In this sense, the children's centre is not only a place where education and learning takes place in timetabled sessions or events, but is also a *moral* space that seeks to educate and to promote learning for the widest audience through its material form and practices. We might, therefore, say that its very fabric is *didactic*, that is, it is delivering lessons to us about what is and what should be. This is not to say, however, that the lessons it seeks to teach children, parents and other users are necessarily consistent, welcomed universally by all or, indeed, what those working in the centres intend.

As we have seen, one of the powerful discourses at the heart of Sure Start, Every Child Matters and the children's centre is the idea of early 'upstream' interventions in the life of young children to prevent later pathologies. This has been viewed as an extension of the idea that poor families are caught in a vicious cycle of poverty and deprivation whereby impoverished children inevitably become impoverished parents and pass their deprivation on to their children, and so on, without any real hope of breaking the cycle unless help and guidance intervene. This diagnosis appears plausible and, in principle, intervention makes strategic sense. However, critics have expressed unease about what they see as an unwelcome and probably unworkable cultural, social and moral agenda through which this

childhood and education

strategically plausible principle actually seeks to realise its goals. These critics (see Gidley 2007) suggest that the children's centre has what philosophers would call an in-built *telos*, that is, a clearly defined end-point, in the form of a completed person or human subject, towards which its work is directed. Clearly, any organisation or agency must be directed by goals; however, critics argue that it is unacceptable when those goals impose standards of behaviour and value on people either without consulting them or without reference to and appropriate respect for their social or cultural circumstances. They suggest that the children's policy agenda can be seen as more about meeting the needs and interests of the state, through the production of children as liberal citizens who are 'set free of the state, autonomous but required to act responsibly towards themselves and others – for example eating healthily, not smoking, and parenting well'. Furthermore, the 'normative model of successful parenting promoted by initiatives like Sure Start closely tallies with the values of white middle-class parents, which implicitly suggests that parents from other backgrounds by definition need intervention' (Gidley 2007: 150).

For these critics, what can be seen as a measure providing help and support is actually underlaid by an assumption that it is the poor and their impoverished social habits that are the problem. Indeed, for them the shiny new institutional affordances of the children's centre can mask a much older judgement that it is impoverished families who are to blame for their children's poverty and the children's centre's mission is to offer redemption from their self-imposed shortcomings.

Others, including Wendy Stainton Rogers (2009), challenge the somewhat pessimistic conviction that children's life-chances are determined by their early experience. She rejects the notion that 'history is destiny' and points to the manifest resilience that children can exhibit under challenging conditions, notably when positions are reversed and children become carers. Stainton Rogers' criticisms are part of a wider challenge to what she regards as dominant discourses of the child, with their roots in modernity and the Enlightenment. For her, modernity cast the child as a passive object to be understood through scientific observation and theorisation – much as David Attenborough might observe a natural history specimen in one of his marvellous programmes about the natural world. In contrast, Stainton Rogers proposes that children should be seen as active, responsible and fully human agents in their own right and able to account for their lives. The ease of access to the nation's children offered by mass schooling enabled researchers to gather a huge amount of data about children at all stages through their childhoods and condense this data into developmentally driven theories and idealised norms of what children are like and childhood should be (Foley 2001). The bulk of this data was derived from physical, medical and psychological observation and examination, and so the model of the child that emerged and that has dominated our thinking about how children grow and learn has been a medical and psychological one, with social factors, such as class, gender and cultural identity, relegated behind more universal and objectified themes. Stainton Rogers suggests that this medicalised and objectified child offers us a list of needs and rights that can be read off and translated into the policies and practices of institutions of childhood such as the children's centre, but that this list may not represent how children live their lives or what *they* seek from their lives. Stainton Rogers is keen that we seek to find out more about what children mean and understand by their well-being, rather than assume that this can be identified by external expert opinion.

7.6 Summary

In this chapter we have explored some social problems of childhood, along with policy responses to some of these problems. Along the way we have questioned whether many of these problems can be 'ring-fenced' as solely belonging to childhood or whether they are particular manifestations of wider phenomena. As social scientists, we have adopted a social construction approach that is concerned to understand the ways in which we make sense of childhood and the meanings we ascribe to it. This has not been undertaken merely as an academic exercise; rather, we have adopted this approach because it is argued that powerfully influential human meanings find expression in what social scientists refer to as discourses, and these discourses shape and inform the institutions that we build for children to live, learn and grow in. These institutions can be made from bricks and mortar and other materials, such as schools and nurseries, but many social scientists think about institutions in a broader and, at times, less apparently tangible form, so that institutions can also be the language and concepts we expect to use about children, or they can be 'ideal forms' (that Weber talks about) around which rules and routines are designed to regulate and direct their lives. Almost certainly, we have all experienced the way that institutions like school shape our experience of childhood, e.g. what we wear, when we must be in one place rather than another, how we address others, how we walk up and down stairs, what we do when bells are rung. However, we have seen that the discourses informing these institutions are frequently ambiguous, or dualistic, and we do not seem to be able to decide or agree on what we think and should do with any clarity. Should children work for their upkeep, or be protected from adult cares? Should children be reasoned with when they are naughty, or be punished physically? Is children's nature fundamentally 'apollonian' (sweetness and light/innocent and virtuous) or 'dionysian' (chaotic and disordered/sinful and needing to be tamed)? Should childhood be about preparation for adulthood (a process of becoming), or about living in the moment (a state of being in its own right)? In an obvious sense, these dualisms make it difficult to frame policy responses with confidence; furthermore, we inhabit societies that are increasingly characterised by diversity in traditions, values, beliefs and practices, and this challenges the conviction that there are simple truths to determine and follow. Social construction tells us that human societies make what they regard as reality, but also, by implication, that any particular social reality could be different. Furthermore, as Prout and James suggest, this all seems to presume that children lack active agency and do not construct views of their own about their lives – how often do we ask children what they think? Social construction could be very useful as we face an increasingly uncertain future.

There is, however, one very important idea about children and childhood that shapes many of the ways we see and respond to social problems. I started this chapter by suggesting that children and schooling hold a unique position in relation to so many of the social problems that you will explore through this book. I am sure you have heard the idea expressed that 'children are our future' many times, and it frequently passes for unquestioned 'common sense' that this is the case. However, what is being expressed here is much more than the truism that we all grow older and adult society in the future will comprise people who are children now. Rather, it suggests something about the need to 'get childhood right', in the belief that if we can do this the world of the future can be transformed for good. Petrie and Moss (2002) explore this idea in relation to two key discourses that they suggest inform our thinking about children. The first discourse is that childhood should be a golden age characterised by innocence, optimism and hope; the second is that children are in the process of becoming adult. In the authors' view, when these discourses combine, children are constructed as a 'vehicle of redemption'. We have seen how many of our ideas about children have their origins in the European Enlightenment and its convictions about the possibility of human progress through reason and science. The idea that children can be a 'redemptive vehicle' combines Enlightenment optimism with older ideas that are deeply rooted in Christianity and the belief that the world can and must be redeemed, or made new. Although on the one hand society frequently seeks to marginalise children and shield them from what are seen as adult concerns, the idea (or ideal form) of 'the child' plays a central role in our faith that society can be transformed and its problems solved. However, we live in deeply uncertain times and, under these conditions, the meaning of a good childhood is likely to be shaped as much by fear for the future as by optimism. It seems entirely valid to ask whether the requirement to redeem the world places too great a burden on our children and might help to explain why so many seem to be so unhappy with their lives.

childhood and education   135

Revision notes

Children are subject to social problems and are also seen as problematic. Further, childhood is seen as a time when social problems can be addressed through what are described as 'upstream interventions' that can not only change, even transform, society but, in the process, save expenditure on rectifying social ills later on. Education and schooling frequently occupy a pivotal position in addressing social problems, both because of children's youthfulness – as above – and, also because since the advent of public schooling in the nineteenth century, the vast majority of children can be reached through their schools.

The quality of contemporary childhood is the focus for a series of ongoing 'moral panics' about children's lives. Concerns are variously expressed about the effects of new digital media and television, spending too much time indoors and alienated from the natural world, obesity and well-being, the threat posed by strangers and paedophilic activity, gangs and 'feral' youth cultures. We asked, are these problems of childhood and youth per se, or do they have roots in broader social problems such as poverty, changes in social structures and in working lives or in new media and communications? Does the emphasis on something called *childhood* cause us to overlook the role of other sociological variables, such as gender, class, ethnicity, disability or sexuality, that may impact more significantly on young people's lives?

Social construction may help us. This is because it turns our attention away from the idea that there are universal and essential truths about children and childhood to be discovered – for example, truths that are constant for all people at all times and in all places – and towards the idea that societies and cultures construct shared social realities. These social realities are informed and structured by discourses that mediate powerful ideas as well as the ideas of the powerful. Conflicts can occur when very different social realities collide, but this can also lead to change and constructive adaptation – in short, social construction suggests that things do not have to be the way they are and they can be different.

Many of our dominant ideas about children, childhood and education have their roots in a period called the European Enlightenment and embody western assumptions about progress, individuality and what it means to be human. They are also powerfully informed by ethical principles and the idea of redemption that comes from the Christian tradition. These ideas continue to shape the way that institutions identify what children need and what it means to grow and learn. They also impose a particular burden of hope on children that they can contribute significantly to the solution of society's problem and transform human fortunes. This may not have been

childhood and education

beneficial to children themselves and frequently ignores what children actually think about their own lives and what they want.

Seminar tasks

Childhood and education

1 Issue:
Despite deliberate policy interventions and measures since 1997, child poverty has not been abolished and the gap between the richest and poorest members of society in the UK is growing.

EXAMPLE:
Tony Blair's New Labour government set out measures designed to eliminate child poverty by 2015. Some inroads were made but they fell well short of their target. The Coalition government that came to power in 2010 pledged to continue with the Children's Agenda that was central to reducing child poverty and enabling parents, especially women, to take up paid employment. There have been changes to welfare benefits as part of the Coalition's deficit-reduction strategy and there is debate about how far and in what ways these impact on children.

EXERCISE:
To what extent is child poverty a problem of children and childhood or a problem with wider social roots and ramifications? Set out lists under the respective headings of 'Childhood' and 'Society'.

2 Issue:
This chapter has argued that children frequently occupy a unique position in relation to social problems in that not only are they subject to the impacts of these problems, but also through education and schooling they are regarded as vital to addressing and solving social problems. The discourse of the child as a redemptive vehicle has been discussed.

EXAMPLE:
A frequent response to any number of social crises is to address them through the school curriculum – obesity and fitness, gangs and knife crime, hate crimes, early pregnancy, money management, social cohesion and voluntary activity, sporting decline and so on. This is at a time when teachers and schools are also under increasing pressure to deliver competence in basic educational areas such as literacy, numeracy and scientific understanding. The chapter has discussed how our discourses of childhood might shape these responses and also that schools occupy a unique position in the access they offer to the nation's children.

> **EXERCISE:**
> In small groups of around four people discuss one of the following statements and, whatever your personal views, develop arguments designed to defend and advocate the position. Now take your arguments to a group that has been working on the other statement; present your arguments to each other and then discuss: (a) what you think about each position, (b) whether you can discern any underlying discourses of childhood that inform and shape each position.
>
> **Position 1:**
> 'Schooling is fundamentally about equipping young people with basic skills such as literacy and numeracy that they can carry forward into their lives and that will equip them to become confident and successful adults – take care of the skills and the social problems will take care of themselves.'
>
> **Position 2:**
> 'Education is about changing the world, and this is something that children care about as much as anybody else – make education relevant to children's social worlds and the problems they face and the skills will take care of themselves.'

Coursework questions

Who should take responsibility for solving social problems and creating the world of the future?

Should social policy address child poverty, or poverty per se?

Has childhood changed and become a source of problems for our children? If so, why is this?

Critics of the children's centres and the Children's Agenda say that they seek to impose middle-class values and expectations on children and their families, whatever their background. Does this make it impossible for professionals working within them to do otherwise, or can they 'row against the tide'?

References

Alexander, R. (ed.), *Children, Their World, Their Education*, Final report and recommendations of the Cambridge Primary Review, London: Routledge, 2010

Benjamin, J., *Grounds for Play*, London: Bedford Square Press, 1974

Blundell, D., *Education and Constructions of Childhood*, London: Bloomsbury, 2012

childhood and education

The Children's Society, *The Good Childhood Report*, 2012, www.childrens
society.org.uk

Foley, P., 'The Development of Child Health and Welfare Services in England
(1900–1948)', in P. Foley et al. (eds), *Children in Society: contemporary
theory, policy and practice*, Basingstoke: Palgrave, 2001, pp. 6–20

Gidley, B., 'Sure Start: an upstream approach to reducing health inequalities',
in A. Scriven and S. Garman (eds) *Public Health: social context and action*,
London: McGraw-Hill, 2007

Jenks, C. *Childhood*, (2nd edn), London: Routledge, 2005

Louv, R., *Last Child in the Woods: nature deficit disorder and what we can do
about it*, New York: Algonquin Books, 2005

Moss, S., *The Natural Childhood Report*, London: The National Trust, 2012

Palmer, S., *Toxic Childhood: how the modern world is damaging our children
and what we can do about it*, London: Orion, 2006

Petrie, P. and Moss, P., *From Children's Services to Children's Spaces: public
policy, children and childhood*, London: Routledge, 2002

Postman, N., *The Disappearance of Childhood*, London: W.H. Allen, 1983

Prout, A. and James, A., 'A New Paradigm for the Sociology of Childhood?
Provenance, promise and problems', in A. James and A. Prout (eds) *Constructing and Reconstructing Childhood*, London: Routledge, 1997

Stainton Rogers, W., 'Promoting Better Childhoods: constructions of child
concern', in M.J. Kehily (ed.), *An Introduction to Childhood Studies*, Maidenhead: Open University Press, 2009

—, *Child Well-being in Rich Countries: a comparative overview*, Innocenti
Report Card 11, Florence: UNICEF, 2013

Further reading

Blundell, D., *Education and Constructions of Childhood*, London: Bloomsbury,
2012

James, A., Jenks, C. and Prout, A., *Theorizing Childhood*, London: Polity
Press, 1998

Jones, P., Moss, D., Tomlinson, P. and Welch, S. (eds), *Childhood Services
and Provision for Children*, London: Pearson/Longman, 2008

Kehily, M.J., *An Introduction to Childhood Studies*, Maidenhead: Open University Press, 2009

Prout, A., *The Future of Childhood*, London: Routledge, 2005

chapter 8

Organised crime and its policing

Dan Silverstone

8.1 Introduction

This chapter will explore the social construction of organised crime, and its policing as a social problem. This is far from straightforward, as it is immediately evident that what we mean by 'crime' is often not at all clear. For example, if a 'gang' member were to scrawl the initials of their postcode onto a wall in a rival area and they were to be arrested by the police service, they might be charged with vandalism and they would start on a journey into the criminal justice system which could end in them being declared a criminal. However, if they were to draw on the same wall a parody of the police, they could embark into the world of street art which could end in fame and fortune (like Banksy!).

Equally, we are aware that some actions that we now consider as an expression of our legitimate desires and part of our basic freedoms or human rights, such as expressing our sexuality with whomever we choose, man or woman, have until recently been illegal and are still illegal in some countries. In the UK, for example, it was not until 1967 that having homosexual sex was declared legal. Finally, most if not all of us have broken the law at some point, whether it is by driving too fast or by taking illegal drugs, or legal ones too soon. Yet, if we are not actually caught for any of these crimes, in what sense are we really a criminal?

It is at this point that social construction, as a methodological approach to crime, can be most insightful. It helps us to point to the historical and social processes that make an act a criminal one. Social construction indicates that no crime is fixed or simply given, but it relates to social norms and values. As Tannenbaum argued in the 1930s, using language which resonates today, the process of making a criminal is a process of 'tagging, defining, identifying, segregating, describing, emphasizing, making conscious and self-conscious' (1938: 20).

What, then, of organised crime? Surely organised crime is less complicated in its 'construction', as it is more obviously criminal, morally dubious and more visible. At the level of fiction, which informs much of our 'common sense' views on crime, this seems to be so, as organised crime has provided a persistently popular cinematic or televisual backdrop in the US and the UK, from *Scarface* to *Taken* to *Essex Boys* and from *Miami Vice* through to *The Sopranos*, *The Wire* and *Top Boy*. Yet, in the UK it was not until the 1990s that government, regardless of political persuasion, felt that the threat from organised crime was such that it merited exceptional policing at a national level. Since this decision, there has been a steady escalation in the powers and scope of specialist organised crime policing. In 1992, the Conservative government elected to set up the National Criminal Intelligence Service (NCIS), and with the 1997 Police Act created the National Crime Squad (NCS), which took over from existing regional crime squads in 1998. Eight years later the New Labour government founded the Serious Organised Crime Agency (SOCA), an intelligence-led agency with law-enforcement powers and national and international reach. In 2013 the Conservative-Liberal Coalition government replaced SOCA with the National Crime Agency (NCA), an institution with unprecedented policing authority. It seems that all political parties are convinced of the threat from organised crime.

Indeed, as the scope and powers of policing agencies have expanded, so has the fervour of the rhetoric. In 2004 the White Paper *One Step Ahead: a 21st Century Strategy To Defeat Organised Crime* describes organised crime as reaching, 'into every community, ruining lives, driving other crime and instilling fear'. Similarly, the Serious and Organised Crime Strategy (2009: 1) states that the global reach of serious organised crime, 'can undermine and corrupt economies, societies and governments; and can cause or exacerbate state failure, in some cases leading to civil war and violent conflict'. Most recently, according to the latest report by Europol (the European Union's law enforcement agency which assists states in dismantling large-scale criminal and terrorist networks), Britain was one of the countries with the most 'high-priority cases requiring in-depth Europol analysis', with London 'a big green spot compared with everywhere else in Europe....the largest one' (Moon 2013).

But can we be sure that governments and law enforcement agencies are to be trusted in their drawing of the green spots, which point to large areas of organised crime? Don't they have a vested interest in promoting the problem to justify their funding and their pleas for wider criminal justice powers? Can we be sure that the biggest green spot should be London, when the methodology of constructing the size of the problem is often secret? As

Woodiwiss and Hobbs (2009) point out, on both sides of the Atlantic the threat from organised criminals, be they the so-called 'Russian Mafia' or the so-called 'Yardies', has frequently been a chimera which has failed to appear.

This chapter will review the definition of organised crime, examine the dimensions of the British organised crime threat and subject to scrutiny the institutions which are involved in its construction and its policing.

8.2 What do we mean by organised crime?

First, it is important to identify who the organised criminal is, and for this we need a definition. However, academics have struggled to produce anything definitive, for example Professor Van Lampe outlines over 170 attempts on his website (Van Lampe 2014).

FAST FORWARD >>>>> 9.2

For a similar definitional problem in relation to trying to define 'gangs'.

For our purpose, we can abandon 167 of these and concentrate on three recent definitions provided by the Home Office and national policing units tasked with pro-active operations against serious and organised crime. These three definitions are sufficient to illustrate that subtle differences in the way organised crime is defined will have important consequences in constructing it as a social problem.

 Key idea: definitions of organised crime

'An organised criminal works with others for a profit motive to commit an offence which impacts on the UK and for which a person aged 21 or over on first conviction could expect to be imprisoned for three years or more.' (National Criminal Intelligence Service 2000, cited in Levi 2007)

'Those involved, normally working with others, in continuing serious criminal activities for substantial profit, whether based in the UK or elsewhere.' (Home Office 2004)

'Individuals, normally working with others, with the capability to commit serious crime on a continuing basis, which includes elements of planning, control and coordination, and benefits those involved. The motivation is often, but not always, financial gain.' (Serious Organised Crime Agency 2012)

The first definition given above incorporates three key aspects: first, in reference to organisation, it sets out that the organised criminal needs to be working collaboratively. This directs us to groups, be they 'Networks', 'Mafias', 'Triads' or 'Firms'; second, it sets out a motive which is profit; and third, it insists that there have to be serious offences committed. The second definition dilutes the claim that organised criminals always need to be working with others. This raises the possibility that the organised criminal could be one man or woman, a key personality such as the North London criminal 'godfather', Terry Adams or the recently convicted police killer Dale Cregan. However, it adds that the organised criminal needs to commit their activities more than once, so this would rule out the opportunist drug dealer who is involved in only one deal. But it also broadens the definition of the organised criminal by including those who are working outside of the UK, so this would include a fraudster based in Belgium who is making profits from carousel fraud by claiming VAT rebates from the Exchequer which they haven't ever paid. Finally, the third definition is the most recent and inclusive. In reference to organisation, it allows that the organised crime can involve both individuals and groups and it keeps the possibility that the crime is likely to be continuing, but can also be a singular event. In relation to motivation it broadens the definition to include crimes which might not be motivated by financial gain; finally, it keeps the stipulation that the crime committed still needs to be serious, although there is no restriction or mention of where the criminal should be based.

These definitional arguments are not merely academic but have important practical consequences, as, if a group or individual is defined as an organised criminal or their activities as organised crime, this will dictate the level of resource which can be deployed in policing them. So, for example, in relation to motivation, recently there have been several cases of men who have been convicted of grooming vulnerable young girls and women who resided in care homes, raping and then trafficking them within their social circle. Clearly, this is a serious offence and in a recent case in Oxford (BBC News 2013) the men were sentenced to life imprisonment. The crime was organised, as the perpetrators deliberately befriended vulnerable girls and women, and involved more than one person, as the men collaborated with other men who supplied drugs and with yet others who supplied residences where the women could be abused without any disturbance. However, what was their motivation? If the motivation was sexual, under the first two definitions this would not be seen as an organised crime but, rather, as a sexual one and would be policed by specialist sexual units. However, under the most recent definition of organised crime this motivation would not preclude the offence from being seen as organised crime and it might attract the attention of investigators from the NCA. Which outcome is preferable, and for whom?

The classification of a crime's seriousness is also of practical importance. For example, two of our most popular drugs are tobacco and cannabis. Although tobacco is legal, as the cost of buying cigarettes and tobacco escalates there is an increasing illegal market where both can be bought at a reduced price. For example, British American Tobacco in a recent report estimated that more than half of all hand-rolled tobacco in the UK is now either counterfeit or smuggled, and one in five cigarettes smoked is a fake (BAT 2014). Counterfeit cigarettes either are manufactured illegally in countries such as China or are bought legally and cheaply in countries with lower taxes and then imported so that duty is not paid, resulting in them being substantially cheaper than their legal counterparts. In relation to cannabis, the police have observed that the domestic cannabis market has changed (ACPO 2012). It still includes drug traffickers who import cannabis from countries such as South Africa and Holland but it now includes thousands of domestic cannabis cultivators. They, keen to avoid the risk of being arrested for importing what is a bulky and pungent drug, take advantage of a myriad of domestic electricity companies where it is hard to trace where electricity is abstracted and instead cultivate the drug locally (Silverstone 2011). Whilst it is quite possible that you have never tried either, their widespread availability means that most of you will have the opportunity to purchase them, potentially putting you in contact with organised crime!

The question is, does this seem right to you? Are importing illegal cigarettes or cultivating cannabis serious crimes – either objectively, as defined by Crown Prosecution sentencing guidelines (that those caught will be faced with sentences of at least three years), or subjectively, that we (you? the police service? politicians?) think so? If you review the length of sentences for these crimes online, you will see a wide disparity. Take, for example, this recent case: 'Eight men from Nottinghamshire and Yorkshire "flooded" north England with millions of illegal cigarettes' (BBC News 2013a). Several participants were jailed for less than three years. How should we construct the argument concerning whether the crime is a serious one? Should we look at the quantities of the commodity involved or the place of the individual in the conspiracy? For example, is their role vital for the crime to work: the electrician in the cannabis factory or the haulier in the importation of cigarettes? Or should we examine the impact of their offending? How dangerous are counterfeit cigarettes: more or less so than cannabis? Who are they being sold to: children or adults? How addictive are these drugs? How much harm is caused by these activities?

8.3 Measuring the harm from organised crime

The question of the harm caused by organised crime and how to measure it is a complex one which is key to the social construction of this problem.

organised crime and its policing

Table 8.1 Crime

Type of crime	Estimate (£ billions)	Main uncertainties
Drugs markets (Dubourg and Prichard 2006)	15.4bn	Based solely on studies by Godfrey et al. (2000) and Gordon et al. (2006).
Drugs markets (Cabinet Office 2009)	17.6bn	Costs of drug-related crime form the majority of these costs, but it is difficult to estimate the intangible costs of victimisation by drug-related crime, and also to estimate the proportion of crime that is drug related.
Fraud (Prichard 2006)	2.7bn	Consists mainly of direct financial losses, so caveats attached to market size apply equally to economic costs. Very conservative estimate of organised crime involvement. Relies on industry and HMRC data. Private sector data often thought to be poor, because of low reporting.
Fraud (Cabinet Office 2009)	7.8bn	It is impossible to calculate precisely the extent of undetected fraud. The proportion of fraud that is committed by serious organised criminals is also difficult to estimate.
People smuggling (Prichard 2006)	1.4bn	Based mainly on the costs of running the asylum system, so again, limitations apply.
People smuggling (Cabinet Office 2009)	1.4bn	The number of undetected people who were smuggled is impossible to quantify precisely.

It is a question taken seriously by law enforcement and one of the key strategic innovations of SOCA, which heralded a departure from traditional policing models of arrest and prosecution. Instead, the organisation had the explicit goal of 'harm reduction'. One of the ways governments try to measure harm is to put losses caused by crime into financial terms, and large figures are used by the government to construct organised crime as a significant and growing problem. For example, in 2011 an attempt by Her Majesty's Government (HMG) to add all the harm together, and the numbers of people who participated in organised crime, arrived at the following: 'between £20 billion to £40 billion a year. It involves around 38,000 individuals, operating as part of around 6,000 criminal gangs' (HMG 2011: 5). As we are studying the construction of the social problem we ought not to accept these figures at face value but, rather, examine them carefully. What do these large numbers tell us? Please review two estimates provided by

Dubourg and Prichard (2006) and the Cabinet Office (2009) in Table 8.1. Consider the figures; have they gone up or down? Consider the types of crimes and think about the main uncertainties.

Can it seriously be considered, as the table suggests, that people smuggling is an organised crime which is causing over a billion pounds of loss to the UK? And that this figure has stayed static for three years? Certainly there are costs in relation to maintaining the asylum system, as stated above, but are there not benefits to immigration too?

REWIND <<<<< 6.4

For a discussion about the benefits, or otherwise, of economic migration.

Many illegal migrants work in the UK in low-paid jobs, in service industries such as the restaurant and takeaway sector, or in cleaning or in the provision of services such as nail bars or farming, all roles which are supportive of the UK economy. When calculating the costs to the UK economy, politicians can argue that illegal migrants will not pay tax, but may use the health service and/or education services and, therefore, are an economic drain. However, it might be countered that those in low-cost labour still spend their wages locally and, without their industry, the businesses they work for would collapse, contributing to higher unemployment and further financial deficits for the UK. These costs and benefits are tangible, as conceivably one can measure them, but what of the more intangible effects in relation to the smuggling of people? How do we account for them? So, for example, if illegal migrants are able to bypass border controls and to essentially defraud the asylum system and other migration controls, at what point do the public see these systems as fundamentally unfair and discriminatory? On the other hand, what is the value of the UK remaining a place where poor migrants can successfully earn a living and support their extended families in their country of origin? And when weighing up these costs and benefits do we have to automatically respond with more enforcement and more controls? Couldn't we consider relaxing our migration controls as a way of reducing the costs of people smuggling? Clearly we could, but we do not. And one of the reasons for not doing so is the putative threat from organised crime.

8.4 The social construction of British organised crime

'The idea that criminal groups and organizations migrate or extend their powers across geographical locations has been a recurrent theme in organized

organised crime and its policing

crime and general criminological research for over a half century' (Morselli, Turcotte and Tenti 2010: 6).

This view is commonly referred to as the 'alien conspiracy thesis', the theory that a virgin America was despoiled by the arrival of Sicilian migrants who brought with them an established Mafia culture and organised crime. According to Woodiwiss (2001: 97–99, cited in Wright 2006), this feeling of resentment towards Italian migrants originated in the nineteenth century but gained widespread currency only in the late 1950s, when the theoretical advocate of this hypothesis, Donald Cressey, argued that there existed a nationwide alliance of 24 tightly knit criminal 'mafia families'. It was alleged that these crime families were large, were connected to each other and back to their country of origin and presented a structured threat to the state. In Cressey's words, 'the structure of formal organisations are rational. They allocate certain tasks to certain members, limit entrance and influence the rules established for their own maintenance and survival' (Cressey 1972: 11).

Returning to the UK, before the 1950s, in the absence of prohibition and with a relatively liberal tradition of prescribing drugs, there was very little mention of organised crime as a social problem at all. However, what did exist was presented in a similar way as in America. In the inter-war period, a nascent drug scene in London was blamed on Chinese migrants, whilst illegal betting activities at horseraces were blamed on the actions and alliances of Jewish and Italian criminals, in particular the Sabini brothers. After the Second World War, public attention focused even more intensely upon the role of foreigners in the provision of vice, with Maltese criminals featuring heavily in law-enforcement accounts (Hobbs 2013).

A brief hiatus from a preoccupation with foreign criminals occurred in the late 1950s and early 1960s, with the arrival of key crime families such as the Krays and Richardsons, before public attention returned to them in the 1970s. As the drug trade exploded, law enforcement and politicians became preoccupied with organised crime threats from countries where the drugs were produced or were most often smuggled from, and the threat again became 'foreign', in the form of Irish, Turkish and Jamaicans criminals. Most recently, academics and journalists have updated these views, arguing that perhaps crime groups in the UK and US have united, becoming global in their reach, sometimes working in conjunction with each other. This argument is known as the 'Pax Mafiosa' thesis and was first put forward by Sterling (1994). Her hypothesis was that, with the fall of communism, global Mafias were able to cooperate and to trade commodities most efficiently (be they people or drugs) by working together. Another variation on the idea of a global Mafia is found in Glenny's (2009) *McMafia*. Here the author rejects the simple notion of global conspiracies but perpetuates the idea that there exist large global crime organisations that operate globally, outsourcing risky parts of their business, generating billions in profits.

> In sum, our assessment of past research maintains that while many claim that criminal organizations are intentionally or strategically mobilizing themselves to seize opportunities in various geographical locations across the world, empirical demonstrations supporting such claims are lacking, with most restricted to anecdotal illustrations.
>
> (Morselli et al. 2010: 10)

As the quotation above illustrates, there is a large gap between the popular and established social construction of the threat from organised crime and the evidence available to justify this claim. Morselli et al. (2010) argue that the threat from mobile, global organised crime groups is, in fact, exaggerated. They engage critically with the 'alien conspiracy thesis' and draw on empirical support from a study by Wortley and McCalla (2008). This study illustrated that there was no link between immigration and crime. Furthermore, no correlation or even negative relationship was found between the two variables. We therefore need to consider why this tendency to blame the outsider is so often repeated.

REWIND <<<<< 6.4

For a discussion relating to the social construction of migrants and the racism that may be associated with some of these debates.

British criminologists also challenge this traditional narrative of linking organised crime to ethnicity. Instead they most commonly situate any involvement by diaspora groups in organised crime with their structurally excluded position in both the labour and housing markets. A key thinker in this regard is Dick Hobbs (1995). He challenges the proposition that organised crime in the UK is made up of large, mobile groups. Instead he argues that the reality of British 'organised' crime is better characterised as 'dis-organised' crime. Criminal activity, he argues, tends to be fluid and chaotic, made up of contingent and transgressive groups and individuals who are not so dissimilar to you and me. Supporting evidence for this claim is the way drugs markets are localised, with different groups competing to control different parts of the drug market, with no one group able to maintain a monopoly on the supply of a drug. Consider as evidence for this the constant supply of illegal drugs. If they originated from one source, then it might be possible for law enforcement to conclusively prevent it by closing down the key organisation. Yet, this has never happened.

organised crime and its policing

The argument that in the UK even so-called organised crime often consists of small and fluid criminal networks is based on two key sociological claims. First, that globalisation, the unprecedented movement of goods, people and money, has shattered the ability of organised crime groups in the UK to grow organically and retain monopolies within their localities. In Hobbs' words, criminals have 'moved from an occupational foundation of neighbourhood-oriented extortion and individualistic craft-based larcenies towards an entrepreneurial trading culture driven by highly localized interpretations of global markets' (Hobbs 1995: 115). The second claim is that the enormity and accessibility of the global drugs trade has meant that involvement in it has become commonplace, with participants no longer needing highly specialised criminal skills. The wider economy of late capitalism has reduced the availability of traditional working-class labour, making involvement in the drug trade a popular alternative for the global poor.

REWIND <<<<< 5.8

For a discussion on unemployment, poverty and crime.

An even more fundamental challenge to the traditional view of the organised criminal is to explore the similarities rather than the differences between organised crime activities and the behaviour of those employed in the legitimate economy. It is useful to refer here to Becker's well-known definition of deviance: 'Social groups create deviance by making the rules whose infraction constitute deviance and by applying those rules to a particular group of people and labelling them "outsiders"' (Becker 1963: 9).

From this point of view, 'deviance is not a quality of the act the person commits but rather the application by others of rules and sanctions to an "offender"'. As Hobbs (2013: 229) has more recently argued, it is 'unwise to disregard hedonism as an aspect of illegal market engagement, as it would be to ignore the coke-addled helicopter riding lifestyles of hedge fund traders in a consideration of the occupational culture of financial service workers in the City of London'.

An example of the way the legitimate and illegitimate economies could be understood as similar, rather than distanced, is to look at the motivations of upper-level drug traffickers. A recent review of the available literature on this subject constructed a four-fold typology of their motivations. First, politico-military groups who were often involved with criminality for political reasons, such as supporting an insurgency; second, business criminals who were motivated by enrichment; third, adventurers, who were opportunistic and sought out fun and risk; and finally, 'mixed cases', who possessed a mixture of motivations (Dorn et al. 2005: 36).

organised crime and its policing

Now consider some of the key actors among those involved in the recent banking crisis. If you were going to explore and create typologies to explain bankers' motivations, would you see similar groupings? It could be argued that that some individuals were also driven by politics or ideology, holding neo-liberal views regarding the primacy of the market and the importance of making money. Second, there are those who are just enamoured by wealth and enrichment, and finally, there are those traders who seem to be little more than risk takers, wildly speculating with little regard for the consequences.

To conclude, recent authors take issue with the portrayal of British organised crime as consisting of large organisations mainly constituted by ethnic minorities. Instead, they draw attention to the excesses which occur in the legitimate economy and highlight that it is as important to examine our demands for illicit services and goods, such as cheap labour, drugs or sex, as it is to study and demonise those who provide those services. Rather than accept a 'common sense' view of British organised crime groups as large, mobile and hierarchical, they argue that this is not accurate but a fantasy – an imagined, symmetrical fit to the way law enforcement is structured.

8.5 Trafficking

The trafficking of women and children into the UK for sexual or labour exploitation is an issue which exemplifies the preceding debate regarding the social construction of organised crime. Trafficking is different from smuggling. Smuggling is the transport of willing migrants who consent to and are aware of the conditions of their travel illegally into the UK. They are also free to do as they wish when they arrive. Trafficking involves the movement (recruitment, transportation or receipt) of a person by the threat of force, deception or fraud, and leads to their exploitation. According to law enforcement, non-governmental organisations and some academics, trafficking is a growing threat. A report by Davies (2009) has summed up some of the statistical evidence that illustrates the extent of the problem. He cites a study of the issue undertaken in 1998 which estimated that as many as 1420 women could have been trafficked into the UK for the purposes of constrained prostitution (Kelly and Regan 2000), although he acknowledges the authors' own honesty in stating that these figures are very speculative. Further figures from the Home Office in 2003 estimated that there were 4000 women and girls in the UK at any one time who had been trafficked into forced prostitution. And in 2007 a figure of 25,000 sex slaves was given in Parliament (Davies 2009: 1).

Those involved as perpetrators and victims, overwhelmingly foreign nationals, and the sheer scale of the trafficking figures and revenue generated

organised crime and its policing

by this illegal trade, have led to accusations that the supply of people is orchestrated by organised crime. In particular, attention has been aimed at vulnerable migrants working in exploitative conditions in cannabis factories, domestic labour and, in particular, prostitution. A recent report by the inter-departmental ministerial group on human trafficking has revealed that 1186 victims were referred to the authorities in 2012, with the largest number being from Nigeria, Vietnam, Albania, Romania and China (HMG 2013).

The suspects orchestrating the trafficking are alleged to be organised crime groups from Eastern Europe and South-East Asia. This in turn has led to a succession of national police operations (Operation Pentameter 1 and 2), new laws which broaden the scope of trafficking legislation, such as section 53a of the Sexual Offences Act 2003 (as inserted by section 14 of the Policing and Crime Act 2009), and demands for tougher sentencing, including a new, maximum life sentence for the worst cases of human trafficking and exploitation.

However, as has been argued previously in the chapter, we need to be cautious in accepting the construction of trafficking as a growing organised crime threat and instead evaluate the robustness of the evidence. Ronald Weitzer (cited in Zhang 2009: 179) points out that in 'no area of the social sciences has ideology contaminated knowledge more pervasively than in writings on the sex industry'. Furthermore, criminologists have argued for some time that, although it might be difficult to conceive, people do voluntarily work within the sex industry. This is an argument that has been consistently supported for a number of years, coming from direct interviews with sex workers (Mai 2009; Zhang 2009).

A key author in this regard is Mai (2009), who has conducted several studies in the UK with both male and female sex workers and concludes that there are significant definitional issues regarding the label of trafficking and that the numbers of trafficked victims are far lower than those given above. He argues that personal dynamics are the key to understanding the process of trafficking, exploring notions of romantic love and economic uncertainty rather than stressing the pervasive involvement of organised crime. Certainly, if we review the numbers of people prosecuted for trafficking, they are low and do not reach beyond 25 a year (HMG 2012: 9). This could be due to the robustness of criminal organisations or it could be due to the fact that trafficking is far less common than the authorities think, with the influence of organised crime even less so.

To conclude, the debate over the prevalence of trafficking in the UK is an evolving political and academic issue which can lead to diametrically opposed policy decisions. On the one hand, if it is accepted that trafficking is rare, and instead that several thousand migrants work in exploitative conditions voluntarily, this ought to mean that resources should be deployed to make their lives more bearable. This may entail the decriminalisation of what is currently criminal activity or the offering of support and training so that workers are able to gain more palatable employment. On the other hand, if it is the case that thousands of people are being trafficked in and through the UK by organised crime groups, clearly there is a real need to boost the law-enforcement response, and if we do not, tragedies will occur.

8.6 The policing of organised crime

The policing of organised crime is also contested territory. As mentioned in the introduction to the chapter, successive governments have expanded the powers and budgets of those tasked with policing organised crime, due to the perception of an increased threat. However, critical sociologists from a Marxist background argue that this rise in state power is less to do with any objective threat and is, rather, an attempt by the state to reassert itself and to control marginal communities, usually with high ethnic minority populations, whose labour is surplus to the economy. These new punitive measures exaggerate the threat from organised crime, or other criminal threats such as gangs or paedophiles, and in so doing allow the state to extend its legitimacy and reach, whist simultaneously cutting back on other areas of social spending such as welfare or education (Wacquant 2009). This critical line of thought originated from American theorists. However, as Andreas and Nadelmann observe, 'The internationalization of law enforcement is thus far from equal or reciprocal. For the most part the United States provides the models and sets the priorities and other governments do the accommodating' (2008: 242). It is unsurprising that this line of argument can also be explored in the UK (Hallsworth and Lea 2011).

In the UK, we have documented that successive governments have argued that organised crime poses a significant threat to the state. There are several examples of the state reasserting its powers in ways that critics feel are controversial. First, in contrast to a more general drive for accountability within British policing, heralded by the Police and Crime Commissioners, voted for by the general public, the head of the newly established NCA will have the power to issue a direction to a police force in England and Wales if it is expedient. His officers will also retain what were unprecedented powers of SOCA officers, holding the combined powers and privileges of a constable, a customs officer and an immigration officer. They will be able to use laws such as the Proceeds of Crime Act 2002 and Serious Crime Prevention Orders. These powers diverge from the traditional understanding of 'due process' protected by the British justice system. For example, the Proceeds of Crime Act, designed to confiscate the gains of crime, reverses the burden of proof, and those accused of benefiting from crime have to prove to the courts that they are not guilty, rather than the other way round. The burden of proof is also lower than that demanded in

organised crime and its policing

the criminal courts, and if the accused cannot prove their innocence on the 'balance of probabilities', rather than 'beyond reasonable doubt', they will lose any purported profits from crime.

Beyond this formal court process it is also possible, under the same legislation, for a forfeiture order to be obtained against a person at a Magistrates Court. This is made only against cash which is believed to be the proceeds of crime or intended for use in crime. However, an order can be made even if someone has not been charged or convicted of criminal offence.

Second, it has been argued that the government has instigated a policy of pre-emptive criminalisation, anticipating criminal conduct rather than investigating its occurrence. For example, Serious Crime Prevention Orders do not apply to past offending but are there to deter future conduct. It is argued that, such is the danger from organised criminals rather than wait for them to offend and then prosecute them, it is safer to impose conditions on their conduct in the future, such as requiring them to surrender their passports or restricting their future use of communication devices. Critics contend that individuals are now punished with prison sentences for what are otherwise noncriminal acts such failing to declare their purchase of a gym membership!

Most controversial is the Metropolitan Police's decision to instigate armed stops of criminal suspects in London. These stops are known as 'hard stops' and are intelligence-led interceptions and searches of suspected serious criminals by firearms officers. This tactic has led to the death of two black men, Azelle Rodney in 2005, whose shooting precipitated a public inquiry (Holland 2013), and the shooting of Mark Duggan in 2011, whose death precipitated the Tottenham riots.

The stakes are high. The Metropolitan Police Service (2014: 1) claims that these tactics are necessary, as 'Armed criminals have shot dead more than 50 people in London in the last three-and-a-half years'. It argues that, given the numbers of hard stops each year, these tragic deaths are an inevitable consequence of the threat they routinely face. However, the number of operations (over 700 in 2011) (Holland 2013: 20) threatens to overturn the long-standing commitment of the British police service to remain unarmed. Second, the deaths of black men are part of a pattern of disproportionate deaths at the hands of the police, especially in police custody, and the lack of convictions against any officers involved gives the police service impunity. The overall consequence is a worsening of community and police relations and a widening division between those who support the imposition of law and order at any cost and those who fear the consequences of an increasingly militarised and unaccountable police service.

Whether or not you think the above changes in law and tactics are justifiable will depend on your view of the threat from organised crime. This is why it is so important to unpack its construction and to carefully evaluate the evidence used to support it. On the one hand, if you think there has been an increase in the global threat from organised crime, you will think these and other measures are justified. On the other hand, if you think the threat is exaggerated you will percieve the state's efforts to appear tough as not only forlorn but having negative implications for justice. Therefore, you have to look at the social research together with the social construction of crime and decide which side of the debate you are on.

8.7 Summary

The beginning of this chapter has argued that organised crime has been presented by successive governments of all political persuasions as an ever-growing and ominous social problem. This problem has several dimensions and includes enormous fiscal losses, threats to social order and the exploitation of the most vulnerable groups in our society. However, in deconstructing the social construction of organised crime, from definition to policing, it has been argued that at an empirical and theoretical level the concept of organised crime needs careful scrutiny and challenge.

At the definitional level it is important to recognise that what is defined as crime and, indeed, what is defined as organised crime is in flux. The array of crime threats facing the UK changes as priorities change, and new technologies create and indeed reduce criminal avenues. Meanwhile, successive law-enforcement agencies are prone to adjusting and expanding their definitional remit of organised crime, which in turn has a direct impact on the way the threat from organised crime is measured. In the second section it was argued that measuring the harm caused by organised crime is also socially constructed and complex. In the absence of a large amount of reliable data generated by academics, policy makers and economists are liable to resort to fiscal estimates of harm. These are interesting in that they offer direct comparisons to other harms caused by other 'social problems'. However, it is argued that fiscal estimates should be treated with the utmost caution. Their assumptions concerning what is harm are not straightforward and should be contested.

The next part of the chapter outlined the general view of the structure of organised crime and introduced the alien conspiracy thesis. It was argued that there is a long-standing tendency, borrowing from the literature in the US, to exaggerate the structure and potency of individual organised crime groups and to blame their existence on new migrants who compromise otherwise saintly social landscapes. This section encouraged readers to reconsider the established way of characterising organised crime and to ponder the similarities between the excesses of the legitimate economy and the motivations of key actors within it, and the actions and motivations of so-called organised criminals.

The penultimate section introduced the issue of trafficking, as this exemplifies the current debates on organised crime. In the established narrative, there is a growing threat of trafficking in the UK, orchestrated by the actions of organised crime groups, whose members and victims are mainly foreign nationals, prompting demands for more punitive legislation. In contrast, the chapter then deconstructed this narrative to argue that the empirical evidence for the existence of a growing trafficking problem is weak – raising the question, however unpalatable it may be, that trafficking could be another example of blaming the 'outsider'. If this is the case, then a more liberal rather than punitive legislative response could be warranted.

Finally, the chapter turned to the policing of organised crime, where it was argued that the threat from organised crime has been used to justify significant and long-lasting punitive changes within the criminal justice system. Some of these changes are to legislation and some are to operational law enforcement tactics. All of these changes have increased the power of the state and law enforcement and it is argued they have had and will continue to have a discriminatory impact on those without economic power, especially those who are from minority backgrounds. The section points out that this direction of travel is often driven by policies in the US, regardless of their success and, by illustrating this, also raises the prospect of whether a more liberal approach might be justified in the future.

Revision notes

The social construction of crime. Crime is historically and socially constructed. Crimes come and go as part of the flux of social change. The process that makes an act a criminal one is not fixed or given, but relies on the social context in which acts are determined to be legal or illegal, normal or deviant, moral or immoral.

Defining organised crime. There is no clear and single way of defining 'organised crime'. Definitional arguments are contested and the kind of definition we accept will have important consequences for resourcing, policy and policing decisions.

The 'alien conspiracy thesis'. This is the idea that criminal groups and organisations migrate or extend their powers across geographical locations. It has been a recurrent theme in the study of organised crime for a number of decades. However, there is evidence to suggest that this view is exaggerated and can be used to discriminate against particular minority ethnic groups. Furthermore, studies of UK organised crime have found it anything but 'organised'. Structures tend to be loose and the individuals who make up its members are neither fixed nor homogenous.

Seminar tasks

1 Shoot to kill

Issue:

There are a number of high-profile cases where the police have been accused of having a 'shoot to kill' policy. This was the accusation by family, friends and supporters of Jean Charles de Mendez, who was shot in July 2005 following the London terrorist bombings. The argument is whether or not the police have the right to kill someone if they believe there is a much wider public danger. In the case of terrorism, the police maintain that they have this right, but there are examples of this accusation in relation to organised crime.

EXAMPLE:

On 4 August 2011 Mark Duggan, a suspected organised criminal, was shot dead by police while they were arresting him inside a taxi. His family have seen this as a cold-blooded murder and argued he was not a 'gangster'. His death was a trigger for the London riots, and what followed was a great deal of debate about organised crime in the UK.

EXERCISE:

Do you think the tactic of 'hard stops' is a justified response to the use of firearms by organised criminals? An inquest recently declared the killing of Mark Duggan a 'lawful killing'. Do you agree or disagree. Please list your reasons.

2 The threat from organised crime

Issue:

The National Crime Agency (NCA) attempts to provide a rationalised model of organised crime by devising a list of organised 'crime threats'. This is not unusual among international crime agencies. However, given the argument of this chapter, which concentrates on the difficulties of defining and measuring organised crime, we have to question whether categorising these threats really helps us to assess their harm.

EXAMPLE:

One of the categories that the NCA uses relates to drugs. They state that drug smuggling 'costs' the UK £10.7 billion a year. However, as we have seen, it is not easy to assess what is meant by 'the cost', nor how this figure was arrived at. The social construction of drug smugglers as 'foreign nationals' with 'cultural and familial ties' across the world is also asserted. Such statements seem to fit the 'alien conspiracy thesis' that has been challenges here as highly questionable, given the research evidence.

organised crime and its policing

Coursework questions

Trafficking has been described by the Coalition government as 'modern day slavery' and by others as a 'moral panic'. What is your view and why?

Why do you think it was necessary for the government to replace SOCA (the Serious Organised Crime Agency) with the National Crime Agency (NCA)? Do you think this new institution will reduce the risk from organised crime? And are its powers justified?

References

ACPO, *Cultivation of Cannabis*, UK National Problem Profile Commercial, 2012, http://www.acpo.police.uk/documents/crime/2012/20120430CBA CCofCPP.pdf

Andreas, P. and Nadelmann, E., *Policing the Globe: criminalization and crime control in international relations*, Oxford: Oxford University Press, 2008

BAT, *Illicit Trade in the News*, 2014, http://www.bat.com/group/sites/UK-3 MNFEN.nsf/vwPagesWebLive/DO8BSMRB?opendocumentandSKN = 2

BBC News, 'Eight-man £26m Cigarette Smuggling Gang Jailed', 2013a, http://www.bbc.co.uk/news/uk-england-23086833

—, 'Oxford Grooming Sex Case: brothers jailed for life', 2013, http://www.bbc.co.uk/news/uk-england-oxfordshire-23079649

Becker, H., *Outsiders*. New York: The Free Press, 1963

Cabinet Office Strategy Unit, *Extending Our Reach: a comprehensive approach to tackling serious organised crime*, Norwich: The Stationery Office, 2009, http://www.official-documents.gov.uk/document/cm76/7665/7665.pdf

Cressey, D., *Organized Crime and Criminal Organizations*, Cambridge: Heffer, 1972

Davies, N., 'Prostitution and Trafficking: the anatomy of a moral panic', *Guardian*, 20 October 2009, http://www.theguardian.com/uk/2009/oct/20/trafficking-numbers-women-exaggerated

Dorn, N., Levi, M. and King, L., *Literature Review on Upper Level Drug Trafficking*, London: HMSO, 2005

Dubourg, R. and Prichard, S., *The Impact of Organised Crime in the UK: revenues and economic and social costs.* London; Home Office, 2006, https://www.gov.uk/government/uploads/system/uploads/attachment_data/file/99094/9886.pdf

Glenny, M., *McMafia: a journey through the global criminal underworld*, New York: Random House, 2009

Greenwood, C., (2011) *How a £7,500 facelift and £7,000 at the dentist landed crime lord back in prison.* www.dailymail.co.uk

Hallsworth, S. and Lea, J., 'Reconstructing Leviathan: emerging contours of the security state', *Theoretical Criminology*, 15: 141–57, 2011

HMG, *Local to Global: reducing the risk from organised crime*, 2011, https://www.gov.uk/government/...data/.../organised-crime-strategy.pdf

HMG, *Report on the Internal Review of Human Trafficking Legislation.* May 2012. London: HM Stationery Office.

HMG, *Second report of the Inter-Departmental Ministerial Group on Human Trafficking*, 2013, https://www.gov.uk/government/uploads/system/uploads/attachment_data/file/251487/9794-TSO-HMG_Human_Trafficking.pdf

Hobbs, D., *Bad Business: professional criminals in modern Britain*, Oxford: Oxford University Press, 1995

Hobbs, D., *Lush Life: constructing organized crime in the UK*, Oxford: Oxford University Press, 2013

Holland, C., *The Azelle Rodney Inquiry*, London: The Stationery Office, 2013, http://azellerodneyinquiry.independent.gov.uk/docs/The_Azelle_Rodney_Inquiry_Report_%28web%29.pdf

Home Office, *One Step Ahead: a 21st century strategy to defeat organised crime*, 2004, http://www.archive2.official-documents.co.uk/document/cm61/6167/6167.pdf

Kelly, L. and Regan, L., *Stopping Traffic*, Police Research Series, Paper 125, London: Home Office, May 2000

Levi, M., 'Organised Crime and Terrorism', in M. Maguire, R. Morgan and R. Reiner (eds), *The Oxford Handbook of Criminology* (4th edn), Oxford: Oxford University Press pp. 771–809, 2007

Mai, N., *ESRC Project: Migrant Workers in the UK Sex Industry: final policy-relevant report*, 2009, https://metranet.londonmet.ac.uk/fms/MRSite/Research/iset/Nick%20Mai/Migrant%20Workers%20in%20the%20UK%20Sex%20Industry%20Project%20Final%20Policy%20Relevant%20Report.pdf

Metropolitan Police Service, 'Statement from Assistant Commissioner Mark Rowley following Conclusion of Mark Duggan Inquest', 2014, http://www.youtube.com/user/metpoliceservice

organised crime and its policing

Moon, T., *Britain Is Organised Crime Capital of Europe, Says Europol*, International Business Times, 2013, http://www.ibtimes.co.uk/crime-europol-gangs-adams-family-cartel-delta-441511

Morselli, C., Turcotte, M., and Tenti, V., *The Mobility of Criminal Groups*, Research and National Coordination Organized Crime Division Law Enforcement and Police Branch Public Safety Canada, 2010, http://publications.gc.ca/collections/collection_2012/sp-ps/PS4-91-2010-eng.pdf

RCMP, *Sleipnir Version 2.0 Organized Crime Groups Capability Measurement Matrix*, 2010, http://jratcliffe.net/research/sleipnir/SLEIPNIRv2_unclassified.pdf

Serious Organised Crime Agency, *Annual Report and Accounts 2012/13*, London: The Stationery Office, 2012

Silverstone, D., 'The Policing of Vietnamese Organized Crime within the UK', *Policing: a Journal of Policy and Practice*, 5(1): 41–8, 2011

Sterling, C., *Crime without Frontiers*, London: Little Brown & Co., 1994

Tannenbaum, F., *Crime and the Community*, New York: Columbia University Press, 1938

Van Lampe, K., *Definitions of Organized Crime*. 2014, http://www.organized-crime.de/organizedcrimedefinitions.htm

Wacquant, L., *Punishing the Poor: the neoliberal government of social insecurity*, Durham, NC and London: Duke University Press, 2009

Woodiwiss, M., *Organized Crime and American Power*. Toronto, ONT: University of Toronto Press, 2001

Woodiwiss, M. and Hobbs, D., 'Organized Evil and the Atlantic Alliance: moral panics and the rhetoric of organized crime policing in America and Britain', *British Journal of Criminology*, 49(1): 106–28, 2009

Wortley, S. and McCalla, A., 'Explaining the Immigration–Crime Connection: a review of competing models and associated policies', *Journal of International Migration and Integration*, 2008

Wright, A., *Organised Crime*, Cullompton, Devon: Willan, 2006

Zhang, S., 'Beyond the "Natasha" Story. A review and critique of current research on sex trafficking', *Global Crime*, 10(3): 178–95, 2009

Further reading

Becker, H., *Outsiders: studies in the sociology of deviance*, New York: The Free Press, 1963

Hobbs, D., *Lush Life: constructing organized crime in the UK*, Oxford: Oxford University Press, 2013

Wright, A., *Organised Crime*, Cullompton, Devon: Willan, 2006

chapter 9

Youth gangs

Tara Young

9.1 Introduction

On a Sunday evening in 2011, a young teenager named Negus McClean lay dying in the street from multiple wounds to his chest and thigh. His fatal injuries had been inflicted by a group of seven or eight teenagers in a frenzied assault after he had fallen off his bike. The attack on Negus occurred two weeks before his sixteenth birthday and in front of the 12-year-old brother he was trying to protect. According to media sources (Dodd 2013; Fagge et al. 2011), McClean's death was the result of a 'postcode' feud between two rival gangs locked in a tit-for-tat, retributive and violent melée that had left one young male seriously injured and two others, including Negus, dead in one week.

On the day of his death Negus was set upon by a 'hunting posse' of 'Get Money Gang' members who had ridden into N9 (Edmonton) from EN3 (Enfield) looking to avenge a previous attack. They happened upon Negus, aka 'Young Chops' and a reported member of 'Dem Africans' and his brother as they went to purchase a chicken and chips supper from the local shop (Fagge et al. 2011). The gang allegedly ran down and brutally attacked Negus with an assortment of weaponry including knives and a metal pole. Onlookers, including his brother, watched helplessly as the group of teenagers mercilessly set upon him. Negus was left dying in a pool of blood as the group took off on their mountain bikes (Dodd 2013; Fagge et al. 2011).

Negus's murder was one of 152 teenage fatalities that occurred in London over a seven-year period from 2005 to 2011 (Citizens Report 2013). The deaths of these young men and women, and many more across the UK, have been attributed to a rise in a sub-cultural phenomenon called 'gun, gang and knife' culture. It has been extensively argued that young people who adhere to this culture, who belong to 'gangs' and are involved in 'gang-related' offending, are responsible for the significant increase in the number of serious violent offences amongst young people. Indeed, 'gang members' were accused of being the primary orchestrators of the national riots that erupted in August 2011, although there was evidence against this point of view (Lewis et al. 2011).

That 152 young people have lost their lives and the riots occurred is not in doubt; that these young people were victims of 'gang-related' crime or that 'gangs' started, and executed, mass civil disturbance in the UK *is* questionable. One reason why this is debatable is partly because identifying a group as a 'gang' as distinct from other collectives is difficult, as is disaggregating 'gang-related' offending from 'non-gang' or individually motivated criminality.

This chapter discusses 'gangs' and 'gang culture' as a social problem. One of the overarching aims of this section is to illustrate how the problem of the gang has been constructed in contemporary society. Here we will review how collections of individuals come to be defined as 'gangs', and by whom. You will see how political viewpoints influence the way in which information on gang, gun and knife culture is disseminated in society and how the construction of 'gang culture' in the UK has led to widespread fear of young people and a growth in punitive sanctions against them.

9.2 What exactly is a gang?

What is a gang? You may think that this is an easy question to answer, but there is no common understanding of what a gang is. Is a group a gang when it engages in particular types of behaviour? Are groups defined as gangs only when they are visible on the street? Does a group have to reach a certain size before it is classified as a gang? Does the ethnicity of a group determine whether a group is labelled a gang? Who decides what a gang is? These questions have influenced research on youth crime and delinquency for nearly a century.

The gang as commonly known is an American construct (although the UK has a long and colourful history of problems related to street-based delinquent youth groups; see Mayhew 2008; Pearson 1983; Davies 2009), so it is not so surprising that the first influential definition of it emanated from research conducted in Chicago by sociologist Frederic Thrasher.

 Key thinker: Frederic Thrasher (1892–1962)

Frederic Thrasher worked in the Sociology Department at Chicago University alongside distinguished scholars such as Robert Park and Ernest Burgess. The focus of this core group of academics, famously known

as the 'Chicago School', was on human ecology and urban development. Thrasher's ethnographic study of street-based groups led to the
production of his seminal text, *The Gang: a study of 1313 gangs in
Chicago,* which was published in 1929. What Thrasher found was that
'gangs' started out as 'playgroups' and transformed, through a process
of interaction between group members and non-group members, into
'gangs' (Thrasher 1927). Adopting this framework, Thrasher believed
that all youth groups had the potential to become gangs and it was the
social conditions of Chicago at the end of the nineteenth century that
played a significant part in gang formation.

Principally, when Thrasher spoke of the gang he made reference to a peer
group in crisis. He saw the gang as a youthful response to the 'social disor-
ganisation' apparent in Chicago during the 1920s. Accordingly, gangs
emerged when playgroups met hostile forces (e.g. other youth groups or
law enforcement) that enabled group members to cast themselves as different and so to formulate a separate identity on the basis of 'us' and 'them'.

Essentialising difference was, perhaps, necessary for survival in the melt-
ing pot that was Chicago in this period when children from diverse ethnic
populations (e.g. Irish, Italian, African American, Polish etc.) sought to
carve a niche for themselves and protect their cultural identity. In ethnically
diverse environments, Thrasher conceptualised the gang as a vehicle
through which young people resolved cultural conflicts and constructed
new identities, forged by rules, loyalties and rituals, in order to affirm their
own alternative lifestyle and agenda (Thrasher 1927).

Thrasher's exploration of Chicago produced a definition that influenced
discussion in the US for a long time. In his seminal study of 1313 juvenile
gangs in the slums of Chicago he defined the gang as:

> an interstitial group originally formed spontaneously and then inte-
> grated through conflict...and characterised by meeting face-to-face,
> milling, movement through space as a unit, conflict and planning. The
> result of this collective behaviour is the development of tradition, unre-
> flective internal structure, esprit de corps, solidarity, morale, group
> awareness and attachment to a local territory.
>
> (Thrasher 1927: 46)

For Thrasher, gangs were no more than anti-social youth 'playing' at being
bad and criminal. Their anti-social behaviour brings them into conflict with
the local community and the wider society. His study points to the disen-
gagement of young people from the broader community. In this sense

youth gangs

there is a broader sociological point at play, identifying gangs as a symbol of social change and generational tensions. The gang provides refuge for marginalised minority youth and provides them with a sense of belonging and safety; in essence, it is a substitute for what society fails to give (Thrasher 1927: 33). Gangs therefore can be seen to provide a short-lived space for youthful transition into adulthood where individuality, cultural values and social customs are tested out. In this sense they can provide a useful function for transition into adulthood. However, on the other hand, they can involve a step towards criminality.

9.3 From classic 'playgroups' to speciality gangs

Whilst being one of the first influential definitions of the gang to be published, Thrasher's was by no means the last and, as concern over the deviant behaviour of youngsters and gangs intensified, so did the search for answers and solutions to the gang problem. Scholars like Malcolm Klein (1971) and Walter Miller (1975, cited in Saunders 1994) were at the forefront of the administrative drive to tackle gang-related offending and their independently published research was equally as influential as Thrasher's; however, the lens through which these scholars viewed the 'playgroups' of Thrasher's study was different.

Malcolm Klein's definition grew out of an evaluation of a gang project in Los Angeles. In fact, much of the early US data on gangs was an accumulation of state-funded research work that began in the 1950s and continued on into the late 1970s. Public policy dictated that gang membership was a problem that needed to be dealt with and so a number of 'gang' projects were created and then evaluated. This radically altered the way in which gangs were thought of and dealt with by the state. With Klein's definition there was a move away from seeing the gang as just a peer group in crisis *within* society to seeing it as a group *separate* from society.

 Key definition: Klein on gangs

'...any detonable adolescent group of youngsters who a) are generally perceived as a distinct aggregation by others in the neighbourhood, b) recognise themselves as a detonable group (almost invariably with a group name) and c) have been involved in a sufficient number of delinquent incidences to call forth a consistent negative response from neighbourhood residents and or law enforcement.' (Klein 1971: 13)

Klein's tighter focus on delinquency rendered the term 'gang' synonymous with 'criminal'. This represents a departure from Thrasher's broader socio-structural definition, towards one more suited to law enforcement. In Klein's work there is a greater emphasis on crime, deviance and legal sanctions; perceptions of the community are now given prominence in how groups are defined.

With Walter Miller's concept of the gang we see the enduring idea of the gang as deviant, as developed by Klein. However, it is refined and narrowed from that offered by Klein by introducing some structural and behavioural characteristics that you may be familiar with.

> A gang is a group of recurrently associating individuals with identifiable leadership and internal organisation, identifying with or claiming control over a territory in the community, and engaging either individually or collectively in violent or other forms of illegal behaviour.
>
> (Miller 1975: 9, cited in Saunders 1994)

Miller's definition attaches as much, perhaps a little more, importance to offending and criminal behaviour, to organisation and leadership, to instrumental violence as a functional and purposive part of gang life, and to violence as a central aspect of a gang's *raison d'être*.

Contemporary definitions such as those offered by Klein, Miller and latterly Jankowski (see Jankowski 1991) give centrality to the notion that collective identity is of utmost importance in gang life and it is the shared criminal interests of its members that bring them together. The gang is now largely viewed as a deviant, anti-social violent group. Gone are the 'childish play' elements of the gang, as is the organic construction of it put forward by Thrasher – who suggested that, if left alone and ignored, 'gang' members would grow up and away from the gang. These aspects have been replaced with calculation and purposefulness, suggesting that young people decide to get involved in gangs. Few contemporary definitions of the gang offer an alternative viewpoint (see Hagedorn 1998; Moore 1991; Kontos et al. 2003) and the majority point to the criminogenic nature of street-based groups.

In 2001, Klein developed his early work and proposed a typology of street gangs. From the analysis of US police data on gangs, Klein, along with his colleague Cheryl Maxson, identified the existence of five different gang types: Traditional, Neo-traditional, Compressed, Collective and Speciality gangs, each with its own unique structure, membership, leadership and behavioural characteristics (Table 9.1) (Klein and Maxson 2001).

According to Klein and Maxson, providing such detail on street gangs is necessary for the combating and suppression of crime and violence engaged in by these groups, since more are emerging not only in the US but also in Europe and other parts of the world. Indeed, Klein and Maxson are not the only scholars to highlight distinctions between youth and gang groups.

Table 9.1 Compressed, collective and speciality gangs

Type	Subgroups	Size	Age range	Duration	Territorial	Crime versatility
Traditional	Yes – (e.g. original gangsters, Seniors, Juniors, wannabes)	Large (>100)	Wide (9–30+ years)	Long (>20 years)	Yes	Yes
Neo-traditional	Yes	Medium (>50)	No pattern	Short (<10 years)	Yes	Yes
Compressed	No	Small (<50)	Narrow (<10 years)	Short (<10 years)	No pattern	Yes
Collective	No	Medium–large (>50)	Medium–wide (>10 years)	Medium (10–15 years)	No pattern	Yes
Speciality	No	Small (<50)	Narrow (<10 years)	Short (<10 years)	Yes	No

Source: Adapted from Klein and Maxson (2001: 5).

In his study of criminal organisations as part of the Greater Vancouver Gang Study, Canadian scholar Robert Gordon (2000) distinguishes between six types of youth groupings. These groups run along what could be considered to be a severity spectrum that ranges from, at one end, social collectives such as youth movements (e.g. Punk Rockers) and small clusters of youth groups, through to semi-structured, criminally motivated violent street gangs and criminal business organisations, at the other end.

In the UK, John Pitts's London-based research on gangs has identified violent youth gangs (Pitts 2007, 2008) and Hallsworth and Young's (2005) study on delinquent formations is at pains to outline the disjuncture between peer groups, street gangs and organised crime groups that make up the crime network. Whilst there are a number of political and theoretical differences between these scholars, what unites them is the belief that in order to produce effective policy responses to the crime and violence associated with such groups, law-enforcement agencies must recognise and appreciate the differences.

9.4 Gangs and subcultures

The question regarding why young people form gangs is one that takes us into the territory of classic theories of deviancy and, indeed, the emergence of criminology itself as a branch of sociology. You will perhaps already have spotted the influence some socio-cultural factors play in creating gang groups in the narrative above. Indeed, the impact of youthful relationship to the urban environment features in the conception of the gang in many of the ideas expressed above.

In *Delinquent Boys: the culture of the gang* (1955) Albert Cohen argued that the formation of sub-cultural groups like gangs was driven by frustration. He maintained that westernised societies like the US and the UK are dominated by middle-class values and norms: academic success, education, wealth and status. These norms and values were transmitted through society (at that time) through the media of the TV, radio, magazines and, in particular, through schooling. Individuals were exposed to these values and internalised the desire to achieve them. They became the measure by which people were judged by others and judged themselves. Because of inequity in society, working-class boys, in particular, realised that they were destined, by virtue of their birth and socialisation, to lose status in a social system that was organised around middle-class values. Consequently, some working-class young men experienced frustration at not being able to compete with middle-class boys to achieve these internalised social goals. They therefore experienced problems adjusting to the fact that they were not going to 'make it'.

Boys who had internalised the middle-class message experienced what Cohen termed 'status frustration', which involved unpleasant feelings of shame (Cohen 1955: 110). Cohen believed this to be especially acute in the school system. The experience of not being able to win out in the terms that schools establish as legitimate (such as obtaining high grades in exams) created 'status frustration' among some young working-class men. The only way this psychological condition could be resolved socially was in the form of a 'reaction formation', such as establishing new ground rules through gang membership. In other words, in order to deal with the anxiety caused by the prospect of failing at school some working-class boys reacted by belittling the importance of middle-class aspirations. Furthermore, they sought out other like-minded individuals and formed groups whose values differed from those of the middle class. They were actively hostile to the mainstream norms, rejecting the rules and behaviour set out by this group. In fact, any action came to be deemed 'right' when it opposed the dominant culture. In this way, the group embraced activities (criminality, fighting, anti-social behaviour) that went against middle-class values and norms, and these activities became justified in the context of their way of understanding the world.

Cohen's findings resonate with Paul Willis's seminal work on how working-class kids in 1970s Britain passed through the education system into paid employment (Willis 1977). While not seeking to explain the formation of gangs or youth delinquency directly, Willis argued that working-class boys questioned education as a way out of restrictive working-class culture. Like Cohen's (1955) delinquent boys and Walter Miller's lads (1975), they created and reproduced an oppositional culture that celebrated masculinity, immediate gratification and toughness in order to survive in a working-class working environment.

The overriding theme of Miller's and Cohen's analysis is that the formation of gangs offers young people (particularly young men) the opportunity to become 'somebody' where, in a society that is experienced as unequal and hostile, they are a 'nobody'. Indeed, all the theories that we have looked at here develop the idea that young people form gangs as an alternative to mainstream culture and argue that this is provoked by limited life opportunities based around social and economic class divisions.

Cohen's analysis of gang formation and delinquency places great emphasis on individual characteristics and responses when explaining the emergence of gang groups. Extending and developing from Cohen's work, Richard Cloward and Lloyd Ohlin (1960) point to more structural features. Influenced by the work of Edwin Sutherland, Robert Merton and Emile Durkheim, their chief concern was to examine the social conditions under which people experienced strain, their response to this and how delinquents found solutions to this condition.

Like Merton (2009), Cloward and Ohlin argued that delinquency occurs because there is a structural disjunction between what society codes as success and the social means made available to realise it. As the capitalist system in the US and the UK is organised in ways that systematically preclude the poor, who simply cannot compete equally for success, it is inevitable that some young people will defer from complying with its norms and rules. Although they may experience strain, these young people are, according to Cloward and Ohlin, free (by virtue of structural inequality) from moral constraints such as guilt and anxiety and thus do not experience 'strain' or 'status frustration'. With a relatively free conscience young people organise themselves into sub-cultural units that provide support, approval and ultimately a rationale for delinquent behaviour. The question of where young people turn for affirmation is of the utmost importance here, since both peer groups and the wider adult community inevitably influence the behaviour of youngsters. Sutherland suggested that crime occurs when there is more social support for being deviant/criminal than for obeying the law. In addition, since deviant behaviour, like all forms of behaviour, is learned from wider social relationships (Sutherland et al. 1991), the type of delinquent/criminal behaviour selected will be dependent upon the peer groups and other criminal networks operating within a given locality.

In other words, the criminal underworld is as inequitable as the legal economy and young people are differentially associated in relation to both social systems. Cloward and Ohlin believed that whilst poorer people lacked access to legitimate ways of making money and achieving success or status, they did not have equal access to illegitimate ways of making money or achieving success. Opportunities are blocked for some and open to others; therefore unconnected individuals find it just as hard to 'make it' illegitimately as legitimately. According to Cloward and Ohlin, this inequality results in three distinctive types of gang: the Criminal gang, the Conflict gang and the Retreatist gang.

Key idea: Cloward and Ohlin's three types of delinquent sub-culture

Criminal gangs are collectives of established older gangsters operating in an existing (illegal) gang economy. They develop in areas with gang legacies where generations of established and, importantly, successful criminals act as role models. These older 'business men' pass on their criminal knowledge to youngsters. In other words, they teach chosen youngsters the 'tricks of the trade'. Consequently, these young people acquire the knowledge/skills/contacts needed to develop criminal careers and perhaps into an organised crime group.

youth gangs

Conflict gangs develop where illegitimate and legitimate opportunities are non-existent, so young people with nothing of any value to attach themselves to band together. These groups are more likely to emerge in areas that lack a social structure with a common value system. They emerge more readily in the areas with the highest transient and migrant population. Violence is more likely to be a common feature of this group.

Retreatist gangs emerge when young people who have no access to legitimate opportunities to achieve goals etc. fail, or choose not, to attach themselves to established illegitimate ones. The group is characterised by drug usage and dealing and petty crime.

Cloward and Ohlin found a greater proliferation of gangs in working-class communities and agreed that collective forms of delinquency occur when aspirations are blocked.

9.5 Criticisms of sub-cultural theory

Subcultural theories of the kind outlined above help us to try to explain gangs by thinking of them in terms of the ways in which they are anomalous to mainstream society. By drawing on sociological concepts, such as social norms and social class, these authors point to some fundamental characteristics that we still associate with gang membership today. Such theories also point to the way that gangs are socially constructed as 'deviant' by mainstream opinion. This is, arguably, problematic because, in some respects, gangs can be seen as an alternative (rather than a completely opposite or different) expression of the *same* kind of values that most people aspire to, such as status, wealth and respect.

Sub-cultural theories rest on the premise that gangs have an alternate and distinct core set of values that are adhered to and distinctly separate from wider mainstream cultural values. However, as we have seen, even in some of these arguments there are already the seeds of a criticism that this is not always and necessarily the case and that there are features of gang formation and behaviour that point to a connection with broader, mainstream cultural values. Sykes and Matza (1957), and latterly David Matza (1964), argued against the idea of a delinquent sub-culture. They maintained that there is little difference between juvenile delinquents and their law-abiding peers. Rather, young people 'drift' into and out of delinquent behaviours. This process is greatly affected by the particular kind of criminal, or deviant, act they are engaged in and also by their own understanding of society and its values. Sykes and Matza argued that most young people, including juvenile delinquents, are aware of the rules and norms governing society, which they have internalised and have some moral responsibility to uphold. But, in the absence of effective forms of social control, some youngsters, particularly those who feel they have been let down by societal institutions (e.g. the family, education, law enforcement) 'switch off' or neutralise this knowledge in order to commit deviant acts. In other words, young people use 'techniques of neutralization' to justify their offending behaviour in an attempt to maintain some connection to the wider society (Sykes and Matza 1957: 234). This means that they find an acceptable way to justify a particular crime to themselves in relation to social norms. Five techniques are adopted by delinquents to neutralise their deviant or offending behaviour: 'the denial of responsibility', 'the denial of injury', 'the denial of the victim', 'the condemnation of the condemners' and 'the appeal to higher loyalties'. In common parlance these could equate to 'it was an accident!' or 'it wasn't my fault', 'they weren't hurt that badly'; 'he was from the other "endz" and shouldn't have been "slippin" in our manor', 'the olders were just as bad back in the day', and 'they robbed my boy, innit!; we have each other's back' (see Sykes and Matza for a fuller account).

According to Sykes and Matza, it isn't that some people are delinquent and others are not. There is an overlap. The techniques of neutralisation are justifications used by juvenile delinquents to defend their behaviour in ways that are broadly intelligible to mainstream society. That young people, including those in gangs, adopt this method to explain their actions suggests not an adherence to commitment to an alternative sub-culture but, rather, an appeal to a pre-existing one. For example, if loyalty to family or friends means breaking the law, this could be justification that attacking someone is the right thing to do. This is not random or based on a sub-cultural code, but the particular acceptance that a situation is 'different' from others. Consequently the individual who commits this act can later feel guilt or remorse, as he or she may come to realise that the 'technique of neutralisation' that they deployed (in this case a higher loyalty) was actually wrong.

Sub-cultural theory understands delinquency as a *collective* endeavour side-stepping the individual within the group. As such, sub-cultural theory generalises about the gang as a whole without taking account of the differences between the individuals who constitute it.

These individuals may have very different levels of socialisation and capabilities. Furthermore, sub-cultural theory presupposes that individuality is subsumed into the group and socialisation within the group, and collective action takes precedence over individual ability to understand the difference between 'right and wrong'. But this may not be the case. Finally, it assumes that individuals are fully socialised into an alternative deviant value system, but this is too totalising a theory. Recognising that individuals within a gang may have different levels of socialisation, and are capable of reflecting on

youth gangs

their behaviour and learning their actions may have been 'wrong', holds out the possibility that through education and awareness gang members can be integrated into law-abiding forms of behaviour.

Key point: sub-cultural theory

Sub-cultural theories require the presence of two conditions: a) that lower-class young men are discontented with the dominant social system and b) that they adhere to a different normative and value structure. For a fuller critique of the subcultural position, see S. Box (1981) *Deviance, Reality and Society* (2nd edn), London: Holt Reinhart and Winston, and D. Matza (1964) *Delinquency and Drift*, New York: Wiley.

9.6 The 'gang' phenomenon in the UK

The concept of the gang and its existence in the UK is much contested. As illustrated above, the US academy has dominated viewpoints about gangs, but some have argued over differences in the culture, style, composition and behaviour of delinquent youth groups that have emerged in Britain. In other words, the US literature on gang culture has never quite satisfied the social conditions found in the UK.

David Downes argued in *The Delinquent Solution* (1966) that gangs as conceptualised in North America did not exist on British soil, thus challenging sub-cultural ideas from a British point of view. He maintained that there was no evidence of structured US-style gangs in his study of adolescents in the East End areas of Stepney and Poplar.

Key quote: Downes

'Delinquent groups in the East End lacked both the structure and cohesion of the New York gangs described by Cloward and Ohlin and the fissile impermanence of Yablonsky's "near group". If the definition of delinquent gang is that of a group whose central tenet is the requirement to commit delinquent acts – i.e. "delinquent subcultures" as defined by Cloward and Ohlin – then the observation and information combined point to the absence of delinquent gangs in the East End, except as a thoroughly atypical collectivity...The groups responsible for the bulk of delinquency were simply small cliques whose members committed illegal acts sometimes collectively, sometimes in pairs, sometimes individually, in some cases regularly, in others only rarely.' (Downes 1966: 198–9)

What Downes found was not gangs per se but what could be more appropriately understood as 'street corner groups' of youngsters socialising to alleviate boredom and create excitement denied in the labour market, engaging on an individual and collective level in crime and anti-social behaviour. In other words, at that time, the social structure of the UK was not producing 'gangs' per se but rather, youth sub-cultures.

Other British scholars pretty much thought the same, preferring to write about sub-cultures, not gangs. For example, sociologists at the Birmingham School argued that the US sub-cultural model was not useful for understanding the formation of new UK youth sub-cultures. They understood these to be a means of 'resistance through rituals' (see Hall and Jefferson 2006). That is, youth sub-culture in post-war Britain was largely a response to the material contradictions experienced by young people. Most famously, Stan Cohen, in his study of Mods and Rockers in *Folk Devils and Moral Panics*, maintained that sub-cultures were as much the product of the media as they were constructed by youth. The media 'demonise' youth subcultures, creating 'moral panics'. In the terms of the methodology outlined for this text they were held to be socially constructed, their actions exaggerated through 'deviancy amplification', and this process engendered a social myth of teenage 'folk devils' (Cohen 1980).

REWIND <<<<< 2.2

For a short discussion of 'moral panics' and how they fit into the social construction approach.

That is not to say that gang-type groups were historically entirely alien to Britain prior to the twentieth century. Gangs are a perennial feature in British culture and history. Their existence is not new, nor is the concern about them (Cohen 1980; Patrick, 1973; Pearson, 1983; Davies, 2009). Indeed, literary scholars such as Charles Dickens writing in the Victorian period (mid nineteenth century) referred to a fictional gang of juvenile pickpockets headed by the 'Artful Dodger' under the watchful leadership of the miserly 'Fagin' (Dickens 1994). Dickens was a journalist writing at the time and it is arguable that in his novels he mirrored the lived realities of the Victorian era.

In academic terms, historians Pearson (1983) and Davies (2009) drew attention to the criminal and violent exploits of groups of 'Hooligans' (Pearson 1983) and 'Scuttlers' (Davies 2009) engaged in street fighting, robbery and stealing, amongst other delinquent and criminal activities. Similarly, Patrick (1973) referred to a history of gangs in Glasgow, the infamous 'City of Gangs'. Patrick's conical ethnography of a Glaswegian gang known as the 'Young Team' located in a working-class neighbourhood in

Maryhill points to the endurance of street groups as a feature of certain neighbourhoods. What's more, in the preface to the newest edition of Patrick's work (2013) he, following the Chicagoan sociologists of the 1920s, posits that the gang will remain a perennial feature of city life unless the structural inequalities facing the many working-class young people born to multiply-deprived families living in overcrowded conditions on 'sink estates' with little prospect of social mobility and destined for a life of menial, low-waged jobs are radically altered (Patrick 2013: xi).

The (re)discovery of the gang

Key point: media headlines

'It's lawless out there' (*Guardian*, 2000)

'The rise of the Muslim boys' (*Evening Standard*, 2005)

'Kids killing kids. Families in fear. It's time to say no more!' (*Sun*, 2008)

'"We should have had the victim raped", said girl gang thug after stripping and whipping rival, 16, in the street' (*Daily Mail*, 2009)

'London gangs using children as drug mules as they seek to expand markets' (*Guardian*, 2014)

In more recent times the gang has become a cause for concern and the topic of much social discourse. A steady increase in official recording of serious violence involving guns and bladed weapons was hailed as illustrative of a change in the offending profile amongst young people. Between 2005 and 2008 serious violent crime amongst young people was reported to have risen by one third (Leapman 2008). In the period between 2007 and 2008, 57 young people were killed in crimes involving knives and guns (Hallsworth and Young 2008). A number of media reports, like those listed above, attributed these deaths to a burgeoning 'gun and knife culture' and pointed to one distinctive social menace: gangs.

Key event: the Damilola Taylor case

Damilola Taylor was the victim of two brothers, Danny and Rickie Preddie, who were reputed to be members of a notorious gang called the 'Young Peckham Boys' and Letisha and Charlene were caught up and gunned down, in a gang-related 'drive-by' between longstanding rivals the Burger Bar Boys and the Johnson Crew on New Year's Eve 2003.

Indeed, some academics claimed that gang groups were the 'new face of youth crime' (Pitts 2008). The terrible murder of 10-year old Damilola Taylor in Peckham, London in 2000 and cousins Letisha Shakespeare, aged 17, and Charlene Ellis, aged 18, in Birmingham were arguably the catalyst for understanding rising violence as gang-related, and the continuation of such deaths throughout the mid to late 2000s was testament to a real social problem.

A number of localised studies attempting to quantify the problem of gangs (see section 9.8 below) have been published since 1998. What emerged from this material was a relatively confused picture, but a central message appeared to advocate the view that there was a growing and serious gang problem in the UK. For example, the Metropolitan Police identified 169–70 gangs (depending on source) operating in the London area; a comparable number, 171, has been identified by Strathclyde Police (Centre for Social Justice 2009). West Midlands Police force claims 42 urban gangs in the area and Nottinghamshire Police cites 15 known gangs, both areas reporting that 400 individuals are involved (Home Office 2011). Such figures added fuel to the media fire and sparked claims of hyper-violent, territorial, hierarchical and American-style gangs in British cities (The London Paper 2007). John Pitts's research connected such groups to serious organised crime and argued that street gangs dominate the illegal drugs market. His research in Waltham Forest discovered 13 gangs in the borough, including two highly organised, articulated 'super-gangs'. Rough estimates placed the number of young people involved in gang groups at 600–700 (Pitts 2007). Groups in Waltham Forest, and elsewhere, were involved in the Class A illegal drugs market and associated violence; they had a fearsome reputation for coercion and recruited reluctant individuals into gang life with threats of physical and sexual violence (Pitts 2007; 2008).

These findings chimed well with media accounts and fitted the Americanised version of street gangs. Waves of media reports constructed urban violence by young people, especially incidences involving guns and bladed weapons, as gang-related. Stabbings and shootings were down to gangs. The *Daily Mail* attributed the five children shot or stabbed each day in London as 'victims of gang violence' (*Daily Mail* 2008). In Manchester and Liverpool half of all shootings were deemed to be 'gang-related' (Bullock and Tilley 2002: 33) and a number of the major cities in the UK were, because of connections with gang groups, dubbed 'Sin cities' crawling with warring gang members (McLagan 2005). Indeed, the threat posed by new-style gangs was reputed to outstrip that of established historical foes, leading to the conclusion that gangs were connected to terrorist organisations (Travis 2008) that were 'tougher than the IRA' (Hill 2007).

youth gangs

9.7 How many gangs are there in the UK?

Despite the seeming rise in US-style gangs in the UK, it might be more salient to consider that the furore around gangs might not reflect the truth about the existence of gangs. Rather, these reports can be understood as a social construction catalysed around a 'moral panic' in the public reaction to the presentation of the gang phenomenon in contemporary society. Certainly, a closer look at the evidence suggests this alternate reading.

To date there is no clear picture of how many gang groups exist in the UK. This is primarily because the Home Office does not systematically collect and collate these data. There are a small number of research studies that have sought over a number of years to quantify the issue. The picture that emerges, however, is a little confusing.

Stelfox (1998) – conducted research on gangs across UK police forces. A national total of 72.

Bullock and Tilley (2002) – research based on police data and interviews (40) with current and ex-gang members. Estimated 470 gang members in Manchester. Less than 10 per cent of total sample (40) were gang members.

Shropshire and McFarquhar (2002) Manchester Council report – estimated 1000 gang members in Manchester.

Bennett and Holloway (2004) – 15 per cent (n = 408 of total sample 2725) had experience of gang life, but only 4 per cent (n = 109) claimed to be gang members.

Communities that Care (2005) – 4 per cent (n = 440 of total sample 11,400) of school-aged children (11–15) defined themselves as gang members.

Smith and Bradshaw (2005) – 20 per cent of young people sampled belonged to a gang at age 13, falling to 5 per cent by age 17.

Home Office Offending Crime and Justice Survey (Sharp et al., 2006) – found that 3827 (or 6 per cent) of 10- to 19-year-olds surveyed were members of delinquent youth groups (DYGs) or 'gangs'.

Metropolitan Police Pan-London Gang Profile (2006) – estimated 169–71 gangs in London totalling around 50,000 members.

Pitts (2008) – 600–700 gang members in Waltham Forest.

Home Office (2008) – four area assessment to establish the existence of gangs. Estimated the number of gang members in Birmingham, Liverpool, Manchester and London to be 127, 96, 96 and 356 respectively.

Strathclyde Police – identified 170 gangs within its jurisdiction, with nearly 2000 gang members based in Glasgow (Centre for Social Justice, 2009).

HM Inspectorate of Constabulary (2009) estimated 2800 'criminal gangs' in the UK.

We can see from the above that available evidence does not present a straightforward picture but one of complexity. What these figures show is a rather unclear picture from which to make a concrete assessment of the gang situation. The variation is perhaps due to a lack of consistency in regard to definition, with each study adopting its own interpretation. For example, some surveys like the Communities that Care Project utilise a self-definition approach whereby the respondent is asked to declare whether they are in a gang, while others provide a definition for the respondents to consider and then use additional 'filters' to attribute gang membership (Bennett and Holloway 2004; Sharp et al. 2006). Further still, criminal justice agencies use different criteria for gang membership, utilising this term to describe teen groups on the streets and organised crime groups involved in serious criminality. Whatever the definition used, however, what these surveys show is that while gangs exist, they are relatively rare and represent no more than 3–7 per cent of the sample population. You might be thinking, 'this number is relatively small, so why the concern?'

9.8 It's gang crime, but not as we know it – what do gangs do?

Some scholars have argued that even though the proportion of gang members is small, the threat and damage caused by such groups is significant. Research suggests that gang members are more likely than non-gang members to hold pro-delinquent views and engage in delinquent behaviour (Battin-Pearson et al. 1998) and that gang membership facilitates criminal behaviour (Thornberry et al. 1993). Gang youths have a higher participation rate in delinquency than do non-gang members (Sharp et al. 2006). Gang members are also more likely to engage in violent crime than are non-gang members (Bennett and Holloway 2004).

The Metropolitan Police Service (MPS) analysis of recorded crime found that gang members were responsible for 48 per cent of all shootings and 22 per cent of all serious violence (Home Office 2011: 18). What do these figures tell us? At first sight they suggest that nearly half of all shootings are attributable to gangs, which could be cause for concern, but how much is 48 per cent in numeric terms? This information is not available to us in the Home Office document referenced. The figures suggest that whilst nearly half of shooting are 'gang-related', 52 per cent are not. Although gun-related crimes are of serious concern they represent a small proportion of reported crime in the UK, and according to recent figures 'gun crime' is falling. The Office for National Statistics figures for 2011/12 shows a 60 per cent decrease (from 24,094 to 9555) in gun crime since its peak in 2003/4 and a 16 per cent reduction during 2011/12 (ONS 2013: 1) The number of recorded gun-enabled crimes committed in London (over the 12-month period from February 2011 to February 2012) decreased by 16 per cent on the previous year. This trend is mirrored in other forms of criminality and overall crime rates.

According to the *Crime in England and Wales* survey (Chaplin et al. 2011), overall crime is at its lowest level since the survey was first introduced in 1981 and the underlying trend for violent crime was downward. The British Crime Survey stated that the number of crimes involving guns or knives was 'relatively low' and the number of victims 'too few to produce reliable trend estimates' (Chaplin et al. 2011: 17). Knife crime fell by 3 per cent between 2009 and 2010, following a drop of 7 per cent the previous year. Yet the majority of people (60 per cent) believe that crime has risen across the county in the last few years, although interestingly the proportion who think that crime has risen locally is much lower, at 28 per cent. (Chaplin et al. 2011: 23).

Studies like the *Crime in England and Wales* survey present figures on the rate of crime amongst the general population, and so might not represent an accurate picture of 'gang-related' offences. As noted by Hallsworth and Young (2008), research in the UK has uncovered similar types of criminality to those undertaken by gang members in the US (Communities that Care 2005; Bennett and Holloway 2004; Bradshaw and Smith 2005; Sharp et al. 2006). Similarly, studies have noted a higher rate of engagement in delinquency and violent crime amongst gang members than amongst non-gang members (Bradshaw and Smith 2005; Sharp et al. 2006; Bennett and Holloway 2004). Whilst these findings indicate a propensity towards crime and violence amongst gang members, other studies paint a less inflammatory picture that challenges the stereotypical offending profile associated with gangs, particularly in relation to young people (i.e. children and young adults).

The only national 'gang' survey to be implemented in the UK (Sharp et al. 2006) shows that whilst members of DYGs (aka gangs) engage in violence, most collective offending involves non-violent offences. Drug use, threatening or frightening people, graffiti and criminal damage were amongst the most common offences (51 per cent, 40 per cent, 36 per cent and 31 per cent, respectively). Only a small minority of DYG members had committed a serious offence such as theft from a vehicle, robbery and assault (Sharp et al. 2006: vi). Drug dealing and possession of weapons, activities most commonly associated with gang life, were even less prominent in the offending profile of respondents. Few people (4 per cent) had possession of a gun, slightly more (17 per cent) admitted to possessing a knife and roughly the same proportion (18 per cent) – or almost one in five – had sold drugs (Sharp et al. 2006: 13). However, the report does show that members of DYGs (age 10–19) were responsible for about one fifth (21 per cent) of core offences committed and were disproportionately involved in serious offences (23 per cent) and violent offences (20 per cent). That DYG members are more criminogenic than non-involved young people should be taken seriously, but before accepting this as evidence of a growing gang crisis it is, as Jankowski (1991) notes, important to recognise the difficulty of distinguishing collective offending from individual endeavour. He argues that 'violence may be committed by gang members, but it is not gang related if it is not enacted as part of a gang's efforts to further its own achievements, productivity and objectives' (1991: 140).

Despite the complexities in analysis of evidence for weapons use amongst 'gang' members, such use is frequently reputed to be high (Centre for Social Justice 2009). If this were always the case, however, one would expect that a proliferation of gangs would translate into higher recordings of violent crime in recent years. That the crime rate is going down in the face of rising gang numbers and gang members poses a bit of a conundrum. One could argue that either the numbers don't add up, or there is a lack of robust evidence to link gangs to rising violence, or the 'gang' phenomenon isn't occurring in the way it is presented.

Notwithstanding the lack of concrete evidence, over the past few years successive governments in the UK have implemented a number of policy and legislative initiatives to combat and eradicate gang groups. In 2006, the New Labour government commissioned what could be considered to be one of the first 'gang' studies conducted in England and Wales (Sharp et al., 2006). The Violent Crime Reduction Act, passed in the same year, imposed tougher sentences for weapons-related offences often associated with 'gang members'. The Tackling Gangs Action Programme (TGAP) was announced in the following year, 2007, and £1.5 million was allocated to four areas experiencing serious gang-related offending (Dawson 2008). A few years later, in response to a persistent gang problem, the Conservative-Liberal Coalition government pledged the construction of the Ending Gang and Youth Violence Team, with a remit to support local areas with a gang or serious youth violence problem (Home Office 2011: 8). A larger sum of £10 million was supplied for this task, in addition to an extra £1.2 million earmarked for tackling the issue of gang-related sexual offences against girls and young women identified in several policy reports (see Firmin 2010, 2011; Berelowitz et al. 2012; Beckett et al. 2013).

It should be clear to you that gangs in the UK are thought to be associated with a catalogue of criminal offences ranging from anti-social and delinquent behaviour through to serious violent crime such as murder, rape and the proliferation of dangerous dogs (Harding 2010, 2012). Indeed, the English riots of 2011 were attributed to gangs by the Prime Minister,

youth gangs

David Cameron, who stated that there was evidence to suggest that gangs were behind the coordination of attacks on the police and the looting that followed. In a speech delivered in Oxfordshire on 15 August 2011, Mr Cameron concurred with John Pitts's analysis of the gang phenomenon and placed gangs 'at the heart of all the violence' conducted in England and Wales. He defined these groups as 'territorial, hierarchical and incredibly violent' and asserted that 'they are mostly composed of young boys, mainly from dysfunctional homes' (Cameron 2011).

However, even though David Cameron identified gang members as the main protagonists in the English riots, academics have since provided evidence that this was not the case (Densley and Mason 2011; Hallsworth and Brotherton 2011). Densley and Mason's analysis of court disposals found that, although gangs of young people were blamed for orchestrating and participating in the riots, almost 80 per cent of participants were adult males with no gang affiliation (Densley and Mason 2011: 14); a similar viewpoint was espoused by Hallsworth and Brotherton in their analysis of the evidence of the riots for the Runnymede Trust. These authors conclude that, in view of the lack of robust evidence, the narrative around the gangs in relation to the rioting is a 'disturbing fantasy that has no explanatory power' and is spun by people who have no real understanding of street life (Hallsworth and Brotherton 2011: 17). In fact, Hallsworth and Brotherton claim that the government and other policy makers have relinquished evidence-based analysis in favour of 'gang talk' (Hallsworth and Young 2008) in their efforts to tackle youth crime and violence. The central argument of this report and other work (Aldridge and Medina 2008; Hallsworth and Young 2008; Fraser 2010; Alexander 2008) is that the issue of youth violence stretches beyond the narrow concept of 'gang'.

9.9 The criminologists' gangs: 'believers' vs 'sceptics'

We can, broadly speaking, separate contemporary commentary on gang-related crime in the UK into two opposing camps: the 'sceptics' and the 'believers'. Using the available quantitative evidence, these construct different perspectives on gang behaviour in contemporary Britain. The 'believers' argue that gangs are a new threat to society; they are organised, and violence is a prolific and uncontrolled part of their character. It is largely violent gangs that are responsible for the growth in violent crime amongst the young (Pitts 2008; Centre for Social Justice 2009).

In contrast 'the sceptics' (Aldridge and Medina 2008; Hallsworth and Young 2008; Alexander 2008; Fraser 2010) have an opposing view. They focus on the discourse through which gangs are being constructed and argue that the gang phenomenon is largely a social construction built around a moral panic that, as we have seen, stretches back at least to mid-twentieth century fears around the first modern youth sub-cultures. Their argument *does not* deny the existence of gangs, as they recognise 'gang' groups as a historical feature of modern UK society, but, rather, the principal argument proposed is that, by and large, it is difficult to determine a rise in gangs or gang membership from current figures, as they are unclear and the moral panic surrounding the gang makes it difficult to see the phenomenon as it is. Moreover, ethnographic work has indicated that gangs in the UK, far from being the organised, hierarchical structures with the coherent membership, rituals, insignia and codes of conduct as illustrated in Pitts's and US research, are 'messy networks' (Aldridge and Medina 2008) of individuals with fluid membership and a negligible normative foundation. Much of the behaviour reported by young people involved in street-based groups is benign and mundane (Young et al. 2007).

The perspective on gangs set out by the 'believers' is, therefore, challenged by the 'sceptics'. Labelling groups of teenagers and young adults as 'gangs' might often be a misnomer. The sceptics argue that collectives of delinquents, with fluctuating membership and sporadic low-level offending, must be distinguished from an analysis of gangs and gang-related crime where this is understood to be structured and organised; indeed this point was argued by Hallsworth and Young (2004) when offering their heuristic typology of street collectives.

9.10 Where are the girls at? Girls and gangs

So far, much of this chapter has been taken up with talk about the male gang experience. As we have already mentioned, gang studies typically refer to male experience; understanding the gang from the perspective of female experience is not prevalent in early gang literature. There isn't much information on the girl gang experience, especially in the UK; much of what we do know comes from, again, the US.

The majority of classic studies on gangs failed to consider the female experience and, whilst Thrasher (1927) and Cohen (1955) did mention girls, they were relegated to a sideshow on the male main event. You may be wondering why. The absence of females from sociological research, and latterly criminology, was primarily because both disciplines were the domain of men researching the criminal motivations and behaviours of men for a majority male readership. More importantly, it is a commonly known fact that the offending rates of males far exceed those of females across all crime categories (Heidensohn and Silvestri 2012: 336). Because males commit more crime than females, their behaviour has commanded the lion's share of criminological and sociological attention from government officials, law enforcers and academics. The social sciences largely considered females to be an unworthy social subject; that was until feminism emerged and questioned the ways in which masculine experience was generalised and normalised within the social sciences.

Considered through the stereotypical and sexist lens of male researchers, gang-involved females were considered to be 'bad', 'mad' or 'sad' because, according to convention, 'good' girls were essentially 'law-abiding' citizens and far removed from the male culture that bred gangs (Sutherland et al., 1991). When girls are mentioned in this early literature, they are either portrayed as sexual chattels (something the boys fight over), maladjusted, violent 'tomboys' or sex toys or both. In other words, they are 'nuts' or 'sluts' (Campbell 1984; Young 2009; Chesney-Lind 1997). All this changed around the 1980s when rising levels of female crime and women's involvement in street-based groups brought attention to, and much discussion of, why young women were in gangs and their roles within these groups. As such, girl gang members were (re)discovered by feminist scholars and researchers who attempted to understand the female gang experience.

9.11 Female gangsters in the UK?

Feminist scholars writing in the 1980s drew attention to the role of girls and women in gang groups. In the early part of the decade Anne Campbell investigated the phenomenon of violence amongst girls and young women (Campbell 1981) and female gang membership (Campbell 1984). Although Campbell's work was situated within a context of rising concern about female offending, she concluded that dominant conceptualisations of female (gang) violence were exaggerated, effectively comprising a 'moral panic' (Cohen 1980). Indeed, Campbell argued that the female gang phenomenon in the UK was, in essence, a social construction. She observed that since female gangs tend to follow (rather than precede) male gangs and since there was little evidence to suggest a significant problem with these groups it was very unlikely that young women in the UK were organising into gangs in any great numbers (Campbell 1995).

Since Campbell's seminal work on girl gangsters much criminological research has explored the involvement of women in gangs (Young 2009, 2011; Batchelor 2011; Pitts 2007; Chesney-Lind 1997; Joe Laider and Hunt 2001; Miller 2001; Moore 1991). Much of this work has centred on the engagement of women in violent crime and also their victimisation. A large proportion of this work points to a bleak existence for girls and young women. In the UK, the work of Pitts (2008) and Firmin (2010, 2011) has established that women are at an increased risk of violent victimisation as a consequence of having a gang-involved relative, associating with or dating gang members. Both Firmin and Pitts have argued that women are frequently cajoled (or ordered) into committing criminal activities, hiding weapons and drugs and assaulting other women. They are beaten, abused and passed around like chattels by male gang members (Pitts 2007), who use rape as a weapon to keep them in line (Firmin 2010). This research, however, has been heavily criticised by Hallsworth and accused of reconstructing lived realities into a 'gang-talking fantasy' (2013: 102).

Running concurrently with the view of gang girls as being victims is one that conceives them as calculated, violent protagonists capable of inflicting the same damage as their male counterparts. In fact, in an attempt to understand male gang membership a separate discourse emerged which focused specifically on the role females played in facilitating gang criminality and the threats they posed as a distinctive group. Archer's conference paper for the British Society of Criminology was one of the first scholarly explorations of the UK girl gang phenomenon (Archer 1998).

Marrying data from North American research with media reports from the UK, Archer's article focused on the new and distinctive type of femininity displayed by girls who join gangs, in comparison with other female sub-cultures (see Archer 1998). In the process of identifying female sub-cultures Archer found evidence of a female gang called the 'Peckham Girls', a three-strong group with all the characteristics and offending profile of the girl gangsters found in US research. The Peckham Girls were rough, with a fearsome reputation and skilled in the use of knives (ibid.: 2). Like their US counterparts (see Campbell 1984, Miller 2001 for a fuller account), the Peckham Girls claimed a territory and illustrated their claim over it by tagging their monikers. They had a distinctive dress code which included 'wearing gold sun visors, pink fluorescent leggings, red blouson jackets, baseball caps and lots of jewellery including nose studs, several earrings on each ear and rings on every finger' (ibid.: 3). These girls had criminal reputations as colourful as the boys', with offences such as robbery, snatch/ theft, shoplifting and fighting.

Set against the backdrop of US research and theory, Archer's portrayal of the Peckham Girls exposes female rational decisions to 'join' gangs. She concludes that female involvement in gangs enables marginalised young girls to establish an identity, reputation and respect (motivations often cited in relations to male gangsters) where violence and offending could be used by adolescents as a method through which to garner some sense of self-worth.

Since Archer's study much has been written in the press about girl gangsters. As Young notes, a considerable proportion of this has, until recently, focused on the violent and destructive aspects of female involvement in male groups and criminality (Young 2009; 2011). Gang-involved girls have been constructed as violent 'She Male gangsters' capable of robbery, rape, murder and 'deadlier than the males' (Young 2009). Branded as 'the feral sex' and 'natural born killers' this new breed of gangster is deemed to include some of the most aggressive, violent and menacing young people in the world (ibid., 2009: 1).

The headlines purported to reflect the true and changing characteristics of female offending. Whilst official statistics historically portrayed female crime as relatively low and non-violent in 2003/4, government office figures indicated a change in profile which illustrated a rise in violent crime amongst young women. Studies like the Offending, Crime and Justice Survey 2003 (Budd et al. 2005) suggested that females were committing a larger proportion of the total number of violent crimes than previously, a trend that was apparently replicated in Scotland (Batchelor 2005). At roughly the same time, violent crime amongst teenage girls had increased by 38 per cent (Smith 2005). Arrest data for violent crime showed an increase in females apprehended for the traditionally male crime of 'violence against the person' (Young 2011). Coupled with the media reporting of extraordinary 'gang' cases such as the 'happy slap' murder involving 14-year-old Chelsea O'Mahoney and 'honey trap' killer Samantha Joseph, this material added weight to the construction of the female gangster as a sociopathic actor devoid of morality and as violent as any male counterpart. Moreover, it added weight to the believers' (see above) gang thesis of a new crime wave spearheaded by gang boys but underpinned by equally competent gang girls. For social commentators, gang girls were, as noted by Young (2009), viewed as Lombrosian women, atavistic throwbacks, out of control and capable of gratuitous brutality. Such girls not only mete out violence directly but, indirectly, they also 'aggravate the violence of young boys' (Razaq 2008: 6) and initiate 'intergang' violence by facilitating 'shootings and deaths' when 'dissed' (disrespected by others) (Centre for Social Justice 2009: 74–5).

9.12 What isn't being said?

There has been a tendency to associate the apparent increase in the antisocial and violent activity of young women in general with a rise in female gangs and female gang membership. Arguably, this association was driven by dominant discourses relating to male gangs and 'gang culture' in the UK. However, the evidential foundation for the existence of the violent female gangster is more flimsy than for males. The exact number of girl gangsters is not known. From the few studies which dedicated some research time to investigating the number of 'girl gangsters' the number ranges from, at the lowest, 18 (Bennett and Holloway 2004), through 2500 (Home Office Gangs Evidence 2006), to an estimated 12,500 females 'closely involved in gangs' (Pearce and Pitts 2011).

Whilst official reports highlight a year-on-year increase in a range of offences committed by girls and young women during the period 2000–6 (including violence against the person, robbery, criminal damage and arson, public order and breach), they state that a greater number of girls, aged 10–17, engage in acquisitive crimes (such as 'theft and handling of stolen goods' and fraud) rather than in 'violence against the person'. Youth Justice Board figures (and those of the Ministry of Justice 2012) on girls' offending patterns indicate that the majority of young female offenders are still significantly more likely to engage in traditionally 'female' crimes (Youth Justice Board 2009: 46). Furthermore, closer examination of such data reveals that the majority of 'violence against the person' offences are likely to be low-level in nature and not resulting in serious injury. The Youth Justice Board study also suggests that there is not a rise in the number of girls committing serious offences, but more girls are entering the youth justice system at a younger age and for offences that would have received a caution or some other sanction in earlier times.

With regard to group offending, the Offending Crime and Justice Study (Sharpe et al. 2006) found that 'co-offenders' were primarily male (81 per cent of incidents involved men only); only one in five (17 per cent) offences involved male and female co-offenders. Co-offending amongst female-only groups accounted for a very small percentage of the total, 2 per cent of the overall number of total of offences (Budd et al. 2005: 60). A further study showed that boys were more likely than girls to be involved in these types of offences and that girls' group offending was significantly lower than boys'. According to Sharpe et al. (2006) the co-offending profile for girls is similar to individual offending, perhaps with the exception of fighting.

9.13 Summary

We began this chapter by looking at the contemporary situation in Britain in relation to fatalities and riots and went on to problematise the concept of the gang, which has been mobilised to explain these phenomena of youth violence. We looked at the origins of the concept of the gang in the classical tradition of US sociology of the early twentieth century, which saw gangs as groups that forged themselves in resistance to mainstream norms and values. We then went on to consider developments within this tradition which see gangs as a more criminogenic phenomenon, which poses a problem calling for social control in a context of law enforcement.

We then considered the context of the UK and questioned whether the gang as conceptualised in the US was applicable to the UK. In doing so we looked at the work of a range of sociologists and criminologists who attempted to paint a different picture. The chapter went on to raise some problems with sub-cultural theory, particularly the idea that gang groups adhere to a separate normative value structure, focusing especially on Sykes and Matza's conception of techniques of neutralisation and the degree to which sub-cultural and mainstream values overlap.

youth gangs

We moved on to draw attention to the important contribution of the Birmingham School in developing the idea of resistance through rituals often attributed to sub-cultures and Cohen's conceptions of folk devils and moral panics.

We then focused on the contemporary rediscovery of 'the gang' as manifest in the 2000s and drew attention to the hyper-violent, ghettoised, territorial and structured gangs to which the media commonly refer, problematising this construction.

Finally, we considered the marginalisation of the female experience in discourse on gangs, and recent feminist work which has sought to illuminate and recover this experience.

Revision notes

Defining gangs. There are no easy ways to define gangs. The US tradition began with Thrasher arguing that gangs were a stage of maturing into adults that some (male) youths passed through and, eventually, moved away from. However, more contemporary American definitions such as those put forward by Klein, Miller and Jankowski maintained that the collective identity of gang life was held together by the shared criminal interests of its members. So it was that the gang became viewed as a deviant, anti-social and sometimes violent group.

Gang formation. Sub-cultural theorists like Cohen argued that the reason why young men join gangs is because of 'status frustration', that is, the realisation that they are not able to achieve middle-class social goals by legitimate means, such as through education. Instead they seek to form groups whose values differ from those of the mainstream. In so doing, they actively reject social norms and conventional behaviour. Criminality, fighting, anti-social behaviour and so on, that go against middle-class values and norms become legitimised in their way of understanding the world.

Criticisms of sub-cultural theory. Authors like Matza argue that sub-cultural theory generalises too much about gang behaviour, as if all gang members were the same. Rather, there are always differences between the individuals who constitute a gang. Furthermore, it has been argued that sub-cultural theory assumes that individuality is subsumed by the group and socialisation within the group is 'total'. However, individuals within gangs may differ in terms of how they understand 'right' and 'wrong' and what they are prepared to do. Finally, sub-cultural theory also assumes that individuals are fully socialised into an alternative deviant value system, but this too is an overly totalising theory.

The social construction of gangs. The US debates about gangs are not necessarily easily transferable to a UK context. Much of the reporting and political discourse sensationalises gangs and might not reflect the truth about their character or frequency. Public debates can be understood as a social construction underpinned by a 'moral panic' about youth in contemporary society.

Girls and gangs. Most of the literature on gangs is centred on male behaviour. The role of girls in gangs was not 'rediscovered' until the 1980s, when feminists began commenting on female gang members. Some studies highlight how gang girls are often victims within gang culture. But there is also a body of work that conceives them as calculated, violent protagonists capable of inflicting the same damage as men. Either way, the newsworthy reporting of girls in gangs often misrepresents their position.

Seminar tasks

Youth gangs

1 Issue:
In this chapter we have looked at a range of theoretical issues that deal with the definition of gangs, gang formation and the degree of socialisation in gangs. Although the study of gangs is a very seductive subject it is the site for some very serious and detailed academic study. This is because the consequences of this research, through its potential influence on policy, could fundamentally affect the lives of many young people.

EXAMPLE:
Government policy towards gangs in London since the riots of 2011 has focused on the Ending Gang and Youth Violence programme, which has had £10 million of public funding poured into it. It relies on local initiatives to try to cut gang-related crime. However, as the government's Ending Gang and Youth Violence Review 2012/13 stated, the biggest problem in trying to assess the programme's success was that 'there is no reliable national measure of gang-association to use to test impact on gangs' (Home Office 2014: 4). In other words, a reliable definition of gangs has yet to be agreed upon to underpin studies of this kind.

EXERCISE:
In small groups write a list of the features associated with a) classical and b) contemporary concepts of the gang. Do you think that classical theories of the gang apply to the female experience? Outline your reasons for and against the application of these theories.

2 Issue:

We have reviewed a range of theories that have analysed the culture of gang membership. It has been argued that gang membership is attractive as a 'playground' for testing boundaries and growing up; that it is substantiated by deviant and criminal activity that is explicitly set against social norms, aspirations and values; or that while the means may be illegal, gang membership actually provides an alternative way of achieving mainstream social aspirations (such as wealth and status).

EXAMPLE:

In Pitts's (2007) study mentioned above, he found that young people in the London Borough of Waltham Forest become 'reluctant gangsters'. That is, the young people who got involved in gangs knew they were taking risks. But they felt that they had no real choice. The gangs exerted an inordinate control over the day-to-day lives of people in the localities where they lived, particularly in large housing estates. In controlling the day-to-day behaviour of residents and tenants living within 'their' territory, controlling who might enter 'their' territory and driving out those whom they believed should not dwell there, some gangs were transforming the estates where they lived into 'totalitarian social space(s)'. This left young people with no option but to join a gang so as to be 'protected', even though they realised it also made them more vulnerable.

EXERCISE:

Consider whether you think it is likely that gang culture has an oppositional value system to mainstream culture.

Coursework questions

What evidence is there to support a rise in gangs in the UK?
How useful are the terms 'gang' and 'gang-related crime' for explaining youth violence?

References

Aldridge, J. and Medina, J., *Youth Gangs in an English City: social exclusion, drugs and violence*, Full Research Report ESRC End of Award Report, RES-000-23-0615. Swindon: ESRC, 2008

Alexander, C. *(Re)Thinking 'Gangs'*, London, The Runnymede Trust, 2008

Archer, D., 'Riot GRRRL and Raisin Girl: femininity within the female gang, the power of the popular', Conference paper, *The British Society of Criminology: select proceedings*, 1998, https://www.martinfrost.ws/htmlfiles/sept2008/riot-grrl.pdf

Batchelor, S., '"Prove Me the Bam": victimization and agency in the lives of young women who commit violent offences', *Probation Journal*, 52(4): 358–75, 2005

Battin-Pearson, S., Thornberry, T., Hawkins, D. and Krohn, M. 'Gang Membership, Delinquent Peers and Delinquent Behaviour', *Juvenile Justice Bulletin*, Washington, DC: US Department of Justice, 1998, https://www.ncjrs.gov/pdffiles/171119.pdf

Beckett, H., Brodie, I., Factor, F., Melrose, M., Pearce, J., Pitts, J., Shuker, L. and Warrington, C., *'It's Wrong ... But You Get Used to It.' A qualitative study of gang-associated sexual violence towards, and exploitation of, young people in England*, London: The Office of Children's Commissioner, 2013

Bennett, T. and Holloway, K., 'Gang Membership, Drugs and Crime in the UK', *British Journal of Criminology*, 44: 305–23, 2004

Box, S., *Deviance, Reality and Society* (2nd edn), London: Holt Reinhart and Winston, 1981

Budd, T., Sharp, C. and Mayhew, P., *Offending in England and Wales: first results from the 2003 Crime and Justice Survey*, Home Office Research Study 275, London: Home Office, 2005

Bullock, K. and Tilley, N., *Shootings, Gangs and Violent Incidents in Manchester: developing a crime reduction strategy*, London: Home Office, 2002

Cameron, D., PM's speech on the fightback after the riots, Cabinet Office and Prime Minister's Office, 15 August 2011, https://www.gov.uk/government/speeches/pms-speech-on-the-fightback-after-the-riots

Campbell, A., *Girl Delinquents*, Oxford: Basil Blackwell, 1981

—, *The Girls in the Gang: a report from New York City*, Oxford and New York: Basil Blackwell, 1984

—, 'Media Myth Making: creating a girl gang problem', *Criminal Justice Matters* 19(Spring): 8–9, 1995

Centre for Social Justice, *Dying to Belong: an in-depth review of street gangs in Britain*, Gangs Working Policy Group, 2009, www.centreforsocialjustice.org.uk/UserStorage/pdf/Pdf%20reports/DyingtoBelongFullReport.pdf

Chaplin, R., Flatley, J. and Smith, K., *Crime in England and Wales: findings from the British Crime Survey and police recorded crime* (2nd edn), Home Office Statistical Bulletin, July 2011

Chesney-Lind, M., *The Female Offender: girls, women, and crime*, Thousand Oaks, CA: Sage, 1997

Citizens Report, *Mapping the Location and Victim Profile of Teenage Murders in London from 2005 to 2013*, 2013, http://www.citizensreportuk.org/reports/teenage-murder-london.html (accessed 10 July 2013)

Cloward, R. and Ohlin, L., *Delinquency and Opportunity: a theory of delinquent gangs*. Glencoe, IL: Free Press, 1960

Cohen, A.K., *Delinquent Boys: the culture of the gang*, Glencoe, IL: Free Press, 1955

Cohen, S., *Folk Devil and Moral Panics*. London: Martin Robertson, 1980

Communities that Care, *Communities that Care*, Findings from the Safer London Youth Survey, 2005, http://www.communitiesthatcare.org.uk/Safer%20London%20Youth%20Survey.pdf

Daily Mail, 'Five Children Shot or Stabbed in London EVERY Day', *Daily Mail*, 16 January 2008

Davies, A., *Gangs of Manchester*, Preston: Milo Books, 2009

Dawson, P., *Monitoring Data from the Tackling Gangs Action Plan*, London: Home Office, 2008

Densley, J. and Mason, N., *The London Riots: a gang problem? Policing Today*, November 2011, http://www.sociology.ox.ac.uk/documents/graduate-research/policing-today.pdf

Dickens, C., *Oliver Twist*, London: Penguin Books, 1994

Dodd, V., 'Gang Feud Victim Killed by "Hunting Posse", Court Told', *Guardian*, 16 April 2013

Downes, D., *The Delinquent Solution: a study in subcultural theory*, London: Routledge, 1966

Fagge, N., Evans, R. and Camber, R., 'Stabbed to Death over a BlackBerry: boy of 15 is killed protecting his younger brother from a gang', *Daily Mail Online*, 12 April 2011 (accessed 15 July 2013)

Firmin, C., *Female Voice in Violence Project: a study into the impact of serious youth and gang violence on women and girls*, London: Race on the Agenda (ROTA), 2010

—, 'This Is It: This is My Life', *Female Voice in Violence Final Report: on the impact of serious youth violence and criminal gangs on women and girls across the country*, London: ROTA, 2011

Fraser, A.D., Growing through Gangs: young people, identity and social change in Glasgow, PhD thesis, University of Glasgow, 2010

Gordon, R., 'Criminal Business Organisations, Street Gangs and "Wannabe" Groups: a Vancouver perspective', *Canadian Journal of Criminology*, 42(1): 39–60, 2000

Hagedorn, J.M., *People and Folks: gangs, crime and the underclass in a rust-belt city*, Chicago, IL: Lakeview Press, 1998

Hallsworth, S., *The Gang and Beyond: interpreting violent street worlds*, Basingstoke: Palgrave Macmillan, 2013

Hallsworth, S. and Brotherton, D., *Urban Disorder and Gangs: critique and a warning*, London: Runnymede Trust, 2011

Hallsworth, S. and Young, T., 'Getting Real about Gangs', *Criminal Justice Matters*, 55, 2004

—, 'On Gangs and Guns: a critique and a warning', *ChildRight*, 220: 14–16, 2005

—, 'Gang Talk and Gang Talkers: a critique', *Crime, Media, Culture*, 4(2): 175–95, 2008

Harding, S. '"Status Dogs" and Gangs', *Safer Communities*, 2010, 9(1): 30–5

—, *Unleashed: the phenomena of status dogs and weapon dogs*, Bristol: Policy Press, 2012

Heidensohn, F. and Silvestri, M., 'Gender and Crime', in M. Maguire, R. Morgan and R. Reiner (eds) *The Oxford Handbook of Criminology* (5th edn), Oxford: Oxford University Press, 2012, pp. 336–69

Hill, A., 'Ja-Ja Should Know How Street Gangs Operate: he runs one', *Observer*, 25 February 2007, p. 9 http://www.theguardian.com/uk/2007/feb/25/ukguns.news

HM Inspectorate of Constabulary *'Getting Organised': a thematic report on the police service's response to serious organised crime*, London: HMIC, 2009

Home Office *Tacking Gangs: a practical guide for local authorities, CDRPs and local partners*, London: Home Office, 2008

—, *Ending Gang and Youth Violence: a cross-government report including further evidence and good practice case studies*, London: Home Office, 2011

—, *Ending Gang and Youth Violence: Review 2012/13*. London: Home Office, 2014

Jankowski, M.S. *Islands in the Street: gangs and American urban society*, California: University of California Press, 1991

Joe Laidler, K. and Hunt, G., 'Accomplishing Femininity among the Girls in the Gang', *British Journal of Criminology* 41(4): 656–78, 2001

Klein, M.W., *Street Gangs and Street Workers*. Englewood Cliffs, NJ: Prentice Hall, 1971

Klein, M.W. and Maxson, C.L., *Gang Structures, Crime Patterns, and Police Responses: a summary report*, London: Department of Justice, 2001

Kontos, L., Brotherton, D. and Barrios, L., *Gangs and Society: alternative perspectives*, New York: Columbia University Press, 2003

Leapman, B., 'Violent Youth Crime up a Third', *Telegraph*, 20 January 2008, http://www.telegraph.co.uk/news/uknews/1576076/Violent-youth-crime-up-a-third.html

Lewis, P., Newburn, T., Taylor, M., McGillivray, C., Greenhill, A., Frayman, H. and Procter, R., 'Reading the Riots: investigating England's summer of disorder', London: The Guardian and London School of Economics and Political Science, 2011

McLagan, G., 'Sin Cities', *Sunday Times*, 25 September 2005, http://www.timesonline.co.uk/tol/life_and_style/article566875.ece?token=null&offset=0

Mayhew, H., *London Labour and the London Poor*, Hertfordshire: Wordsworth Editions Limited, 2008

Matza, D., *Delinquency and Drift*, New York: John Wiley, 1964

Merton, R.K., 'Social Structure and Anomie,' in C. Lemert (ed.), *Social Theory: the multicultural and classic readings*, Boulder, CO: Westview Press, 2009

Metropolitan Police Service *MPS Pan-London Gang Profile*, London: Metropolitan Police Service, 2006

Miller, J., *One of the Guys: girls, gangs, and gender*, New York: Oxford University Press, 2001

Miller, W.B., 'Lower Class Culture as a Generating Milieu of Gang Delinquency', *Journal of Social Issues*, 14: 5–19, 1958

Ministry of Justice, *Arrests for Recorded Crime (Notifiable Offences) and the Operation of Certain Police Powers under PACE England and Wales 2006/7*, London: Ministry of Justice, 2008

—, *Statistics on Women and the Criminal Justice System 2011: a Ministry of Justice publication under Section 95 of the Criminal Justice Act 1991*, London: Ministry of Justice, 2012

Moore, J., *Going Down to the Barrio: homeboys and homegirls in change*, Philadelphia, PA: Temple University Press, 1991

Office for National Statistics *Focus on: Violent Crime and Sexual Offences, 2011/12*, London: Office for National Statistics, 2013

Patrick, J., *A Glasgow Gang Observed*, London: Eyre Methuen, 1973 and 2013

Pearce, J. and Pitts, J., *Youth Gangs, Sexual Violence and Sexual Exploitation: a scoping exercise for the Office of the Children's Commissioner for England, 2011*, www.beds.ac.uk/research/iasr/centres/intcent

Pearson, G., *Hooligan: a history of respectable fears*, London: Palgrave Macmillan, 1983

Pitts, J., *Reluctant Gangsters: youth gangs in Waltham Forest*, Waltham Forest Borough Council, 2007, http://www.walthamforest.gov.uk/documents/reluctant-gangsters.pdf

—, *Reluctant Gangsters: the changing shape of youth crime*, Collumpton, Devon: Willan Publishing, 2008

Razaq, R., 'Girls Are Becoming as Violent as Boys', *Evening Standard*, 14 May 2008

Saunders, W.B., *Gangbangs and Drive-by's: grounded culture and juvenile gang violence*, New York: Walter de Gruyter, Inc., 1994

Sharp, C., Aldridge, J. and Medina, J., *Delinquent Youth Groups and Offending Behaviour: findings from the 2004 Offending, Crime and Justice Survey*, London: Home Office, 2006

Shropshire, S. and McFarquhar, M., 'Developing Multi Agency Strategies to Address the Street Gang Culture and Reduce Gun Violence amongst Young People', Briefing no. 4 in the series Young People, Gang Cultures and Firearms Violence, 2002

Smith, D.J., 'Deadlier than the Male?', *Sunday Times*, 17 April 2005

Smith, D.J. and Bradshaw, P., *Gang Membership and Teenage Offending*, The Edinburgh Study of Youth Transitions and Crime, No. 8, Edinburgh: Centre for Law and Society, 2005

Stelfox, P., 'Policing Lower levels of Organised Crime in England and Wales', *The Howard Journal of Criminal Justice*, 37 (4): 393–406, 1998

Sutherland, E., Cressey, D.R., and Luckenbill, D., *Principles of Criminology* (11th edn), Oxford: General Hall, 1991

Sykes, G.M. and Matza, D., 'Techniques of Neutralization: a theory of delinquency', *American Sociological Review*, 22(6): 664–70, in T. Newburn (ed.) *Key Readings in Criminology*, Cullompton, Devon: Willan Publishing, 1957, pp. 234–6

Thornberry, T.P., Krohn, M.D., Lizotte, A.J. and Chand-Wieschem, D., 'The Role of Juvenile Gangs in Facilitating Delinquent Behaviour', in M.W. Klein, C.L. Maxson and J. Miller (eds) *The Modern Gang Reader* (1995), Los Angeles: Roxbury, 1993, pp. 174–85

Thrasher, F.M., *The Gang: a study of 1313 gangs in Chicago*, Chicago, IL: Phoenix Press, 1927

Travis, A., 'Officials Warn of Terrorist Links to Prison Gangs' *Guardian*, 3 March 2008, http://www.theguardian.com/society/2008/mar/03/prisons.terrorism.uk

Willis, P., *How Working Class Kids Get Working Class Jobs*, Aldershot: Ashgate, 1977

Young, T., 'Girls and Gangs: "Shemale" Gangsters in the UK?' *Youth Justice*, 9(3): 224–38, 2009

—, 'In Search of the Shemale Gangster', in B. Goldson (ed.) *Youth in Crisis? Gangs, Territoriality and Violence*, Cullompton, Devon: Willan Publishing, 2011

Young, T., FitzGerald, M., Hallsworth, S. and Joseph, I., *Groups, Gangs and Weapons*, London: Youth Justice Board, 2007

Youth Justice Board, *Girls and Offending: patterns, perceptions and interventions*, London: Youth Justice Board, 2009

Further reading

Cottrell-Boyce, J., 'Ending Gang and Youth Violence: a critique', *Youth Justice*, December, 13(3): 193–206, 2013

Densley, J.A., *How Gangs Work: an ethnography of youth violence*, Hampshire: Palgrave Macmillan, 2013

chapter 10

Conclusion

As a student it is unlikely, and not necessarily desirable, that you have read the whole of this book from cover to cover – although if you have, well done! We wish that we could offer you a great ending, like a novel: to be able to set out in this conclusion how to solve all social problems. That would be something. Unfortunately, we cannot. However, we hope that whatever you have read in this textbook it has given you some clearer idea about how to think through social problems as a social scientist. Knowing *how* to think, not *what* to think, is at the heart of becoming a critical, reflective undergraduate. You may agree or disagree with some of the arguments given here. You may be confused or unsure about certain topics. None of these positions is at all bad. Doubt and an engaged scepticism are where thinking begins. Hannah Arendt (referred to in 2.2) once summed up her whole life's work – which covered issues about totalitarianism, revolution, the human condition, friendship and love – as simply being about 'thinking what we are doing' (Arendt 1958). What she meant by this wasn't simply thinking in the way that we do in our practical lives: 'what shall I eat for dinner?', 'where shall I go tonight?', 'what do I say to my boyfriend?' and so on. What Arendt was implying was that we ought to develop a capacity to reflect upon an issue in an intelligent, informed and ethical way. To do this as an individual, to take up the challenge of being thoughtful and having the willingness to learn, is the greatest contribution we can make to people around us and our communities. If this book has ever so slightly nudged you to be more like this, then it would have done its job.

One of the main ways that we have tried to make you think about the world differently, through the mind-set of social science, is to present social problems within the framework of social construction. This methodology has been deployed in order for you to try to grasp the idea that social scientists work with certain methodologies, methods and theories to try to analyse the social world. The methodology of social construction may not be the only way of looking at social problems, although its use in the teaching of this subject area is quite common. For those starting out on the process of learning to read society as a sociologist, criminologist, social policy student or within any related discipline, drawing upon social construction is a fairly straightforward way of going about it. Its key point is that we can understand social problems in different ways, that they are contested. From this realisation we are made aware that there are underlying ideological and political assumptions about social problems that need to be analysed (to be 'unpacked') in order to comprehend what are the implications of various arguments. For example, we have seen here that in relation to poverty, migration, crime, work, childhood and education, as well as gangs, there are a myriad ways of constructing these problems. At a general level many of the social issues associated with these problems – such as inequalities, racism, deviant behaviour, educational underachievement and lack of opportunities – could all be constructed as largely the consequence of individual failings and family breakdown. Conversely, they might also be constructed around an argument about misplaced government focus and policy failures. In other words, we might come across micro and macro arguments. The former tend to emphasise what we call an agency approach, where individuals and their families are taken as the main actors responsible for the social problem. The latter tend towards a social structural perspective that highlights the role of social institutions and broader, historically embedded cultural attitudes.

Within each of the chapters of this book there have been many particular social constructions of the issues at stake. Poverty has been deemed to be the fault of the poor or the result of fundamental social inequalities. Problems of migration have been characterised as an issue to do with over-population or associated with racism. Work may be constructed as an economic issue, purely to do with labour market employment, or as a site for the perpetuation of gender equalities. Childhood may be taken as a period of innocence that ought to be nurtured by schools, or as a focus of state intervention in education so as to 'improve' society. Crime can be understood as a policing issue or as a way of life that is not far removed from mainstream social goals and aspirations. Similarly we have seen that gangs can be constructed as an increasing sign of social breakdown or as part of a moral panic about youth.

In all these ways and more the methodology of social construction helps us to think through these issues. In particular, this methodology points to the way that certain groups in society are looked upon negatively, deemed to be 'different', 'unwanted', 'immoral', 'socially corrosive', 'un-British' and so on. This throws light upon the most political and ideological aspect of what we have been discussing. Social construction illuminates the inequalities and artificial barriers that are drawn up between sets of people and communities. These dividing lines may be drawn around prejudices about wealth, lifestyle, nationality, age, 'race', gender and any other of a number of socially divisive criteria. But they are all similar in that they emerge as discourses of power, often serving one or more particular social group. Although it is not necessary, especially if you are a first-year undergraduate, to go much beyond an awareness of this at this stage, it is worth pointing out that it may be here that the usefulness of the methodology of social construction ends. When we begin to get into the terrain that takes us into discourses of power and ideology, we begin to enter a much broader set of methodological debates. It may take us from social construction to other theoretical approaches. These approaches may be more theoretically sophisticated and more controversial. But all that is for further study and, perhaps, the sequel to this book! Suffice to say here that while social construction is an excellent approach to introduce the study of social problems, as you delve into these issues you will see there are other ways of approaching the same subject matter.

For now it remains, as is traditional at the close of a text, to take some poetic licence and speculate about the future. Can the kind of social problems that we have set out here be, at least, partially, 'solved'? As stated in the introduction, the role of the social scientist is not necessarily to solve problems, as such, but to make our thinking about these issues a little clearer. As we have seen, these problems have a relatively long-running historical legacy and are complex in their make-up. Nevertheless, there ought not to be a sense of despair about them. Many social problems have become less significant because of political campaigns, public opinion, government policy and social change. Despite continued inequalities and social injustice there are many successes relating to the social problems that we have looked at here to do with social class, gender, education, work, sexuality, impairment, ethnicity, poverty, young people and the homeless. The rise of the British welfare state did a tremendous amount in the twentieth century to alleviate many of the worst social problems of the nineteenth century. It is now up to students, like yourself, to understand the contemporary issues and build towards diminishing the social problems of the twenty-first century.

Reference

Arendt, H., *The Human Condition*, London: University of Chicago Press, 1958

Index